The Complete Photo Guide to

HOME
DECORATING
PROJECTS

**DIY Projects to Transform Walls, Windows,
Furniture, Floors & More**

Creative Publishing
international

MINNEAPOLIS, MINNESOTA
www.creativepub.com

Contents

The Complete Photo Guide to Home Decorating Projects

Creative Publishing international

Copyright © 2010
Creative Publishing international, Inc.
400 First Avenue North, Suite 300
Minneapolis, Minnesota 55401
1-800-328-0590
www.creativepub.com
All rights reserved

Printed in Singapore

10 9 8 7 6 5 4 3 2 1

Library of Congress Cataloging-in-Publication Data

The complete photo guide to home decorating projects.
    p. cm.
  At head of title: Branded by Black & Decker
  Summary: "Features do-it-yourself information on everything from painting and trimwork to slipcovers and window treatments"--Provided by publisher.
  ISBN-13: 978-1-58923-484-0 (hard cover)
  ISBN-10: 1-58923-484-7 (hard cover)
  1. Handicraft--Amateurs' manuals. 2. House furnishings--Amateurs' manuals. 3. Interior decoration--Amateurs' manuals. I. Black & Decker Corporation (Towson, Md.) II. Title: Branded by Black & Decker.

  TT157.C575 2009
  747--dc22

  2009019965
  Softcover ISBN 13: 978-1-58923-630-1
  Softcover ISBN 10: 1-58923-630-0

President/CEO: Ken Fund

Home Improvement Group

Publisher: Bryan Trandem
Managing Editor: Tracy Stanley
Senior Editor: Mark Johanson
Editor: Jennifer Gehlhar

Creative Director: Michele Lanci-Altomare
Senior Design Managers: Jon Simpson, Brad Springer
Design Manager: James Kegley
Production Managers: Linda Halls, Laura Hokkanen

Compilation author: Betsy Matheson
Page Layout Artist: Danielle Smith

The Complete Photo Guide to Home Decorating Projects
Created by: The Editors of Creative Publishing international, Inc., in coopera-
tion with Black & Decker. Black & Decker® is a trademark of The Black &
Decker Corporation and is used under license.

NOTICE TO READERS

For safety, use caution, care, and good judgment when following the
procedures described in this book. The publisher and Black & Decker
cannot assume responsibility for any damage to property or injury to
persons as a result of misuse of the information provided.

The techniques shown in this book are general techniques for
various applications. In some instances, additional techniques not
shown in this book may be required. Always follow manufacturers'
instructions included with products, since deviating from the directions
may void warranties. The projects in this book vary widely as to skill
levels required: some may not be appropriate for all do-it-yourselfers,
and some may require professional help.

Consult your local building department for information on building
permits, codes, and other laws as they apply to your project.

Cover photograph credits; middle left courtesy of FLOR / www.flor.com;
middle right and lower middle courtesy of Louvolite / www.louvolite.com.

Introduction

Decorating is the key to transforming a functional living space into a comfortable home that is uniquely yours. The nearly limitless variety of decorating techniques, materials, colors, patterns, and accents that can be used in any room in your home provides endless options for customization—and an inherent creative challenge. With so many choices, where do you start?

The Complete Photo Guide to Home Decorating Projects will guide your creative vision and provide the know-how to complete nearly any decorating project with professional quality and designer results. Whether you plan to reinvent your living room with new upholstery, window treatments, decorative painting, and an aluminum-gilded ceiling or you merely want to know the best way to hang artwork and shelving, this volume provides clear, step-by-step instructions with large, easy-to-follow photographs to guide each project from start to finish.

To ensure that you love your completed project, always begin by envisioning the atmosphere and design scheme that best suits your room's needs and your personal style. Also, take stock of the tools, materials, and skills needed to be successful. "Decorating Basics," the first section of this book, is intended for exactly that purpose. Focused on principles of good design and on the basic skills and tools needed to achieve high-quality results, this section is a must for every decorator. With these resources, you can confidently create a home décor that truly reflects your abilities and creative intent.

Each of the remaining sections is composed of a set of projects associated with one element of room design, such as "Wall Paint," "Cabinets & Doors," and "Furniture Refinishing." Projects are widely varied, encompassing both large and small commitments, varied skill levels, and both innovative and time-tested techniques. Let these projects help you complete common tasks—such as installing curtains, applying wallcoverings, or installing a tile backsplash correctly. Or let them inspire you to take on a more challenging project such as installing wainscot frames, sewing a custom-fit slipcover, or applying sophisticated painting techniques to walls, ceilings, and floors.

Successfully completing a decorating project will be one of the most creative, most rewarding, most fun ways you can invest in your home while also achieving a lasting impact on its value. In addition, the beauty and personality you create will become a part of your family's story for years to come. Add the extensive resources of The Complete Photo Guide to Home Decorating Projects to your own creative energy and get started on your first project today.

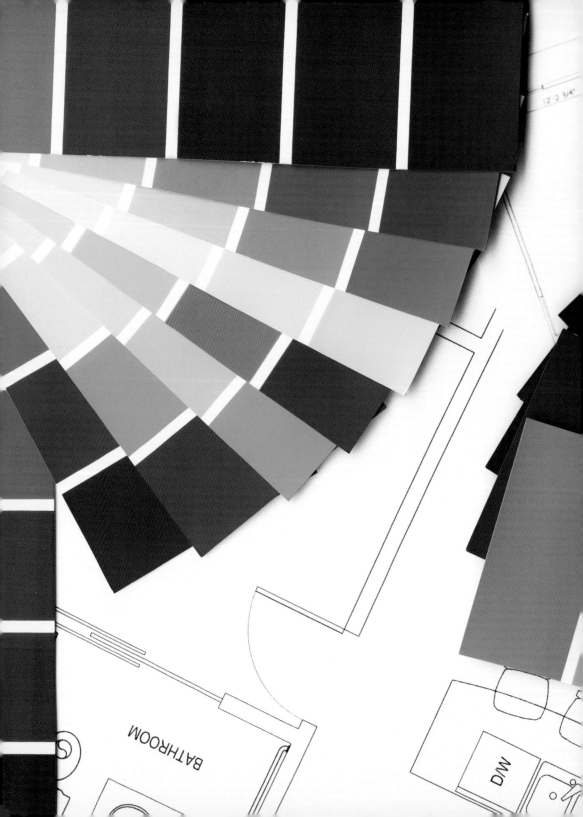

Decorating Basics

Taking on a home decorating project can transform the spirit of your home. Whether completing a small task such as updating a window with new curtains or a major undertaking such as wallcovering an entire room, each project in this book will require you to be familiar with a few basic design considerations, tools, and techniques.

Consider the needs of your room, the interplay of colors and patterns, the desired atmosphere, and the impact of your own personal style when selecting materials and projects for your home. Then, familiarize yourself with the basic techniques and tools you'll need to complete the project—as well as any specific measuring and planning instructions. Review this chapter for tips and techniques to ensure your project is a success from start to finish.

In this chapter:

- Planning Your Project
- Understanding Color
  & Pattern
- Selecting Materials
- Using Décor to
  Create Atmosphere
- Discovering Your Style
- Sewing Techniques
- Painting &
  Carpentry Techniques
- Home Décor Tools

Planning Your Project

The first step in planning any decorating project, large or small, is to analyze the room in which the project will take place. Consider what you like best about this room—and what you would like to change. Make notes about your initial impressions of changes you'd like to see, including key words about how you'd like the room to feel when your project is complete.

Remember, there is no right or wrong way to coordinate the décor of a room. Collect samples of any carpeting, fabric, wallpaper, or paint that will remain in the room and bring them with you when purchasing new materials to help you coordinate the old and new. Page through decorating magazines for additional inspiration. Consult salespeople, designers, websites and friends for helpful suggestions. The general guidelines laid out in this chapter can also help you make good decisions. Ultimately, however, your own preferences and sense of style are the most important consideration in any decorating decision. Each project in this volume can be customized thousands of different ways to suit your taste, so follow your instincts to achieve a decorating scheme you'll love in the end.

A well-thought-out combination of colors, patterns, and texture are presented here. The color scheme is related (see page 10), the patterns work well together (see page 12), and the wainscot wall ties together the overall formal feel (see pages 60 and 64).

Use warm tones such as red, orange, brown, or natural to create a space that is intimate, cozy, or dramatic.

To create an illusion of more space, paint walls and trim white or pale cool colors. Cool colors recede from view, making walls feel farther away than they really are. Cool colors (see page 11) are also calming.

Planning Considerations ▸

Light: Carefully observe the natural light in your project room at various times of the day and the artificial light available at night. Write down where you'd like to create, soften, accent, or utilize light to beautify your décor.

Color: Decide which colors in the room you want to keep, and decide on new colors to introduce to play up the strengths of the room. Consider how color contributes to the overall mood of the room—does the space appear too bland, or are the colors overwhelming the space? Does your color scheme appear outdated? Notice how the colors play off of one another and consider how to modify and/or accent this interplay.

Material selection: Notice the materials currently present in the room that make up the floor surface, walls, trim, ceiling, fixtures, windows, and furniture. Decide what materials you like best, and consider how adding new materials will complement or contrast with the existing elements of the room. Research the techniques you'll need to master to work with new materials.

Pattern: Rooms with several printed or patterned surfaces can appear cozy and small, whereas rooms with many solid surfaces tend to be restful and expansive. Consider the needs of your room and how using patterns with fabrics, decorative painting, ceramic tile, or other techniques could help you achieve your design goals.

Functionality: Your home should be a livable space. Always consider the durability and day-to-day functionality of any design decision during the planning stage. Will your floor surface be subjected to daily wear and tear? Will children be using this space, and are your design decisions child-proof? Select materials and techniques that will fit with your day-to-day life as well as with your decorative taste.

Understanding Color & Pattern

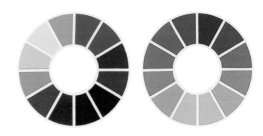

Most home decorators have an instinctive sense of how to choose effective color combinations, but the majority of us could benefit from a little more color theory to enhance our color combination decisions. Basic color theory is illustrated with a color wheel. The color wheel shows how colors are related and can help guide decisions about which colors work best together, and the effect they have on a room's overall décor.

The color wheel illustrates how basic colors are related. Red, yellow, and blue are primary colors. Orange, green, and purple are secondary colors made by combining two primary colors. Neutral colors are shades of white, gray, or beige (image right).

Basic Color Theory

Related colors, sometimes called analogous, are next to one another on the color wheel. Related colors harmonize naturally; many decorators use various shades of two related colors in one room.

Complementary colors are located opposite one another on the color wheel. Taupe and moss (shown here) are complementary colors within a neutral scheme. Decorating with complementary colors adds intensity when used within bold color schemes and adds interest in neutral color schemes.

Monochromatic colors are all within a single family (shown here, green) but are presented in various lightnesses and saturations. This scheme looks clean and elegant, resulting in a soothing effect.

Neutral colors are shades of white, gray, or beige. Most neutrals are tinted slightly with another color, which is good guidance when choosing accessory colors for pillows, curtains, and other accessories. Use the color wheel to choose complementary or related colors based on the tint color of the main shade in the room.

Dimensions of Color

Color is so much more than what the very important, if overly simplistic, color wheel can illustrate. Colors also vary in value, temperature, and brightness.

Value is a color's lightness or darkness (see vertical axis on diagram) and is determined by the amount of black or white that is in a color. Using a mixture of light, medium, and dark values of the same color in one space is called a *monochromatic* scheme. Using color in this way is subtle, sophisticated, and calming. Light color combinations create bright, spacious rooms and can make rooms appear larger and ceilings higher. Light colors reflect light well and can brighten and expand small spaces. Dark color combinations create intimacy, and can make rooms feel small and cozy. Dark colors absorb light, can disguise problem areas, and create drama. Large swaths of dark colors can be very dominant— you may want to break up a dark room with light accents for balance.

Saturation describes the brightness of a color and works around the color wheel (see rounded arrows in the center of the diagram). Bright colors, on the outside of the circle, are intense and undiluted by a neutral color. Subdued colors, closer to the center, are diluted with a neutral color or a complementary hue. Bright colors demand attention and are a great choice for active, creative spaces or in rooms that receive little natural light. Bright colors are often used as accents or can be paired with neutral elements; an entirely bright-colored room can be bold and energetic. Subdued colors are diluted with neutral colors and create restful, relaxing spaces. They are clean and modern and can be effectively accented with one or two bright colors used sparingly.

Temperature describes how warm or cool a color is, according to its position on the color wheel (see horizontal axis on the diagram). Reds, oranges, yellows, and browns are warm colors; greens, blues, and purples are cool colors. Intense warm colors create stimulating social spaces, perfect for dining rooms or kitchens. Research has shown that people actually feel warmer in a room painted in a warm color, so that may be a great choice for warming up homes in cold climates. Cool colors are fresh and tranquil, perfect for rooms that receive abundant sunlight. Using cool colors in warm climates can make a home feel more comfortable year-round.

The orange rug and brown walls add warmth to an otherwise cold, stark loft with steel stairs and concrete floors. The wood stair treads, curvy couch, and oval pendant lights all add natural elements and shapes to further soften the room, resulting in a blend of industrial loft design and a warm atmosphere.

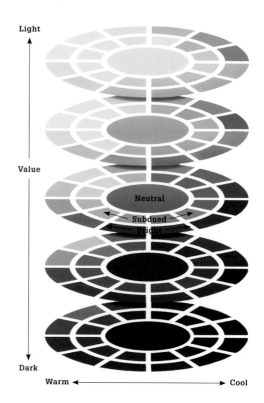

Understanding Patterns

There are six basic categories of patterns in decorating, and any design scheme may use several of them in the same room. Start with an overall plan, taking into account the architecture of your home and the ambiance you'd like to evoke.

Solids are used in flooring, carpeting, walls, wallcoverings, and window treatments. Calm and contemporary, solids are a classic choice that will never go out of style.

Geometric prints are dominant and stimulating, and help move the eye around a room. To prevent a room from looking too busy, balance intense geometric prints with solid-colored accents.

Stripes can be used to great affect all over the home—in window treatments, furnishings, and painted on walls and ceilings. Stripes can expand small spaces and are very elegant in subdued colors.

Combination prints use two or more of the previous patterns and work best in large areas. Six or more patterns can be used effectively in one room if you have a balance of color along with pattern size and scale.

Patterns take up more visual weight than solid expanses of color. Contemporary rooms usually forgo bold or aggressive patterns in favor of solid-color fabrics on large upholstered pieces. Traditional rooms require a minimum of pattern for authenticity. When pattern is desired, choose subtle color combinations such as those featured in tone-on-tone stripes or damask patterns, and use sparingly.

Overall prints and florals are effectively used on wallcoverings, large furniture pieces, or flat window treatments, such as window shades or valances. As accents, overall prints add a spark of interest to quiet spaces. As the dominant decorative element, overall prints create energy and fun and are a great choice for social or creative spaces.

Experiment with pattern scale with sketches or collages of your room. Typically, patterns close together make a room appear cozier, while patterns far apart can make a room appear more spacious. Dense patterns allow accents and furniture in the room to stand out, making it easy to create focal points even if the pattern is large.

Designer Tip: Working with Color and Pattern ▸

- **Repeat one strong-patterned print** at least once or twice in the room. For example, a strong print in a sofa could be repeated in a valance, or in a cushion across the room.
- **Repeat strong accent colors** more than once in a room.
- **More than four patterns** in one room can work, but the effect will be stimulating and eclectic.
- **Mini-prints** can easily be overdone. Do not use more than two very small prints in the same area.
- **Have fun!** Do not be afraid to let the prints and colors you choose reflect your personal taste.

Selecting Materials

Careful material selection ensures that your project will turn out the way you've envisioned it in your mind's eye. Research your options and question your salesperson about differences between materials and brands before you make your final selections.

Selecting Fabric

Selecting the right fabric for your decorating project can affect your success. Always consider how the fabric's durability, formality, weight, and care will affect your project. Use the chart at right as a basic guide to various fabric types and uses. Consult a salesperson at your fabric store before you purchase fabric to determine whether or not the fabric you love will work well for your project.

Always carefully calculate the yardage you'll need to purchase according to your project's specifications before you purchase fabric. It's usually a good idea to buy slightly more fabric than you think you'll need to help accommodate for small mistakes, or to add decorative accents, if possible. Also, remember that fabric bolts often come from different dye lots. To avoid problems of slight color variations or differences in pattern printing, buy all fabric for a large project from only one bolt.

Fabric Terms to Know ▶

Fiber is the basic unit of yarn before it is made into fabric. Fiber content affects durability and care.

Blends are the best qualities of two or more fibers combined in one fabric.

Decorator fabrics are designed for decorating projects. They are usually wider than 48" and often have special finishes that are desirable for home décor projects.

Fashion fabrics are used primarily for fashion sewing; however, fabrics such as calico, poplin, cotton, gingham, sateen, and muslin may also be used for the home.

Repeat is the size (length and width) of the pattern or motif printed on the fabric. You will usually need to buy one extra repeat for each length of fabric you use. The size of the repeat is often printed on the label or selvage.

Selvage is the finished lengthwise edge of a woven fabric.

Grain is the direction in which fabric threads run.

Working with Decorator Fabric

Some decorator fabrics should not be pre-washed. Many are treated with finishes to protect their beauty and resist soiling. Washing may remove this finish, alter the fabric, or fade the colors. Check the care label on the end of the bolt to learn how best to prepare the fabric.

Decorator fabrics are often made of natural fibers, which include cotton, linen, silk, and wool. Natural fibers are breathable, comfortable, and easy to sew. If decorating outdoor areas, however, choose a fade-resistant, acrylic or polyester decorator fabric that looks and feels like a natural fiber fabric. These fabrics will resist stains and mildew and will fade less quickly.

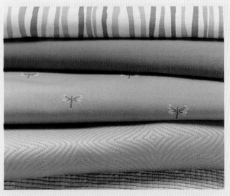

Decorator fabrics are available in countless colors, weaves, and styles. Always carefully choose the right fabric for your project.

Fabric Selection Guide ▸

Fabric	Weight	Formal/Informal	Decorative Uses	Durable	Care
Antique Satin	Heavy	Formal	Draperies, upholstery, cushions, tablecloths, slipcovers	Yes	Dry-clean
Batiste	Light	Formal/informal	Under curtains, casual curtains, balloon shades	No	Machine-wash
Broadcloth	Light to medium	Informal	Curtains, soft shades, bed linens, pillows, cushions, table linens, shower curtains	Yes	Machine-wash
Brocade	Heavy	Formal	Draperies, bedcovers, pillows, cushions, tablecloths, slipcovers	Yes	Dry-clean
Calico	Light to medium	Informal	Curtains, pillows, table linens	Yes	Machine-wash
Chintz	Medium to heavy	Formal/informal	Curtains, draperies, upholsteries, shower curtains, cushions, Roman shades, slipcovers	Yes	Dry-clean
Damask	Medium	Formal	Draperies, upholsteries, bedcovers, tablecloths, slipcovers	Yes	Machine-wash or dry-clean
Dimity	Light	Formal	Under curtains, soft shades	No	Machine-wash
Duck	Heavy	Informal	Draperies, slipcovers, Roman shades	Yes	Machine-wash or dry-clean
Gingham	Light	Informal	Curtains, soft shades, tablecloths, napkins	Yes	Machine-wash
Lawn	Light	Formal	Curtains, under curtains, pillows, napkins	Yes	Machine-wash
Lace	Light	Formal	Curtains, tablecloths	Varies	Machine-wash or dry-clean
Matelasse	Heavy	Formal	Draperies, upholsteries, slipcovers	Yes	Dry-clean
Moiré	Light to medium	Formal	Draperies, curtains, tablecloths	Yes	Machine-wash or dry-clean
Muslin	Light	Informal	Curtains, table linens, linings	No	Machine-wash
Organdy	Light	Formal/informal	Curtains, under curtains	No	Machine-wash
Percale	Medium	Informal	Curtains, bed linens, table linens	Yes	Machine-wash
Sateen	Light to medium	Formal	Curtains, bed linens, table linens, draperies	Yes	Machine-wash
Satin	Medium to heavy	Formal	Draperies, curtains, pillows, bed linens, Roman shades, upholsteries, slipcovers	Yes	Machine-wash or dry-clean
Shantung	Light to medium	Formal	Draperies, curtains	Yes	Dry-clean
Suede cloth	Heavy	Formal/informal	Cushions, draperies, upholsteries, slipcovers	Yes	Dry-clean
Taffeta	Light to medium	Formal	Draperies	Yes	Machine-wash or dry-clean
Velvet	Medium to heavy	Formal	Draperies, upholsteries	No	Dry-clean
Voile	Light	Informal	Curtains, under curtains, balloon shades	No	Machine-wash

Selecting Paint

Interior paints are either water based (latex) or oil based. Latex paint is easy to apply and clean up and suitable for nearly every interior application. Oil based paints sometimes create a smoother finished surface but also require longer drying times and harsh solvents for clean up. For small projects such as stenciling or detailing and for some faux finishes, you may also use specialty craft paints, which are generally water based.

Choosing a quality paint will save you time in extra coats now and in repairs and repainting in the future. Because quality paint is more durable and washable, the pigments will remain bright, even when scrubbed or washed repeatedly. Paint coverage for quality paints should be about 400 square feet per gallon. Bargain paints may required two or even three coats to cover the same area as quality paints. Paint prices are usually an accurate reflection of quality. As a general rule, buy the best paint your budget can afford.

Always purchase a good primer to coat surfaces before painting. Primer is designed to bond well to a bare surface and creates a durable base that keeps the finish coat from cracking or peeling. When using deep colors, use a tinted primer to reduce the number of coats necessary for good coverage. Ask your retailer to help you find the best tint for your project.

Quality paint lasts longer, covers beautifully, and will usually end up costing less than bargain paints in the long run.

Estimating How Much Paint to Buy ▸

1) Length of wall or ceiling (feet)	
2) Height of wall, or width of ceiling	×
3) Surface area	=
4) Coverage per gallon of chosen paint	÷
5) Gallons of paint needed	=

Types of Paint ▸

Paint	Characteristics & Applications
Flat latex	No sheen; for walls and ceilings
Satin latex	Low sheen; for walls, ceilings, trim
Semigloss latex	Slightly glossy sheen; for walls and trim; durable
High-gloss latex	Reflective sheen; for doors, cabinets, trim; washable; durable
Satin-enamel latex	Low sheen; smooth, hard finish; for trim and furniture
Gloss-enamel latex	Very glossy; smooth, hard finish; for trim and furniture
Oil-based enamels	Very glossy sheen; smooth, hard finish; for trim and furniture

Selecting Trim

Before you design your new trim project, choose the style of molding that is most appropriate for your overall home decor. Balance and scale, existing furnishings, and the applied finish will all change the effect your project has on the room. To narrow down your style options, focus on the overall result you'd like to achieve in the room—is your style simple and modern, formal and decorative, or classic and streamlined?

Scale, the size of an object in relation to its surroundings, is a very important consideration in trim selection. Moldings that are too large or small might not impact a room the way you had planned. Moldings that are well balanced create a sense of stability and proportionality. For example, if you have tall base moldings, the crown or cornice treatment should be similar in scale or the room will feel imbalanced.

Playing with Scale ▶

Generally, our eyes do not like surprises when it comes to scale. However, it is possible to create effective illusions by violating the normal rules of proportional scale. For example, the elaborate crown detail shown here makes this standard-height room appear to have a taller ceiling. But use caution—if not handled graciously, the trick can backfire and make your room feel cluttered.

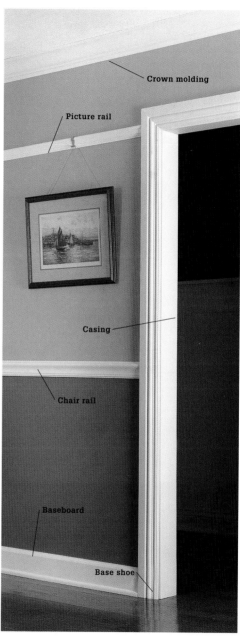

Crown molding

Picture rail

Casing

Chair rail

Baseboard

Base shoe

The style of trim in this example is well balanced. The individual elements are similar in color and molding profile and do not overpower each other with strong differences in size.

Using Décor to Create Atmosphere

A good way to define parameters for color, pattern, and material decisions is to establish the atmosphere or mood you'd like your room to take on. A good way to start is to list five words that describe how you'd like your newly decorated room to look and feel. These words can evoke instincts about color, fabric patterns, texture, furniture styles, and woodwork. For example, a kitchen that is described as sunny, bright, clean, crisp, and cheery will look very different from a kitchen described as rich, warm, mellow, cozy, and traditional.

Return to your chosen descriptive words throughout your decorating process, as you decide on projects, materials, finishes, fabrics, and techniques. Remember that each decision in the design process is completely up to you—so have fun and express yourself!

This neutral, related scheme of blues, grays, and tans is warmed up by adding a subtle yellow tone: notice the warmed wall color, brown throw pillows, and yellow hues in the dresser. Neutral schemes and cool colors are known for being restful and good choices for bedrooms. The white accents allude to a fresh and clean space. All of this surely results in sweet dreams!

Decorating Schemes

Bold schemes are created with high-contrast tones, such as whites and blacks, and complementary colors. Hard-edged geometric patterns and dark walls also contribute to these striking designs. Bold schemes work especially well in entryways and foyers and can also be appropriate in kitchens and living rooms.

Subtle schemes are restful and open, often using subdued complementary colors. They often include a careful balance of warm- and cool-toned elements. Subtle schemes are always a safe choice and are appropriate for any room in your home.

Cheerful schemes are created by using light, saturated colors that make the room seem larger. To maintain an open feeling, use low-contrast, pastel furnishings and minimal window treatments for maximum sunlight. Multiple patterns can be combined to great success in a cheerful scheme; this style works well in any frequently used room and in children's rooms.

Tranquil schemes use cool related colors with low contrast. To unify the room, use coordinating patterns that repeat the color scheme in draperies, artwork, rugs, and other accents. Use a tranquil scheme in rooms that serve as relaxing retreats, such as bedrooms, bathrooms, sunrooms, or living areas.

(continued)

Formal schemes use rich fabrics and classically detailed furniture and window treatments. To create a more intimate atmosphere, choose a rich, dark color for the walls. Guest bedrooms, dining rooms, powder rooms, and parlors are all well suited for a formal decorating scheme.

Natural schemes use neutral colors and fabrics, well-chosen accents and earthy textures. Often, the warmth of brown tones is balanced with light cool colors, such as blue and gray. Libraries, family rooms, and bedrooms often feature a natural scheme.

Guidelines for Creating a Décor Scheme ▸

Atmosphere Key Words	Suggested Colors	Fabrics & Textures	Projects to Consider
Cheerful	Bright, clear colors: pink, yellow, blue, green, orange	Bold florals, geometric or combination patterns, lightweight cotton blends, sateens, laces	Tiling backsplash, painting polka dots, applying sticker art, button-tufting cushion, making tab curtains
Comfortable, casual	Autumn colors: rust, tan, gold	Smooth to lightly textured finishes, sheers, polished cottons, sateens, casements	Installing wood shelves, installing carpet squares, making chair slipcovers, making draped window treatments
Conservative, clean & neat, tidy, crisp	Light colors, warm tones: white, mauve, peach, ecru, maize	Woven fabrics, nubby textures, all-over prints, sheer linens, cottons, suede cloths	Installing wainscot panels, trimming wall openings, applying faux grasscloth, making an upholstered ottoman, making upholstered valances
Contemporary	Neutral tones: beige, gray, ivory, cream	Textured or smooth fabrics: simple designs, solids, casements	Applying veneer plaster, hanging glass shelves, applying a faux stainless steel finish, making a photo montage table, making tent-flap curtains
Cozy, restful	Soft to medium shades: blue, mauve, green	Softly padded or quilted fabrics, inviting prints: sheers, percales, sateens, broadcloths	Applying color-blended bands, upholstering walls, paneling a ceiling, making an upholstered headboard, making a scarf swag
Elegant, refined	Dark, rich colors: taupe, gold metallic, ecru — and clean neutral accents	Shiny fabrics or fabrics with sheen: silks, antique satins, moirés, decorative trims	Installing crown molding, applying a wallcovering panel, applying faux-serpentine finish, aluminum roll gilding, wood graining mahogany, making a cloud shade
Practical	Multi-colors, medium shades: red, blue, orange	Washable or stain-resistant fabrics, over-all prints: sheetings, cotton blends	Installing a basement window casing, hanging pictures and mirrors, installing a bifold door, painting wood floors, painting a furniture piece, making rod-pocket curtains
Romantic	Fresh colors: pastel pink, blue, green, ivory; clean white	Sensory fabrics with texture or elegant prints, florals, laces, eyelets	Installing decorative wallboard panels, installing a built-up cornice, installing two-color meshing, stenciling a floor, making a butterfly shade, making tietop curtains
Tailored, masculine	Earth tones, rich colors: rust, brown, intense blue and green	Geometrics, plaids, stirpes: upholstery fabrics, tapestries	Creating architectural detail with wallboard, applying veneer plaster, installing a tiled fireplace surround, installing a decorative door header, creating a faux leather tabletop, making a buttoned valance
Traditional, classic	Reliable colors: green, white, blue, burgundy	Timeless fabrics: antique satins, jacquards, matelasses, linens, velvets	Installing wainscot frames, installing a chair rail, painting stripes, applying built-up cabinet molding, making reversible seat slipcovers, painting radiators, making roller shades, making bias swags

Discovering Your Style

Even after you've assessed the needs of your room, planned out your projects, and established the atmosphere you'd like to create, the most important factor in your home décor may still be a mystery—your personal decorating style. Focusing on one general decorating style throughout your home will unify your décor from room to room and will help guide many steps in the decision-making process.

There are several ways to discover your style. The first and least expensive is to go to furniture stores—both online and brick-and-mortar. What rooms attract you? What repels you? Do you prefer florals and ruffles or glass and chrome? What do the rooms you like have in common? The rooms you dislike? As you look around, take notes and make sketches.

Looking at magazines and decorating books is another great way to discover your style. As you flip through the pages, ask yourself the same type of questions you asked at the furniture stores and websites. Take note of your responses and look for common threads.

Creating a collage is one of the best exercises to kick off a decorating project. Just find some decorating magazines and cut out images that appeal to you—it doesn't matter what they are or why you like them. The only criteria is that the images strongly appeal to you. Once you've collected several images, paste them together in a collage (poster board works well as a base). When making your collage, don't think or plan too much. Discovering the information hidden inside the images you've selected is what you're after and that only happens when you leave structured thought behind and play with the possibilities. Eventually, patterns will emerge, revealing your favorite colors, shapes, and textures.

Collect design magazines, color swatches, photographs that inspire you, travel books, favorite fabrics, and photographs of treasured furniture pieces or decorative accents to kick off your design challenge.

What's Your Decorating Style? ▶

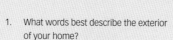

To take this quiz, check the answers that appeal to you most, then count the number of As, Bs, Cs, and Ds you have. Finally, consult pages 24 and 25 to find out what decorating style best suits you.

Minimalist

Romantic

Contemporary

Theme

Formal

1. What words best describe the exterior of your home?
   A. Angular and dramatic
   B. Traditional and elegant
   C. Simple and adaptable
   D. Reflects its setting

2. Which of these descriptions most closely matches the interior of your home?
   A. Streamlined rooms filled with straight lines and angles
   B. Cozy rooms accented with detailed moldings and trim
   C. Rooms filled with a wide variety of colors and shapes
   D. The style is closely tied to the exterior architecture

3. What textures appeal to you most?
   A. Flat matte or shiny surfaces
   B. Smooth surfaces with rich patinas
   C. Some of everything
   D. Natural textures such as rough-hewn wood, sisal, or terra cotta

4. What type of fabrics do you prefer?
   A. Textured fabrics in solid colors
   B. Chintzes and brocades
   C. A little of everything
   D. Hand woven with dramatic colors

5. What color combinations do you prefer?
   A. Muted or monochromatic with dramatic accents
   B. The colors of a garden
   C. Anything goes
   D. Bright, cheerful colors

6. What details draw you to an upholstered piece?
   A. Clean, spare lines
   B. Luxurious fabrics and elaborate trim
   C. You never can tell what might strike my fancy
   D. A dominant theme or motif

7. Which of these do you prefer?
   A. Streamlined shapes with simple details
   B. Button-tufting, nail-head trim, fringe
   C. The more details the better
   D. Homespun or handcrafted accessories

8. When it comes to art, what would you choose first?
   A. Modern or contemporary art
   B. Botanicals, landscapes, and still-life paintings
   C. Mementos and items of personal interest
   D. Wildlife art or pieces with themes related to nature

9. What type of materials would you most like to live with?
   A. Metal, stone, and glass
   B. Painted and stained wood, burnished metal, such as polished brass or nickel
   C. Distressed paint and patina on metals
   D. Terra cotta, rough plaster, and natural materials, such as bamboo

10. The perfect window treatment is:
    A. Nothing at all or the simplest possible shades or blinds
    B. Formal draperies with valances and swags
    C. Layers of fabric with details galore
    D. Simple shutters or flat fabric panels

Total

A = _____

B = _____

C = _____

D = _____

Decorating Style Quiz Results

IF YOU CHECKED MOSTLY As, YOUR STYLE IS LIKELY TO BE CONTEMPORARY.

Contemporary styles are based on furnishings developed from 1900 to the present. Contemporary-style homes embrace the Arts and Crafts, Art Deco, and Art Nouveau movements, as well as Asian, retro, and modern influences. Upholstered pieces have minimal seams and no adornments (such as tufting or buttons) for a streamlined look. Rooms are filled with straight lines and simple angles and typically include natural materials, such as wood, stone, metal, and glass. Color schemes tend to be muted or neutral. A limited amount of bright color is used as an accent. A few vintage pieces or natural elements, such as plants or trees, soften the angles and often strengthen the overall impact of the decor.

IF YOU CHECKED MOSTLY Bs, ROMANTIC STYLES ARE YOUR CUP OF TEA.

Romantic-style homes focus on the types of furnishings and accessories developed before 1900. This style includes Traditional, Victorian, and Country. Furnishings in these homes tend to include pieces upholstered with luxurious fabrics and elaborate trim. Rolled arms and kick pleats abound. So do the colors of a garden, detail-painted millwork, and carefully selected accessories. Window treatments typically include layers of fabrics and lots of details.

IF YOU CHECKED MOSTLY Cs, OR YOUR ANSWERS ARE EVENLY DIVIDED AMONG THE CHOICES, ECLECTIC MAY BE THE WAY TO GO.

Eclectic homes are the style equivalent of wearing your heart on your sleeve. They're a mix of period styles and personal mementoes. Many people refer to this style as Bohemian. *Eclectic* does not mean hodgepodge or Grandmother's attic. Every piece needs to be deliberately selected and carefully displayed to contribute to the whole. Although eclectic types generally follow no style rules but their own, they understand the value of editing their choices to create the best possible mix of styles, shapes, colors, and textures.

IF YOU CHECKED MOSTLY Ds, A THEMED STYLE IS LIKELY TO SUIT YOU.

Themed-style homes reflect a specific aspect of their environment or architecture. Southwestern, tropical, and rustic homes are examples of environmental theme styles. For example, an adobe house with a red tile roof calls out to be filled with rough textures, earth tones, handwoven fabrics, and the colors of the desert. Architectural themes are most successful if derived from the era in which your home was built. Some styles include Vintage, Antique, and the Old West. Every detail should relate back to this era—from trim moldings to rugs and sofas to lighting. It's important that the interiors of themed-style homes complement the exteriors and vice versa.

Sewing Techniques

Home décor sewing requires many techniques, from matching and cutting fabric to stitching seams, ruffles, welting, and hems—both by hand and with a sewing machine. Before you get started, familiarize yourself with these simple techniques, and gather the supplies shown on page 52.

Preparing Fabric

Before you begin, pre shrink your fabric, lining, zippers, and trims so the finished project won't shrink later. Launder everything as you intend to launder the finished item.

1. Check care instructions printed on the end of the fabric bolt before you launder. Machine-washing may remove sizing and other finishes that enhance the fabric's beauty and performance. Many upholstery fabrics should not be laundered.

2. If care instructions aren't available, launder a 6" square. Remove it from the dryer, press, and measure. Is it still a 6" square? Did it fade, ravel, or visibly lose its finish? If the results are good, preshrink the entire length of fabric the same way. If fabric ravels, zigzag-stitch the cut edges before laundering.

3. Press dried fabric to eliminate wrinkles.

4. If fabric can't be laundered, steam to preshrink it or have it dry-cleaned. To preshrink with steam, first steam-press a small scrap to test for damage. Dampen the fabric and press on the wrong side until the water evaporates.

5. If fabric is identical on both sides, choose one side as the right side and mark the wrong side so you won't confuse the sides when sewing.

6. Trim selvages before or after seaming or before hemming sides. Do not use the selvage as an edge.

7. Find the straight grain and straighten the cut ends, using a carpenter's square or T-square. Align one side of the ruler with the selvage and mark the perpendicular side with tailor's chalk.

Cutting & Matching Fabric

Work on a large, flat surface so you can lay the fabric straight and smooth. For most home décor projects, the fabric is cut in a single layer, with the right side up. This layout makes it easy to position and match design motifs. If fabric is directional, mark the top of the fabric and place all pattern pieces or cut all measured pieces in the same direction. For professional results, always match the pattern of a fabric at the seam lines. Extra yardage is usually needed in order to match the pattern.

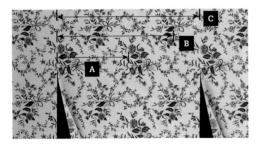

To calculate the amount of fabric you'll need, multiply the cut length by the number of fabric widths required for your project, and then add one pattern repeat. The pattern repeat is the lengthwise distance of one distinctive point on the pattern. This will be the total length in inches. Divide by 36" to determine the number of yards required.

To match patterned fabric, position fabric widths right sides together, matching selvages. Fold selvage back at one end until pattern matches. Press the foldline, and then pin and stitch on the foldline. Trim fabric to finished length (inset).

Machine Stitching

Most home decorating sewing can be done entirely by machine with a straight or zigzag stitch. Although machines vary in capabilities, each has the same basic parts and controls. Consult your machine manual to review threading procedures and to locate the controls that operate the principal parts. Also, select the appropriate needle and thread for your project's fabric to ensure quality stitching, and test your stitching on a scrap of fabric before stitching your project. Learn more about the sewing machine on page 52. There are a few machine-stitching terms you should know:

Tension is the balance between the upper and bobbin threads as they pass through the machine.

When tension is perfectly balanced, the stitches look even on both sides of the fabric because they link midway between fabric layers. Too-tight tension will cause seams to pucker; too loose results in weak seams.

Pressure regulates the even feeding of fabric layers. If too heavy, the bottom fabric layer gathers, causing unevenness. Too-light pressure may cause skipped stitches or crooked stitching lines.

Stitch length is the length of each stitch, and is measured in different scales depending on your machine. For normal stitching, set the regulator at 10 to 12 stitches per inch, or the equivalent.

Straight stitches should link midway between fabric layers so stitches are the same length on both sides of the fabric.

Zigzag stitching is adjusted correctly when the links interlock at the corner of each stitch. Stitches should lie flat.

Machine Stitching Terms

Baste stitching is the longest straight stitch on the machine. Some sewing machines have a separate built-in baste stitch that makes two stitches to the inch. Use it for speed-basting straight seams.

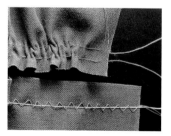

Gathering stitch is done with two rows of baste stitching placed ½" and ¼" from the fabric edge. Loosen tension, use a heavier bobbin thread, and pull up bobbin thread to form gathers. For long areas of gathers, zigzag over cord, string, or dental floss without catching the cord in the stitch. Pull up the cord to gather.

Edge stitching is placed on the edge of a hem or fold. Use a straight-stitch foot and straight-stitch needle for close control.

Gathering Ruffles

Use a ruffler attachment to make a test strip. Adjust ruffler to desired fullness. Before ruffling lightweight fabrics, zigzag ⅜" from the edge with the widest zigzag to give the ruffler teeth something to grasp.

Use a shirring foot, designed to lock fullness into every stitch with evenly spaced shirring. Set stitch length according to fullness desired; the longer the stitch, the greater the fullness.

How to Attach a Ruffle with a Heading

Hem both edges of the strip to be ruffled with a narrow double hem or overlock rolled hem. Gather the ruffle strip the desired distance from the upper edge.

Overlock the edge and press ½" to right side. Or, turn and stitch a double ¼" hem on the right side of the edge.

Place the wrong side of the ruffle on the right side of the fabric, with the gathering line on the hemline. Stitch the ruffle in place. Allow extra fullness at corners.

How to Apply Ribbon

Mark the trim location, using a marking pen. Use a glue stick to hold the trim in position.

Stitch both sides of the ribbon trim in the same direction to prevent diagonal wrinkles.

How to Miter Corners

Place two lengths of trim right sides together and edges even. Fold the top trim at a right angle to form a diagonal at the corner, and then press.

Slip-baste the two pieces together on the diagonal fold. Unfold the trim.

Stitch on the line of the slip basting on the wrong side. Trim the seams, and finish the edges.

Hand Stitching

Almost all home decorating sewing can be done on the machine, but sometimes hand stitching is necessary. Closing seam openings on pillows, attaching trims, and finishing hems are tasks that may require delicate hand sewing.

Running stitch is a straight stitch used for temporary basting, easing, gathering, or stitching seams. Work from right to left, taking several stitches onto the needle before pulling it through.

Slipstitch is a nearly invisible stitch for hems, seam openings, linings and trims. Work from right to left, holding the folded edge in the left hand. Bring the needle up through the fold and pull the thread through. Then, take a tiny stitch in the body of the fabric, directly opposite the point where the thread came out. Stitch every ¼".

Blindstitch makes a hem that is inconspicuous from either side. Work from right to left with the needle pointing left. Take a tiny stitch in the body of the fabric, roll hem edge back slightly, and take the next stitch in the underside of the hem every ¼ to ½". Do not pull the thread too tightly.

How to Sew a Simple Casing

A casing, or rod pocket, is the hem along the upper edge of a curtain or valance. The curtain rod is inserted through the casing so that the fullness of the curtain falls into soft gathers.

Determine the rod-pocket depth by loosely pinning a curtain fabric strip around the rod. Remove the rod and measure the distance from the top of the strip to the pin. Add ½" to be turned under.

Press under ½" along the upper cut edge of the curtain panel. Fold over again at the rod-pocket depth and press.

Stitch close to the inner folded edge to form the rod pocket, backstitching at both ends. If desired, stitch again close to the upper edge to create a sharp crease appropriate for flat or oval curtain rods.

How to Sew Double-fold Hems

Double-fold hems are the most common hem for home decorating projects. Insert drapery weights to help curtains and draperies hang nicely.

Turn a scant 3" to the wrong side on the lower edge of the curtain. Pin along the cut edge. Press fold. Turn under another 3", pin, and press in place. Finish the lower hem using one of the methods below.

Turn a scant 1" to the wrong side for the side hems. Pin and press. Fold under another 1". Pin and press. Tack weights inside the second fold at the side corners, if desired.

Press the side hems in place. When the hems have been pressed, finish them with straight stitching, machine blindstitching, or fusible web.

Basic Seams

All seams in home decorating projects are ½" unless otherwise specified. To secure seams, backstitch at each end.

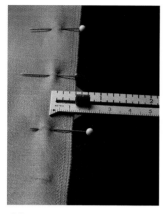  

Plain seams are suitable for almost every fabric and sewing application when you plan to enclose the seam or cover it with lining.

French seams eliminate raw edges in exposed seams. Use whenever a seam is visible on the wrong side or will be laundered frequently.

Interlocking fell seams completely enclose raw edges. Sew on the wrong side of the fabric. Use the narrow hemmer attachment (inset) to save time.

Making Welting

To make welting, cut fabric strips on the bias for greater flexibility around curved edges and corners. Strips do not have to be cut on the true bias; strips cut at an angle less than 45° provide the necessary flexibility but require less yardage.

The width of the fabric strips will depend on the size of the cording. To determine how wide to cut the strips, wrap a piece of fabric around the cording. Pin it together, encasing the cording. Measure this distance and add 1" for seam allowances. Cut fabric strips to this width.

Seam fabric together as necessary for desired length. Fold the fabric strip around the cording, wrong sides together, matching the raw edges. Using a zipper foot, machine-baste close to the cording; smooth the cording as you sew, removing any twists.

Measuring for the Bedroom

One of the simplest rooms to redecorate is the bedroom. Start with fabulous bed linens to set the stage. Easy-care and easy-to-sew fabrics—such as polyester/cotton sheeting, sateen, and cotton flannel—are ideal for bedroom fashions.

If you are decorating a guest room, consider luxurious satin, antique linen, and lace fabrics for bed coverings. If the room has another use—as an office, for example—choose tailored bed linens. Fabrics should be durable, machine washable, and crease, wrinkle, and soil resistant.

Mattresses have standard sizes, but the depth of the box spring and the mattress and the height of the bed frame may vary. Before you begin your project, measure your bed—with the sheets and blankets in place.

Mattress width and length: Measure across the top of the bed from edge to edge.

Mattress depth: Measure from the top edge to the bottom edge.

Full drop: Measure from the top of the mattress to ½" above the floor.

Comforter or duvet drop: Measure from the top edge of the mattress to 3 to 5" below the bottom edge of the mattress.

Dust ruffle: Measure from the top edge of the box spring to ½" above the floor.

Bed pillows: come in standard sizes, but fullness (loft) varies, so you might want to measure each pillow to ensure the best-fitting pillow cover.

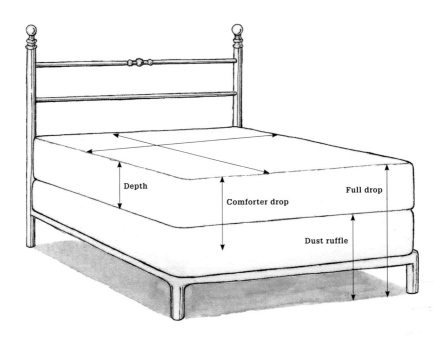

Standard Bed Pillow Sizes ▸

Name	Size
Standard	20 × 26"
Queen	20 × 30"
King	20 × 40"

Fabric Requirements for Bed Covers

Bed covers are large, so you usually need to piece fabrics—unless you work with sheeting, which is available in widths of 90 or 120". When piecing, try to avoid a center seam. It's much more attractive to have one wide center section with two narrower side sections.

Bedspreads and coverlets require only a top fabric. Comforter and duvet covers require a top and bottom fabric, and comforters also need a layer of batting. The amount of fabric you'll need depends on the fabric width and the size of the bed covering—and on the pattern repeat, if there is one.

Finished Bed Cover Length = [bed length] + [desired drop length] + [12 to 15" for pillow tuck, if desired]

Finished Bed Cover Width = [bed width] + [two times desired drop length]

Cut Length = [Finished bed cover length] + 4"

Cut Width = [Finished bed cover width] + 4"

To determine how many widths of fabric you need, divide the cut width by the fabric width. Round up the number.

To determine the total length of fabric you need to buy, multiply the number of widths you need by the cut length.

Painting & Carpentry Techniques

By mastering a few basic painting and carpentry techniques, you can tackle any home decorating project in this volume. Whether painting, cutting and attaching trim, or creating snug joints, familiarize yourself with these steps before you begin.

Paint Safety Tips ▸

Always wear safety goggles when using chemical strippers or cleaning products, or when painting overhead. Paint fumes are often hazardous, so ventilate indoor painting areas by opening doors and windows, and use a fan to move air in and out of the room. Wear a respirator to filter vapors if you cannot ventilate a work area adequately. When you're finished with your project, dispose of leftover latex primers and paint safely. Let the container stand uncovered until the paint dries completely. In most communities, dried latex paint can be put in the trash, whereas alkyd primers and paint must be disposed of as hazardous waste.

Read label information completely before you begin. Chemicals that are poisonous or flammable are labeled with warnings and instructions for safe handling.

Pour paint thinner into a clear jar after use. When the solid material settles out, pour off the clear thinner and save it to reuse later. Dispose of the sediment as hazardous waste.

Make a scaffold to reach ceilings and high spots by running an extension plank through the steps of two stepladders. The plank should be no more than 12 ft. long. Ladders should face away from each other, so the steps are on the inside.

Never stand on the top step, top brace, or utility shelf of a stepladder.

Center your weight on the ladder. Move the ladder often; do not overreach. Keep the ladder in front of you when working. Lean your body against the ladder for balance.

Painting Techniques

Painting a wall is a simple matter of distributing paint evenly and can be a fun and satisfying process as you watch your room transform before your eyes. Try to paint during daylight hours, as it's much easier to see missed areas in natural light. Use high-quality paint and tools, and work with full brushes and rollers to keep lap marks to a minimum.

When painting bare drywall or plaster, apply a coat of primer to the entire project area and let it dry before applying the paint. When applying dark or deep colors, (especially reds), ask your dealer to tint the primer to match the paint; tinted primer reduces the number of paint coats required for full coverage.

Roll one 2 × 4-foot section at a time, cutting in the edges and corners before rolling the main area. Roll the area while the areas that have been cut in are still wet, and start the next section while the edges of the first are still wet. This technique, called painting to a wet edge, keeps lap marks from showing on the finished wall.

Tools & Materials ▸

Paint
3" paintbrush
Paint roller and tray

Paint surfaces in small sections, working from dry areas back into wet paint to avoid roller marks.

How to Paint a Wall

Stir the paint using a variable-speed drill and paint-mixing bit. Set the drill on a low speed and keep the head of the bit in the paint until it completely stops turning. Paint separates quickly, so stir it thoroughly from time to time.

Cut in the edges of a 2 × 4-ft. section of the first wall using the narrow edge of a paintbrush. Press down just enough to flex the bristles. Use long, slow strokes, and paint from dry areas back into wet paint.

Cut in any corners in the section using the wide edge of the paintbrush or a specialty corner roller.

Use a roller loaded with paint to make a diagonal sweep about 4 ft. long on the wall. Roll upward on the first stroke to avoid spilling paint. Roll slowly to avoid splattering.

5

Draw the roller straight down from the top of the diagonal sweep. Shift the roller to the beginning of the diagonal stroke and roll upward to complete the unloading of the roller.

6

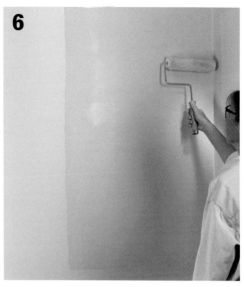

Roll back and forth across the section to smooth the area. Lightly draw the roller down the section from top to bottom. Lift the roller and start again at the top after each stroke. Finally, slide the roller cover slightly off of the roller frame and roll the cut-in areas to minimize brush marks.

7

Cut in and roll the section directly next to the first one. Continue with adjacent areas, cutting in and rolling the top sections before the bottom sections. Roll all finish strokes toward the floor.

Paint Color Consistency ▶

Paint, especially custom-mixed paint, can vary a tiny bit from one can to another. If using more than one bucket for your project, this may result in slight variations between paint colors from wall to wall. To avoid this common problem, mix the cans together in a large pail and stir it thoroughly before you begin. This technique is called boxing.

Painting Trim Moldings

Although you will need to apply a final topcoat after trim is installed, always prime and paint trim before installation. First, prime your trimwork on both sides to seal the piece, balancing the wood movement from humidity and temperature changes. After the primer is dry, apply two finish coats to the face. After the finish coats are dry, install the molding and fill in gaps in joints and fastener holes. The final step is to apply a touchup coat to the filler areas.

Use a high-quality brush to paint trimwork. Straightedge brushes around 2" are the tool of choice for many professional painters when painting moldings. If bristle marks are a concern, consider putting an additive in the paint. Paint additives thin the paint without affecting its durability or sheen. The end result is a paint that flows on smoother and lays out flatter when dry. Using an additive may require that you apply at least one additional coat.

After each coat of primer or paint is applied, carefully inspect each piece for drips or clots. These problems need to be dealt with immediately, or they will mirror through the final coat. Remember that multiple thin layers of paint look better and last longer than one heavy coat. Heavy paint layers will also hide any intricate details or crisp edging and could possibly make installation more difficult.

Tools & Materials ▸

Paintbrush
Paint
Cut bucket
Paint additive

Small paint roller
Mineral spirits
  or warm water

Using Additives ▸

Cut bucket

Pour a paint additive into the mix to reduce brush marks on the finished product. A cut bucket like the one above is easier to handle than a gallon pail and creates a convenient way to mix the products.

This baseboard has a very different appearance when it is painted. The finish you choose will alter the cost of your project as well.

Painting Trim Moldings

Dip the brush into the paint, loading one-third to one-half of its bristle length. Tap the bristles against the inside of the can to remove excess paint. Do not drag the bristles against the top edge, or rub them against the lip of a one-gallon can.

Paint moldings with thin, even coats starting along the deeper grooves of the trim, and moving on to the smooth areas. This sequence will minimize drips into the detail of the molding.

Use a small paint roller to coat long, straight strips of trim material. Rollers make for fast work and don't leave brush marks. If the paint is too thick or you roll too quickly, however, the roller can create an orange peel effect that you may not like.

Clean the brush with mineral spirits when using oil-based paint, or with warm water when using water-based. Shake out the brush and let it dry. Always start subsequent coats with a clean, dry brush.

Clear-coating Trim Moldings

Water-based and oil-based finishes have a few basic differences in application and end result that you should be aware of so that you can make the best decision about which product is right for you.

Not long ago, oil-based polyurethanes were regarded as much more durable and capable of providing more even coverage than water-based products. Today, this is not always the case. The major differences between modern oil and water urethanes are not related to finish quality as much as to secondary (but important) characteristics such as odor, finish appearance, and drying times. The durability of water-based products is no longer an issue. In fact, the most durable urethanes available are water based.

Oil products emit fumes during drying that can linger for weeks. Pregnant women and young children should avoid these fumes altogether. Water-based products create minimal fumes, and are not dangerous under normal conditions with adequate ventilation.

According to most manufacturers, water-based products dry faster than oil varieties. This literally means less time spent between coats. Water-based urethanes also clean up with soap and warm water, rather than with mineral spirits. Easy clean-up can come in handy for large spills.

The biggest factor to consider when choosing a type of polyurethane is finish appearance. Although water-based products offer many more conveniences than oil, the end results can be quite different. When oil-based urethanes are applied, they add a warm amber color to trimwork that creates more visual depth and variety.

Water-based products dry crystal clear. The color of the trim before the product is applied is similar to the finished product. Only a light color change appears. Keep in mind that most of the clear-finished trim in an older house is oil based and water-based finishes will not match.

The following examples run through the steps of successful clear-coat finishing. These steps are a guideline to finishing only. Always follow the manufacturer's specific application directions. Drying times will vary, depending on temperature and humidity.

Tools & Materials ▸

Bristle brush or foam brush	Drop cloth or cardboard
Latex gloves	Sawhorses
Stir sticks	Trim material
Paint can opener	Polyurethane
	Stain (optional)

Arts and Crafts Style trimwork is normally stained rather than painted to show off the grain detail of quartersawn white oak.

How to Apply a Clear Finish to Trim Moldings

Set up the work station area with a drop cloth or sheet of cardboard on the floor and two sawhorses. Place the trim pieces to be finished on the horses. Inspect each piece for large blemishes or flaws, repairing any large splinters.

Sand each piece as necessary, finishing with a fine-grit paper. Wipe the moldings with a clean, dry cloth to remove any leftover dust.

Apply a coat of stain, if desired, to the moldings with a foam or bristle brush. For more even coverage of the stain, apply a pre-stain wood conditioner. Follow the manufacturer's instructions for stain drying time, and remove the excess with a clean rag. Let the stain dry sufficiently.

Apply the first thin coat of polyure-thane with a brush. Stir the polyurethane frequently before you begin, between coats, and during application. Let the finish dry for four to six hours.

Lightly sand the entire surface with 220-grit sandpaper after the finish has dried. This will ensure a smooth finish with a strong bond between layers. If the sandpaper gums up quickly, the moldings need more time to dry. Use a clean, dry rag to remove dust.

(continued)

Apply a second layer of polyurethane. Check each piece for skipped areas and heavy drips of urethane. These areas need to be corrected as soon as possible or they may show through the final coat.

Lightly sand the entire surface of the moldings with 220-grit sandpaper after they have dried for four to six hours.

Apply a third and final coat of polyurethane to the moldings. Keep the third coat very thin, using only the tip of the brush to apply it. Lightly drag the tip across the molding on the flat areas. If the moldings have deep grooves or intricate details, skip these areas; two coats will be sufficient. Try to maintain constant pressure and avoid smashing the brush as this will create air bubbles in your finish. Allow the moldings to dry for a minimum of 12 hours (check manufacturer's recommended drying times).

Removing Old Trim

Damaged trim moldings are an eyesore and a potentially dangerous splinter waiting to happen. Removing trim so that it can be reused is not always easy, especially if you live in a home with intricate moldings. The age of your trim and the nailing sequence used to install it will greatly affect your ability to remove it without cracks or splits. Regardless of whether or not your trim can be reused, however, take your time and work patiently when you remove it so as not to damage the surrounding walls, floor, or ceiling.

How to Remove Painted Moldings

Before removing painted trim, cut along the top seam of the molding and the wall with a utility knife to free the molding from any paint buildup on the wall. Cut squarely on the top edge of the molding, being careful not to cut into the wallboard or plaster behind it.

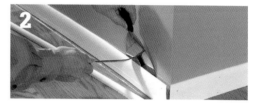

Work the molding away from the wall from one end to the other, prying at the nail locations. Apply pressure to the molding with your other hand to help draw it away from the wall. A wide joint compound or putty knife makes a good guard to insert bwteen the tool and the wall.

How to Remove Clear-finish Moldings

Remove the molding starting with the base shoe or the thinnest piece of trim. Pry off the trim with a flat bar using leverage rather than brute force, working from one end to the other. Tap the end of the bar with a hammer if necessary to free the trim.

Use large flat scraps of wood to protect finished surfaces from damage. Insert one bar beneath the trim and work the other between the base and wall. Force the pry bars in opposing directions to draw the molding away from the wall.

Removing Nails from Trim ▶

Extract nails from the moldings using end nips or side cutters. "Roll" the nails out rather than pulling them straight out. Or use a nail set to drive the nail through the molding from the front (inset).

Planning Trim Installation

Before you start your project, plan the order, layout, and type of joint at each end of the trim. Measure the corners accurately to ensure a snug fit.

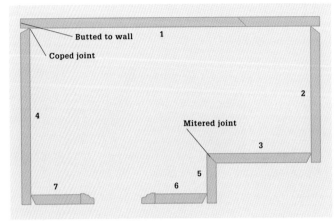

Plan the order of your trim installation to minimize the number of difficult cuts on individual pieces. Use the longest pieces of molding for the most visible walls, saving the shorter ones for less conspicuous areas. When possible, place the joints so they point away from the direct line of sight from the room's entrance. If a piece will be coped on one end and mitered on the other, such as with 3 (left), cut and fit the coped end first. Also keep in mind the nailing points—mark all framing members you'll be nailing into before starting the installation. At a minimum, all trim should be nailed at every wall stud, and every ceiling joist, if applicable. Install door and window casing before installing horizontal molding that will butt into it.

Miter outside corners, cutting each piece at 45°. Use a pattern with mitered ends to help position your workpieces. Fasten the first piece of each joint to within 2 ft. of the corner, leaving some flexibility for making adjustments when you install the adjoining piece.

Use the trim piece as a measuring device, marking the cut line directly off the wall. Eliminating the tape measure reduces errors and makes it easier to visualize the cut.

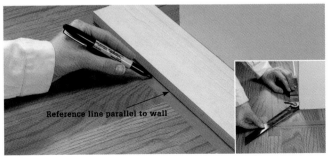

Draw a reference line off each wall of the corner using a straight 1 × 4. Trace along each wall, connecting the traced lines at a point out from the tip of the corner. To find the angle you need to miter your moldings, place a T-bevel with the handle flush against one wall and adjust the blade so that it intersects with the point (inset). Lock the blade in place.

Coped Cuts

At first glance, coping molding appears to be difficult work, but with patience and the right tools coping can be mastered by a DIYer. Coping is essentially cutting back the body of a trim piece along its profile. This cutting is done at an angle so that only the face of the molding makes direct contact with the adjoining piece.

How to Make a Coped Cut

Measure, cut, and install the first trim piece. Square-cut the ends, butting them tightly into the room corners, and nail the workpiece at the marked stud locations.

Cut the second piece of molding at a 45° angle as if it were an inside miter. The cut edge reveals the profile of the cope cut.

Starting with the most delicate edge of the molding, cut along the front edge of the molding with a coping saw, following the contour exactly. Bevel the cut at 45° to create a sharp edge along the contour.

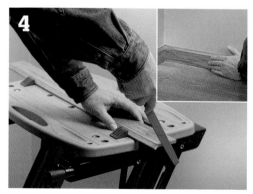

Test-fit the piece (inset photo) and use a metal file to fit the joint precisely. When the joint is properly fitted, nail the coped piece in place.

Tip ▸

Trim components such as this chair rail can be complex to cope properly. A variety of rasps or metal files with different profiles is the key to fitting these joints tightly.

Mitered Returns

Mitered returns are a decorative treatment used to hide the end grain of wood and provide a finished appearance when molding stops prior to the end of a wall. Mitered returns range from tiny pieces of base shoe up to very large crown moldings.

Tools & Materials ▶

Combination square
Utility knife
Power miter saw
Miter box
  and backsaw
Pencil
Tape measure

Pneumatic finish
  nail gun
Air compressor
Air hose
T-bevel
Molding
Wood glue

How to Cut Mitered Base Shoe Returns

Measure and mark the molding to length. Adjust the miter saw blade to 45° and back-miter the molding, cutting the front edge to the desired overall length of the trim. Nail the back-mitered piece in place using a square to line it up flush with the edge of the door casing.

Adjust the blade of the miter saw to the opposite 45° angle and miter-cut the molding using a slow, steady stroke.

Mitered return

Hold the mitered molding against the baseboard at a right angle above the installed base shoe. Mark the molding at the depth of the installed base shoe. Square-cut the molding at the cutoff mark. Because making this cut with a power saw is very dangerous, use a miter box and a back saw. The cut-off piece will be the mitered return piece.

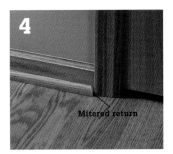

Mitered return

Check the fit of the return against the baseboard. If it is too small repeat step 3, making the piece slightly larger. If the return is too large, trim it to fit with a utility knife or sandpaper. Once the return fits properly, glue it in place with wood glue.

Beveled return

Option: Beveled returns are a quick and simple alternative to mitered returns. They require finish touchups after the trim is installed.

Scarf Joints

Scarf joints are mitered joints used to join two pieces of trim over a long length. This joint should always be laid out over a stud location so it can be properly fastened. Position scarf joints so they point away from the main entry to the room, which will hide the joint from view at a quick glance.

Tools & Materials ▸

Moldings
Miter saw
Wood fence extension
Pencil

Tape measure
Pneumatic finish
  nail gun
Wood glue

How to Cut a Scarf Joint

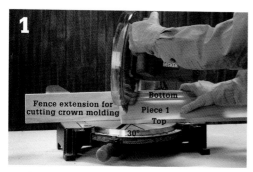

Cut the first piece of molding a couple of inches longer than its planned length at a 30° angle. This angle should be back-beveled or back-mitered so the molding will fit over the open-cut end of the second piece. If you are cutting crown molding and the molding is taller than the fence of your power miter saw, attach a wood fence extension to the fence so you can position the molding properly on the saw table (see "How to Install Wood Crown Molding," page 120).

Measure and cut the second piece of trim to length (so it will fall over a stud when installed), leaving the saw set at its original 30° angle. Make sure the second piece of molding is in the same orientation as the first (bottom edge up in photos above).

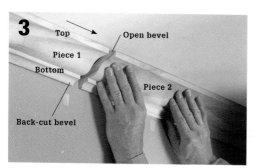

Test-fit the scarf joint on the wall (a helper is a great asset here). Have one person hold the piece with the open bevel (piece 2 above) in position while the other person places the piece with the back-cut bevel over it. Check for a tight joint and then mark the back-cut piece for trimming to final length (if both ends of the run are inside corners, you'll have to overlap the open-cut piece and mark for cutting to length).

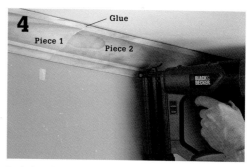

Tack the piece with the open bevel in position and apply wood glue (high-tack trim and molding glue are perfect here) to the open bevel. Reform the scarf joint and tack the back-cut piece in position. Finish nailing around the joint, and then work your way toward each end with the nailer.

Home Décor Tools

The decorating projects in this book will require you to work with a wide variety of materials, including fabric, wallcovering, paint, wood, trim moldings, stain, wallboard, tile, foam padding and polyester batting— even your own photographs. Whatever the project, familiarize yourself with the required tools before you begin project preparations for the highest quality result and easiest application process.

Essential Home Decorating Tools

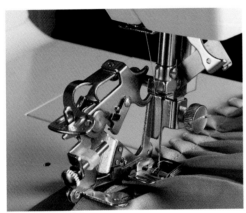

Specialized presser feet for sewing projects increase efficiency and prevent a lot of headache. Shown here is a ruffler attachment, which automatically gathers strips of light or mediumweight fabric. Refer to your sewing machine manufacturer for attachments that may help with your job.

A paint-mixing bit attached to a drill can speed up your preparations for painting projects.

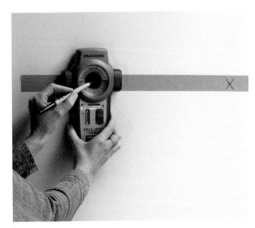

A stud finder takes the guesswork out of decorating projects, such as hanging pictures and mirrors or attaching trim moldings.

Keep multiple cleaning products on hand to prepare surfaces for decorating projects.

Preparation Materials

As each project in this book will remind you, preparation is key to a successful project and a professional-quality finish. Always take the time to prepare your work area before beginning.

Preparation liquids (A): A latex-bonding agent makes plaster repairs more durable; liquid deglosser dulls glossy surfaces so paint can adhere properly.

Wallpaper stripper (B): A chemical agent that loosens wallpaper adhesive so it can be removed easily.

Pressure sprayer (C): Used to apply wallpaper stripper over large areas.

Sponges (D): Used to smooth damp joint compound, which reduces the amount of sanding needed later.

Wood Filler (E): Compound used to fill holes in wood. It can be sanded and painted or stained.

Trisodium phosphate (F): Cleaning agent used for washing walls before painting or hanging wallpaper.

Hole-patching kits (G): Sturdy, self-adhesive mesh and backing materials used to repair large holes in walls.

Easy-release painter's tape (H): Tape designed for easy and clean removal (does not leave an adhesive residue).

Spackle (I): A quick-drying drywall compound. Some types of spackle are pink when wet and turn white as they dry, which makes it easy to tell when the patch is ready to be sanded.

Self-adhesive seam tape (J): Used to smooth drywall compound over joints and cracks.

Safety equipment (K): Rubber gloves, safety glasses, and dust masks or respirators; these are necessary when using strong or caustic chemicals.

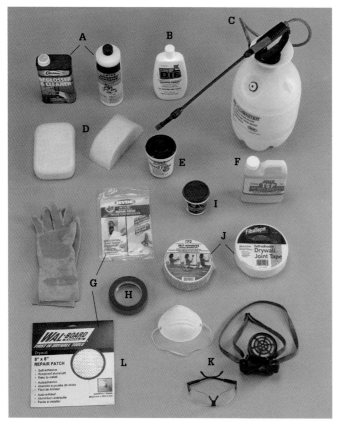

With the help of these tools and materials, project preparation can be smooth and easy.

Sewing Tools

Hand-sewing supplies: A pincushion and pins (A) are an absolute must for any sewing project; a thimble (B) protects your finger while hand sewing; a needle threader (C) makes threading machine or hand needles a breeze; select thread (D) appropriate for the fabric and sewing method you'll be using; beeswax (E) strengthens thread and prevents tangling.

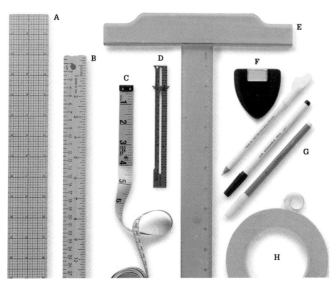

Measuring and marking supplies: A transparent ruler (A), yardstick (B), and tape measure (C) are each essential tools for various sewing projects; a seam gauge (D) helps make quick, accurate measurements; a transparent T-square (E) is used to locate grainlines and measure 90° angles; marking chalk (F), fabric marking pens (G), and narrow masking tape (H) can each be used for marking fabrics during decorating projects.

Cutting tools: Bent-handled dressmaker's shears (A) are ideal for cutting fabric shapes; sewing scissors (B) are used for clipping threads and seam allowances; seam rippers (C) are used to remove stitches and open buttonholes; rotary cutters (D) are perfect for cutting straight lines; pinking shears and pinking rotary cutters (E) cut fabric in zigzag or scalloped patterns and are used to finish seams.

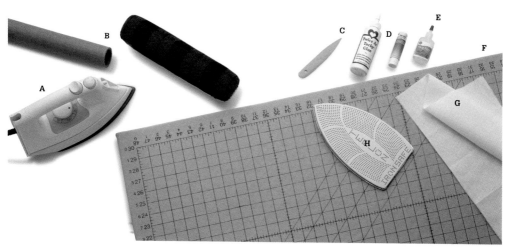

Other sewing supplies: A steam-spray iron (A) with multiple temperatures accommodates all fabrics; a seam roll (B) is used for pressing seams; a point turner (C) safely pokes out stitched corners; glues (D) hold trims or decorative motifs in place; liquid fray preventer (E) stiffens fabric and prevents fraying; cutting boards (F) protect your work surface; press cloths (G) or a Teflon-coated sole plate guards (H) help prevent iron shine on fabrics.

Understanding your sewing machine well will make fabric decorating projects quick and easy to complete. The principle parts common to all modern sewing machines are shown in the diagrams at right. The parts may look different on your model, and they may have slightly different locations, so refer to your manual as well. If you do not have an owner's manual for your machine, you should be able to get one from a sewing machine dealer who sells your brand—or download one from the manufacturer's website.

If you are buying a new machine, consider how much and what kind of sewing you expect to do. Talk to friends who sew and to sales personnel. Ask for demonstrations, and sew on a demo machine before you buy. Many dealers also offer free sewing lessons with purchase of a machine as well, which will be geared to your particular brand and model of sewing machine.

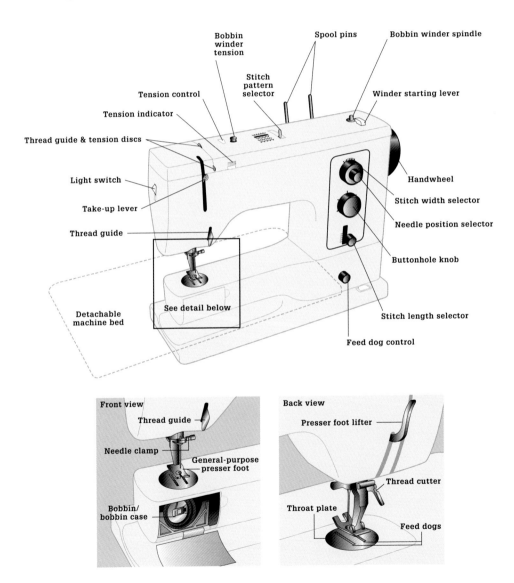

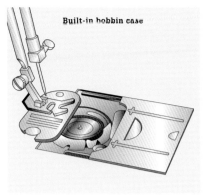

Built-in bobbin case

Removable bobbin case

The bobbin holds the lower thread that locks with the upper thread. Always use bobbins in the correct style and size for your machine. Bobbin thread tension is controlled by a spring on the bobbin case, which may be built in or removable.

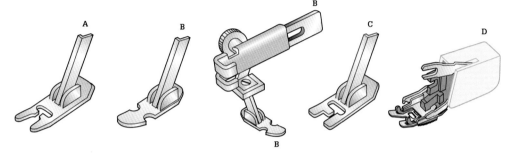

A general-purpose foot (A), probably the one you will use the most often, has a wide opening to accommodate the side-to-side movement of the needle in all types of utility (nondecorative) stitches. It is also suitable for most straight stitching. A zipper foot (B) is used to insert zippers or to stitch any seam that has more bulk on one side than the other. A special-purpose or embroidery foot (C) has a grooved bottom that allows the foot to ride smoothly over decorative stitches or raised cords. Some styles are clear plastic, allowing you to see your work more clearly. A walking foot (D) feeds top and bottom layers at equal rates, allowing you to more easily match patterns or stitch bulky layers, as in quilted projects.

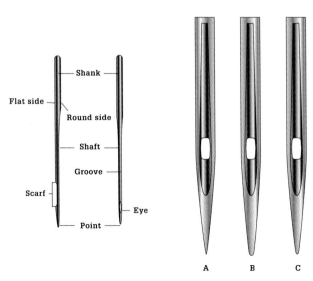

Sewing machine needles come in a variety of styles and sizes. The correct needle choice depends mostly on the fabric you have selected. Sharp points (A), used for woven fabrics, are designed to pierce the fabric. Ballpoints (B) are designed to slip between the loops of knit fabric rather than pierce and possibly damage the fabric. Universal points (C) are designed to work on both woven and knit fabrics. The size of the needle is designated by a number, generally given in both American (9, 11, 12, 14, 16, 18) and European (60, 70, 80, 90, 100, 110) numbering systems. Use size 11/70 or 12/80 needles for medium-weight fabrics. A large number means the needle is thicker, and that it is appropriate for use with heavier fabrics and threads.

Painting Tools

When it comes to painting tools, some people prefer disposable tools while other value traditional versions. The difference between the two are cost and quality.

Paintbrushes: All-purpose brushes are made from a blend of polyester and nylon. Brushes blended with hog or ox bristles should be used only with oil-based paints. Your kit should include a 3" straightedged wall brush, 2" straightedged trim brush, and tapered sash brush. A good-quality brush has a shaped handle, non-corrosive metal ferrule, and several spacer plugs between bristles. Split (flagged) and tapered (chiseled) bristle ends make clean edges.

Roller trays: Sturdy trays are a must. Disposable pan liners minimize cleanup, but they are not substitutes for roller trays.

Standard roller frames: Choose a well-balanced frame with nylon bearings and a comfortable handle. Extensions are available for painting ceilings.

Standard roller covers: Most jobs can be done with ⅜" synthetic rollers. Special corner roller covers allow you to paint corners without cutting in the edges. Good-quality roller covers create an attractive finish without leaving fibers in the paint.

Special containers: Large and small containers simplify large projects. For large projects, some paint manufacturers sell their paint in 5-gallon containers, so you can paint straight from the container. If the paint you choose doesn't come in a container like this, you may want to buy one. For cutting-in and touchups, small, easy-to-hold containers are a good idea.

Paint-mixing bit and drill: Stirring paint is extremely important. The best way to stir large amounts of paint is with a drill and special paint-mixing bit. These bits are easy to use and clean up quickly.

Lead test kit: If your home was built before 1978, it's critical that you test paint before cleaning, sanding, or repainting it. Easy-to-use lead test kits are available at home centers, hardware stores, and paint retailers everywhere. If the test indicates the presence of lead, consult a lead abatement specialist before starting any project.

Choosing a Paintbrush ▸

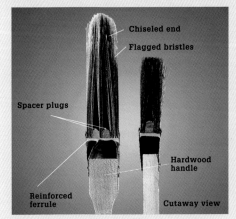

Chiseled end

Flagged bristles

Spacer plugs

Hardwood handle

Reinforced ferrule

Cutaway view

A **quality brush (left),** has a shaped hardwood handle and a sturdy reinforced ferrule made of noncorrosive metal. Multiple spacer plugs separate the bristles. A quality brush has flagged (split) bristles and a chiseled end for precise edging. A cheaper brush (right) will have a blunt end, unflagged bristles, and a cardboard spacer plug that may soften when wet.

A **3" straight-edged brush (top)** is a good choice for cutting paint lines at ceilings and in corners. For painting woodwork, a 2" trim brush (middle) works well. Choose brushes with chiseled tips for painting in corners. A tapered sash brush (bottom) can help when painting corners on window sashes.

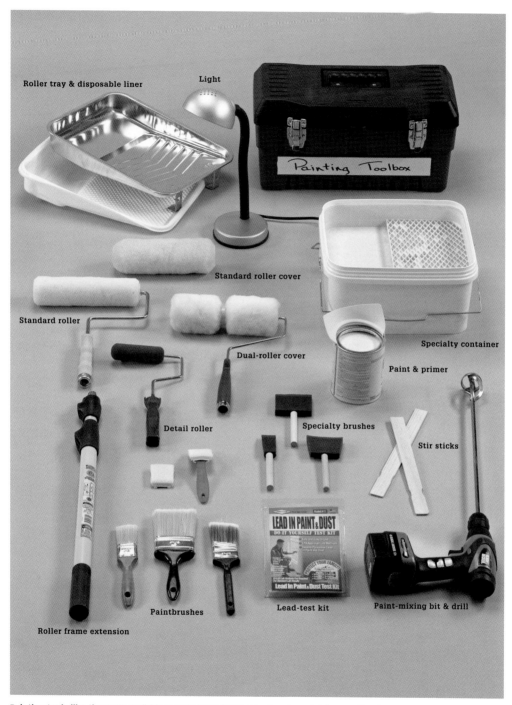

Roller tray & disposable liner

Light

Painting Toolbox

Standard roller cover

Standard roller

Dual-roller cover

Specialty container

Paint & primer

Detail roller

Specialty brushes

Stir sticks

LEAD IN PAINT & DUST
DO IT YOURSELF TEST KIT
Lead in Paint & Dust Test Kit

Roller frame extension

Paintbrushes

Lead-test kit

Paint-mixing bit & drill

Painting tools like these are available at every home improvement center, paint store, and hardware store.

Decorating Tools

Basic decorating tools like the ones shown here are a must for any burgeoning decorator. Before you begin your project, check to make sure that you have all the tools you'll need on hand.

Carpenter's or laser level: A carpenter's level contains two or more bubble gauges used to check the level of work surfaces. A laser level creates level, square lines on any surface.

Hammer: Designed for driving, setting, and pulling nails, hammers are essential. A 16-ounce, curved claw hammer with a high-carbon steel head and a handle made of hickory, fiberglass, or solid steel is a practical choice for typical home repairs.

Drill: Variable-speed reversing drills are handy for driving and removing screws, nuts, and bolts, as well as for drilling holes and stirring paint. For most decorating projects, a medium-voltage cordless drill is a good choice. Look for features such as a keyless chuck, adjustable clutch, and electronic level.

Cordless screwdriver: For small projects, cordless power screwdrivers are a great alternative to standard screwdrivers. These tools come with a universal ¼" drive as well as a slotted bit and a #2 Phillips bit. Other bits, such as Torx and square drive, are also available.

Power sander: Sanders smooth surfaces to be painted or decorated.

Screwdriver: Standard screwdrivers—both slotted and Phillips—are essential. Choose quality screwdrivers with hardened-steel blades and easy-to-grip handles. Insulated handles protect you from electric shock, and oxide-coated tips provide a strong hold on screw heads.

Tape measure: A high-quality, retractable steel tape measure will last for decades. Choose a tape that has a locking mechanism and a belt clip. Make sure the tape you choose has a standout of at least 7 feet.

Stud finder: A stud finder has an indicator that lights up when it passes over a stud.

Awl: An awl is a tool that has a metal shaft with a sharpened end. It is used to poke holes in drywall and other surfaces when drilling a pilot hole isn't necessary.

Nail set: This is a metal shaft with a rounded end that is used to drive finish nails below a work surface.

Drywall knives (putty knives): These knives have a thin, somewhat flexible blade attached to a sturdy handle. They are used to spread spackle and drywall compound and can also be used to scrape away debris before cleaning walls or filling holes.

Razor knife: A razor knife is a sharp, retractable, disposable blade in a sturdy handle.

How to Use Self-drilling Metal Anchors

Drive the anchor into the wall in between studs. As the threads touch drywall, slowly tighten the toggle until it's nearly flush to the wall.

Insert a screw through a rail and into the anchor.

As you drive the screw into the anchor, the metal flange pulls tight against the inside of the wall.

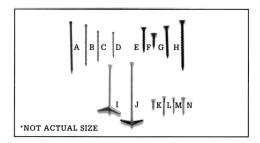

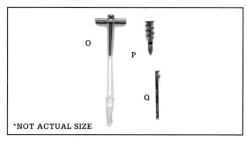

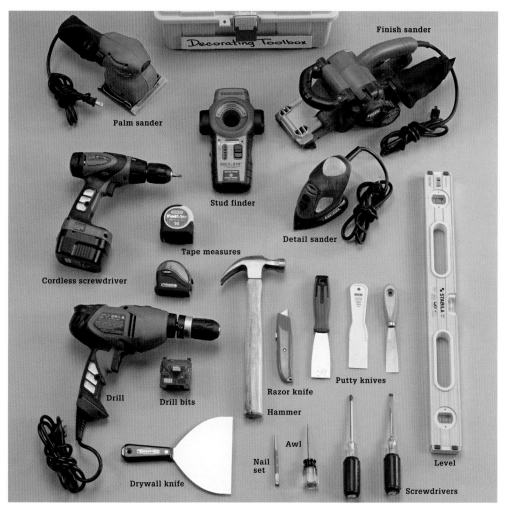

Finish sander

Palm sander

Stud finder

Detail sander

Tape measures

Cordless screwdriver

Drill

Drill bits

Razor knife

Putty knives

Hammer

Awl

Nail set

Drywall knife

Screwdrivers

Level

These tools are available at every home improvement center, paint store, and hardware store. Scour your garage and closets before you buy new tools—you may have many of them in your home already. (Top left): Standard hardware for decorating include (A) 10d finish nail, (B) 8d finish nail, (C) 6d finish nail, (D) 4d finish nail, (E) 1¼" drywall screw, (F) ¾" drywall screw, (G) 1⅝" drywall screw, (H) 2½" drywall screw, (I/J) toggle bolts, (K) ¾" panhead screw, (L/M) wood screws, (N) 1¼" panhead screw. (Top right): (O) Toggler SanToggle ¼–20, (P) self-drilling anchor, (Q) self-drilling toggle.

Wall Panel & Tile

Decorating with substantial materials such as paneling, tile, or glass block results in both a luxuriously appealing finish and lasting durability. As you beautify your rooms, you are also protecting your walls! By using innovative design plans and thoughtfully selecting materials, you can increase the value of your home while you make it your own. Be sure to select your project thoughtfully—and experiment with innovative designs while using time-tested, traditional techniques. Each wall treatment project in this chapter significantly contributes to the overall mood of the space—it helps distinguish the space and reflect personality. The treatments can be mixed and matched in endless ways and are suitable for an entire room as well as specifically chosen accent walls.

Use decorative wallboard, traditional wainscot paneling, and colorful tile backsplashes to define your hallways, add color and usability to your kitchen, and cleanly divide separate living spaces. Each one of these projects will set your room, your home, and your style apart from the rest.

In this chapter:

- Decorative Wallboard Panels
- Architectural Detail with Wallboard
- Wainscot Panels
- Tongue-and-Groove Wainscoting
- Wainscot Frames
- Tile Backsplashes
- Embellishing a Tiled Wall

Wallboard Panels

ld detail and polish
allboard replicates
-consuming work)
gs with detailed
a single pre-designed
to add a wainscot,
r create a coffered
ceiling; they work equally well used on accent walls
or on all the walls of a room, depending on the effect
you wish to achieve.

To install raised panels, plan the layout carefully
to ensure the panels are in alignment across the
entire surface. In our project, standard wallboard is
used to fill strips between or around decorative panels
and all seams are finished using standard techniques.
While you're finishing your project, be careful not
to smudge compound in the raised panel area of
wallboard since it is difficult to remove once dry. If
you do smudge the panels, carefully clean off the
compound immediately with a clean wallboard knife
and a damp towel. If you prefer to add decorative
wallboard directly on top of your existing walls,
consider products or easy-to-install kits specifically
for this purpose.

Decorative wallboard adds a refined finish and the antique
character of formal estates, established residences, and
country cottages.

Planning Your Wallboard Installation

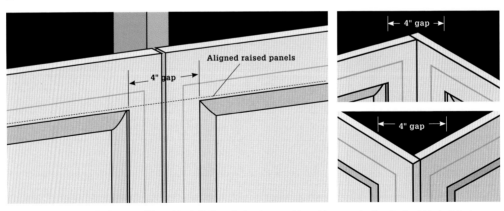

When planning your designer wallboard installation, the key to a good layout is symmetry. Panels should be installed so
the raised areas break at equal distances from the corners. Standard wallboard can be used to fill in between panels to create a
workable layout. Treat both inside and outside corners similarly, so that the raised areas fall the same distance from the corner on
each side of the wall. Panels also can be installed to "wrap" inside corners if necessary (inside corners, opposite page). Take careful
measurements of your walls and ceilings and make accurate sketches to guide your project.

How to Install Decorative Wallboard Panels

Measure and mark the location of the first panel on the framing. At one end of the wall, measure and mark the top edge of the panel's raised area. Drive a nail and run a level mason's line across the wall 1" from the framing. Install the first panel with wallboard screws, so the top edge of the raised area is level with the mason's line. *Note: if your wall is already covered with wallboard, consult a licensed remodeling carpenter to remove the existing wall or consider easy-to-install decorative wall kits.*

Tools & Materials ▸

Wallboard panels
Tape measure
Screwgun or ⅜" drill
Chalk line
Wallboard screws
T-square
Utility knife
Construction adhesive

Inside Corners ▸

To wrap an inside corner, score the back of a panel using a T-square and sharp utility knife, being careful not to pierce the front face. Gently snap back the panel, leaving the face paper intact. Fill the void with a bead of adhesive to reinforce the panel, then install it immediately.

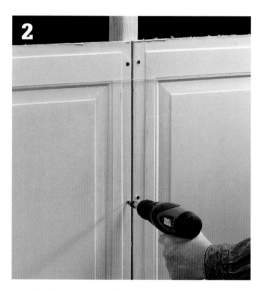

Install subsequent panels not only so the raised top edge is level with the mason's line, but also with an equal distance between the sides of the raised areas of each panel. At corners, make sure to account for panel overlap when making cuts.

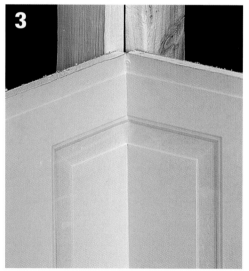

Finish the rest of the wall and fill gaps with standard wallboard of the same thickness. The designer panels can be taped and finished in the same manner as standard wallboard.

Architectural Detail with Wallboard

Wallboard can be installed in creative ways to bring a variety of architectural detail to a room. From a simple series of tiers wrapping the perimeter of the room to curved soffits or raised panels on walls, you can use traditional wallboard to replicate designs in high-end homes or bring your own creation to life.

Use a sharp utility knife and a rasp for cutting, as panel edges must be clean for finishing. Use adhesive to create strong bonds between layers, and type-G screws to hold panels together while the adhesive sets up. Use L-bead to create sharp, clean panel ends. Finish all seams and beads with joint tape and at least three coats of compound.

Tools & Materials ▸

Wallboard	Tape measure	Utility knife	Chalk line
Wallboard screws	T-square	Wallboard rasp	Screwgun or ⅜" drill
L-bead			

A decorative ceiling finish like this requires wallboard and trim finish carpentry skills. By combining built-up wallboard step soffits flanked by trim, a stunning layered effect is created.

How to Add Decorative Tiers to a Ceiling

1

Measure and mark the width of the first tier on the ceiling along each wall, then snap chalk lines to mark the perimeter. Cut pieces of wallboard to size and apply ⅜" beads of adhesive to the backside.

2

Install the wallboard with screws following traditional wallboard spacing recommendations. Snap chalk lines on the first tier for the second tier perimeter.

3

Cut and install the wallboard as in step 2. Stagger all seams at corners and along tier runs.

4

Install L-bead on all exposed edges of each tier, then finish with three coats of joint compound. Edges can also be finished with flexible corner tape.

Variation: Built-up Wallboard ▸

For a more substantial step soffit, build a 2× framework as a base for the wallboard. As you lay out the placement of the new framing, make sure to account for the thickness of the wallboard in all final dimensions.

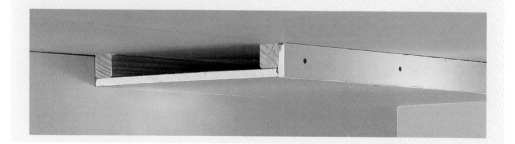

Wainscot Panels

A wainscot is a wall treatment covering the lower portion of a wall and is not only decorative, but also protects your wall against wear and tear in high-traffic areas such as hallways and mudrooms. In most applications, the wainscot is covered along the bottom by a baseboard and along the top by a cap molding, rail, or shelf.

There are two basic methods for installing wainscot panels: sheets and thinner boards (up to ⅜") can be attached to drywall with construction adhesive and nails, or with nails alone. Most wainscot is 30" or 36", but the exact height of the wainscoting is up to each designer. When installed to the height of the furniture in the room, wainscoting provides visual symmetry. It also allows the cap rail to double as a chair rail.

Most paneling is available in 4 × 8, 4 × 9, and 4 × 10 sheets. Before you start, measure the length of each wall in your room and plan the layout of the paneling sheets. The last sheet on each wall should be at least 3" wide, so you may have to trim the first sheet in order to make the last sheet wide enough. Specific installation instructions may vary according to the type of paneling you purchase—be sure to check the manufacturer's instructions for the product you choose before installation.

Tools & Materials ▸

Stud finder
Caulk gun
Tape Measure
Circular saw
Sheet paneling
Compass
Construction adhesive
Chalk line
10d, 6d and 2d finish nails
1 × 6 and 1 × 3 clear pine lumber
Power miter saw
Router with roundover bit
Chamfer bit
Wood glue
Drill
Cove molding
Baseboard
Nail set

Solid and veneer wood wainscot panels can be stained or painted, depending on the look of your room. Synthetic paneling comes in hundreds of colors and styles as well.

Types of Paneling ▸

Solid and veneer wood paneling is durable and easy to clean—and brings a warm, rich tone to any room.

FRP (fiberglass reinforced plastic), extruded plastic, and vinyl panels contain solid material throughout, creating a low-maintenance, water-resistant wall surface. These materials are great for garages, workshops, and commercial applications.

Laminate panels are available in hundreds of colors and patterns, providing a more durable alternative to paint or wallcoverings.

Tileboard is moisture-resistant hardboard coated with melamine—a durable, easy-to-clean plastic finish that replicates the appearance of ceramic tile.

Bamboo (not pictured) is unique and green-friendly. Its unusual construction—strips of bamboo laminated to a fabric backing—allows it to conform to any type of shape or surface.

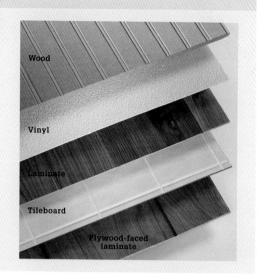

Wood

Vinyl

Laminate

Tileboard

Plywood-faced laminate

How to Scribe the First Panel

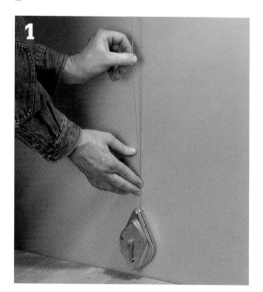

Starting in the corner farthest from the entry, use a stud finder to locate the stud closest to but less than 48" from the corner. Snap a plumb chalk line down the wall at this location. Measure the distance from the corner to this plumb mark and add 1". Use a circular saw to cut your first sheet of paneling to this measurement.

Position the first sheet of paneling against the wall so the cut edge is 1" from the corner and the opposite, finished edge is plumb. Temporarily tack the top of the paneling to the wall. Spread the compass to 1¼" and run down the full height of the wall to scribe the cut line onto the face of the paneling. Remove the paneling from the wall and cut to fit.

How to Install a Wainscot with Sheet Paneling

1

Measure up from the floor and snap a chalk line ¾" below the height you've determined for your wainscot. Use a pencil to mark the stud locations approximately 1" above the chalk line. Scribe and cut your first panel to fit into the corner (see page 65). Measure the distance from this line to 1" above the floor and use a circular saw to cut the first sheet of paneling to length.

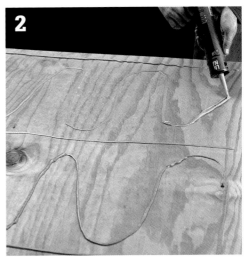

2

Apply construction adhesive with a caulk gun to the back of the first panel. Apply the sheet to the wall so its top edge is flush with the chalk line and its scribed edge is set into the corner. Press the sheet firmly to bond it to the wall.

3

Drive 6d finish nails at the stud locations, spacing them every 16" or so. Use only as many nails as needed to hold the sheet flat and keep it in place.

4

Install the remaining sheets in the wall section. If you are paneling an adjacent wall, check the paneled wall for plumb, and trim the first sheet, if necessary. Install the sheet butted against the end sheet on the paneled wall.

Install the 1 × 6 rail with its top edge flush with the chalk line, fastening it to each stud with two 10d finish nails driven through pilot holes. Butt together rail pieces at inside corners, and miter them at outside corners. *Preparation tip: Before you install the rail, sand the front face and bottom edge smooth.*

Mill the 1 × 3 top cap material using a router and roundover bit. Work on test pieces to find the desired amount of roundover, then rout your workpieces on both front corners. Sand the cap smooth. *Option: Create a waterfall edge by rounding over only the top edge of the cap (top inset), or chamfer the front edges with a chamfer bit (bottom inset).*

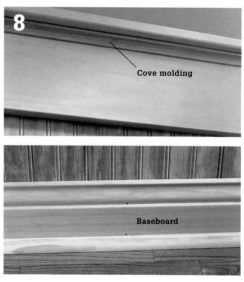

Cove molding

Baseboard

Install the cap with wood glue and finish nails. Glue along the top edge of the rail and drive a 10d finish nail, angled at 45° through the cap and into each stud (drill pilot holes for the nails). Miter the rail at corners.

Add cove molding to the joint between the cap and rail, fastening it to the rail with 2d finish nails. Install the baseboard along the bottom of the wainscot. Recess all nails with a nail set.

Tongue-and-Groove Wainscoting

Typical tongue-and-groove boards for wainscoting are made of pine, fir, or other softwoods, and are ¼ to ¾" thick. Each board has a tongue on one edge, a groove on the other, and usually a decorative bevel or bead on each edge. Boards are cut to length and then attached with nails driven through the tongues of the boards.

If installed over finished wallboard, tongue-and-groove wainscoting will require that nailers be fastened to the wall studs to provide a reliable backing for nailing. You can skip this step if you know there is consistent blocking between the studs to substitute for this backing. However, this is usually difficult to confirm unless the walls were framed with tongue-and-groove wainscoting in mind.

If you plan to stain your tongue-and-groove wainscoting, use oil-based stains before or after installation, since most of the stain will be absorbed into the wood and won't interfere with the tongue-and-groove joints. If painting, choose a latex-based paint, which will resist cracking as the joints expand and contract with changes in the weather.

Tools & Materials ▸

Circuit tester	Level	Pry bar	Tongue-and-groove boards
Circular saw	Miter box	Tape measure	Spacers
Compass	Miter saw	Fine-tooth	Cap rail
Drill	Nail set	woodcutting blade	Cove molding
Hammer	Pencil	Receptacle box	or quarter round
Jigsaw	Plane	extenders, as required	4d and 6d finish nails

Tongue-and-groove wainscoting boards are milled with smooth faces or contoured to add additional texture to your walls. For staining, choose a wood species with a pronounced grain. For painting, poplar is a good choice, since it has few knots and a consistent, closed grain that accepts paint evenly.

How to Prepare for a Tongue-and-Groove Wainscoting Project

1

Measure to make a plan drawing of each wall in your project. Indicate the locations of fixtures, receptacles, and windows. Use a level to make sure the corners are plumb. If not, mark plumb lines on the walls to use as reference points.

2

Condition the planking by stacking it in the room where it will be installed. Place spacers between the planks to let air circulate around each board, allowing the wood to adjust to the room's temperature and humidity. Wait 72 hours before staining or sealing the front, back, and edges of each plank.

3

Remove the baseboard moldings, along with any receptacle cover plates, vent covers, or other wall fixtures within the area you plan to cover. Before you begin, turn off the electricity to the circuits in the area.

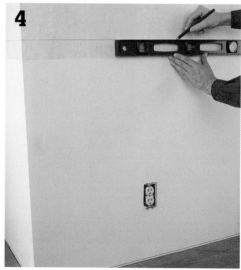

4

Mark the walls with level lines to indicate the top of the wainscoting. Mark a line ¼" from the floor to provide a small gap for expansion at the floor.

Planning Your Project ▸

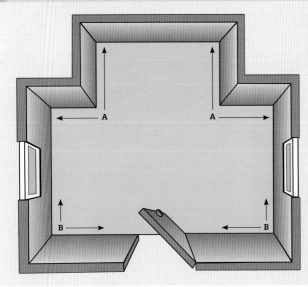

Begin installation at the corners.
Install any outside corners (A) first, working your way toward the inside corners. In sections of a room that have no outside corners, start at the inside corners (B), and work your way toward the door and window casings. Calculate the number of boards required for each wall, using the measurements on the drawing you created earlier (length of wall divided by width of one plank). When making this calculation, remember that the tongues are removed from the corner boards. If the total number of boards for a wall includes a fraction of less than ½ of a board, plan to trim the first and last boards to avoid ending with a board cut to less than half its original width.

How to Install Tongue-and-Groove Wainscoting at Outside Corners

Cut a pair of boards to the widths indicated in the calculations you developed during the planning process.

Position the boards at the corner, butting them to create a plumb corner. Facenail the boards in place, then nail the joint, using 6d finish nails. Drive the nails to within ⅛" of the face of the boards, then finish with a nail set.

Position a piece of corner trim and nail it in place, using 6d finish nails. Install the remaining boards (opposite, steps 5 and 6).

How to Install Tongue-and-Groove Wainscoting at Inside Corners

Hold a level against the first board and hold the board flush with the corner. If the wall is out of plumb, trim the board to compensate: hold the board plumb, position a compass at the inside corner of the wall, and use it to scribe a line down the board.

Cut along the scribed line with a circular saw. Subsequent boards may require minor tapering with a plane to adjust for plumb.

Hold the first board in the corner, leaving a ¼" gap for expansion, and facenail into the center of the board at each nailer location, using 6d finish nails. Drive the top nails roughly ½" from the edge so they'll be hidden from view once the cap rail is attached.

Install a second board at the corner by butting it against the first one, then facenailing in at least two locations. Nail to within ⅛" of the face of the board, then use a nail set to finish.

Position subsequent boards. Leave a ¹⁄₁₆" gap at each joint to allow for seasonal expansion. Use a level to check every third board for plumb. If the wainscoting is out of plumb, adjust the fourth board, as necessary, to compensate.

Mark and cut the final board to fit. If you're at a door casing, cut the board to fit flush with the casing (trim off at least the tongue). If you're at an inside corner, make sure it is plumb. If not, scribe and trim the board to fit.

How to Make a Cutout

Test the receptacle (inset) to make sure the power is off. If tester lights, determine the correct circuit and shut it off before continuing. Then, unscrew and remove the receptacle from the box. Coat the edges of the electrical box with bright colored chalk.

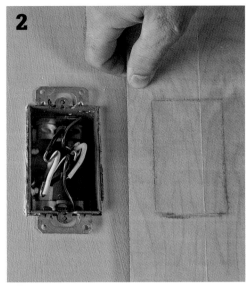

Create a cutting outline by pressing the back of the board that will be installed over the receptacle directly against the electrical box.

Lay the board face down and drill a large pilot hole near one corner of the outline. Use a jigsaw fitted with a fine-tooth woodcutting blade to make the cutout. Be careful not to cut outside the lines.

Facenail the wainscoting to the wall, then reattach the receptacle with the tabs overlapping the wainscoting so the receptacle is flush with the opening. You may need longer screws.

Tip ▸

When paneling around a receptacle with thick stock, you will need to attach a receptacle box extender to the inside of the box, then reconnect the receptacle so it is flush with the opening in the paneling.

How to Install Tongue-and-Groove Wainscoting Around a Window

On casement windows, install wainscoting up to the casings on the sides and below the window. Install ½" cove molding, quarter round, or other trim to finish the edges.

On double-hung windows, remove any window trim and install wainscoting up to the jambs on the sides and below the window. Cut the stool to fit over the wainscoting, then reinstall the apron.

How to Finish a Wainscoting Project

Cut baseboard moldings to fit over the wainscoting, and attach them by nailing 6d finishing nails at the stud locations. If you plan to install a base shoe, leave a small gap at the floor.

Cut the cap rail to fit. At doors and windows, install the cap rail so its edge is flush with the side casings.

Attach the cap rail by nailing 4d finish nails through the flats of the moldings at the stud locations so that the nails enter both the studs and the wainscoting. Set the nails with a nail set.

Wainscot Frames

Frame-and-panel wainscot adds depth and variety to living spaces and can be constructed to match any specifications you determine. Use paint-grade materials, such as MDF, or build with hardwoods and finish-grade plywood if you prefer a clear-coat finish. It's best to prime all of the wainscot parts prior to installing them.

Installing wainscot frames can be done piece by piece, but it is often easier to assemble the main frame parts in your shop. Not only does working in the shop allow you to join the frame parts together using pocket screws driven in the backs of the rails and stiles, it also generally results in a more professional look.

Once the main frames have been assembled, attach them to the wall at stud locations. If you prefer to site-build the wainscot piece by piece, you may need to replace the wallcovering material with plywood to create nailing surfaces for the individual pieces.

Tools & Materials ▸

¾" MDF sheet stock
1¹⁄₁₆" cove molding
½ × ¾" base shoe
⁹⁄₁₆ × 1⅛" cap
 molding (10 feet
 per panel)
Panel adhesive
Paint
Primer
Laser level
Pencil
Tape measure
Router
Circular saw
 or table saw

Straightedge guide
Power miter saw
Clamps
Drill with bits
Carpenter's square
Pocket hole jig
 with screws
Pry bar
Hammer
Pneumatic finish
 nail gun with
 compressor
Caulking gun

Wainscot frames fit in well with contemporary room design, adding a traditional class and craftsmanship to the design. Inset: The wainscot panels shown here, as well as the wall sections within the frames, were painted a lighter contrasting color from the wall for added depth.

How to Install Wainscot Frames

Use a laser level and a pencil to mark the height of the wainscot installation directly onto all walls in the project area. Also mark the height of the top rail (¾" below the overall height), since the cap rail will be installed after the rest of the wainscot is installed. Mark stud locations, using an electronic stud finder.

Test your layout plan by drawing lines on the wall to verify that your design will work in your room. Try to use a panel width that can be divided evenly into all project wall lengths. In some cases, you may need to make the panel widths slightly different from wall to wall, but make sure to maintain a consistent width within each wall's run.

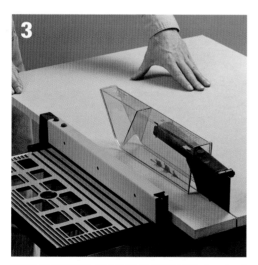

Based on your plan, rip a sheet of MDF into strips to make all of the wainscot parts except the trim moldings. In our case, that included the cap rail (2" wide), the top rail and stiles (3½" wide), and the base rail (7¼" wide). *Note: These are standard lumber dimensions. You can use 1 × 4 and 1 × 4 dimensional lumber for the rails and stiles (use 1 × 2 or rip stock for the cap rail).*

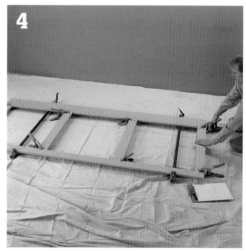

Dry-assemble the cut top rails, base rails, and stiles into ladder frames on a flat surface based on your layout. Plan the layouts so wall sections longer than 8 ft. are cut with scarf joints in the rails meeting at a stud location.

(continued)

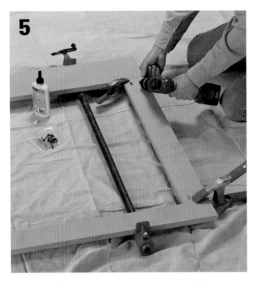

5

Assemble the frames using glue and pocket screws or biscuits. Clamp the parts together first and check with a carpenter's square to make sure the stiles are perpendicular to both rails.

6

Mount a ¾" roundover bit in your router or router table and shape a bullnose profile on the front edge of your cap rail stock.

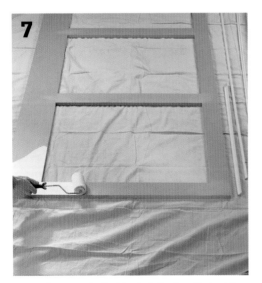

7

Prime all parts on both sides, including the milled moldings and uncut cap rail stock.

8

Position the frames against the wall and shim underneath the bottom rails as necessary to bring them flush with the top rail marks on the wall (¾" below the overall height lines). Attach the wainscot sections by driving 3" drywall screws, countersunk, through the top and bottom rail at each stud location. If you are using scarf joints, be sure to install the open half first. Cut the cap rail.

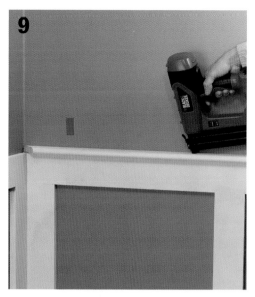

Attach the cap rail to the top rail with panel adhesive and finish nails. Drive a 3" drywall screw through the cap rail and into the wall toenail-style at each location. Be sure to carefully drill pilot holes and countersink holes for each screw. Miter-cut the cap rails at the corners.

Install cove molding in the crotch where the cap rail and top rail meet using glue and a brad nailer. Then, nail the base shoe to conceal any gaps between the bottoms, rails, and floor. Miter all corners.

Cut and install mitered frames out of cap molding to fit around the inside perimeter of each panel frame.

Mask the wall above the cap rail, and then prime and paint the wainscot frames. Generally, a lighter color contrasting the wall color above is most effective visually.

Tile Backsplashes

There are few spaces in your home with as much potential for creativity and visual impact as the space between your kitchen countertop and cupboards. A well-designed backsplash can transform the ordinary into the extraordinary.

Tiles for the backsplash can be attached directly to wallboard or plaster and do not require backerboard. When purchasing the tile, order 10 percent extra to cover breakage and cutting. Remove switch and receptacle cover plates and install box extenders to make up for the extra thickness of the tile. Protect the countertop from scratches by covering it with a drop cloth.

Tools & Materials ▸

Level	Straight 1 × 2
Tape measure	Wall tile
Pencil	Tile spacers
Tile cutter	(if needed)
Rod saw	Bullnose trim tile
Notched trowel	Mastic tile adhesive
Rubber grout float	Masking tape
Beating block	Grout
Rubber mallet	Caulk
Sponge	Drop cloth
Bucket	Grout sealer

A tiled backsplash normally extends all the way from countertop to the bottoms of the wall cabinets. The tile pattern also can be extended to the wall underneath your range hood.

Tips for Planning Tile Layouts ▸

Gather planning brochures and design catalogs to help you create decorative patterns and borders for the backsplash.

Break tiles into fragments and make a mosaic backsplash. Always use a sanded grout for joints wider than ⅛".

Add painted mural tiles to create a focal point. Mixing various tile styles adds an appealing contrast.

How to Tile a Backsplash

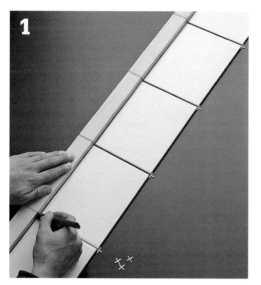

Make a story stick by marking a board at least half as long as the backsplash area to match the tile spacing.

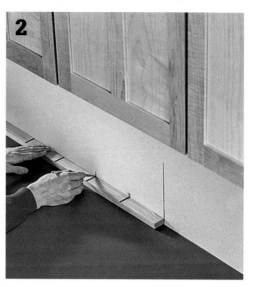

Starting at the midpoint of the installation area, use the story stick to make layout marks along the wall. If an end piece is too small (less than half a tile), adjust the midpoint to give you larger, more attractive end pieces. Use a level to mark this point with a vertical reference line.

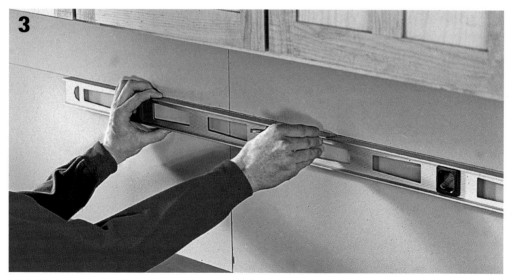

While it may appear straight, your countertop may not be level and therefore is not a reliable reference line. Run a level along the counter to find the lowest point on the countertop. Mark a point two tiles up from the low point and extend a level line across the entire work area.

(continued)

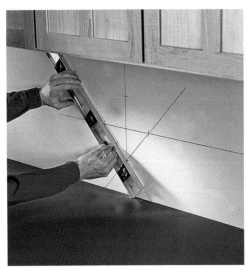
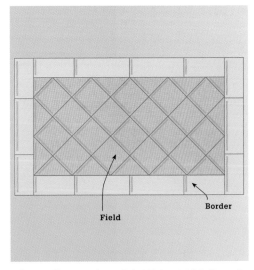

Field

Border

Variation: Diagonal Layout. Mark vertical and horizontal reference lines, making sure the angle is 90°. To establish diagonal layout lines, measure out equal distances from the crosspoint, then connect the points with a line. Additional layout lines can be extended from these as needed. To avoid the numerous, unattractive perimeter cuts common to diagonal layouts, try using a standard border pattern as shown. Diagonally set a field of full tiles, then cut enough half tiles to fill out the perimeter. Finally, border the diagonal field with tiles set square to the field.

Apply mastic adhesive evenly to the area beneath the horizontal reference line, using a notched trowel. Comb the adhesive horizontally with the notched edge.

Starting at the vertical reference line, press tiles into the adhesive using a slight twisting motion. If the tiles are not self-spacing, use plastic spacers to maintain even grout lines. If the tiles do not hang in place, use masking tape to hold them in place until the adhesive sets.

Install a whole row along the reference line, checking occasionally to make sure the tiles are level. Continue installing tiles below the first row, trimming tiles that butt against the countertop as needed.

Apply adhesive above the line
and continue placing tiles, working from the center to the sides. Install trim tile, such as bullnose tile, to the edges of the rows.

Lay a beating block against the tile
and tap it lightly with a mallet. Remove the spacers. Allow the mastic to dry for at least 24 hours, or as directed by the manufacturer.

Mix the grout and apply it with a rubber grout float. Spread it over the tiles, keeping the float at a low 30° angle, pressing the grout deep into the joints. *Note: For grout joints ⅛" and smaller, be sure to use a non-sanded grout.*

Wipe off excess grout, holding the float at a right angle to the tile, working diagonally so as not to remove grout from the joints. Clean any remaining grout from the tiles with a damp sponge, working in a circular motion. Rinse the sponge thoroughly and often.

Shape the grout joints by making slow, short passes with the sponge, shaving down any high spots; rinse the sponge frequently. Use your finger to fill any voids with grout. When the grout has dried to a haze, buff the tile clean with a soft cloth. Apply a bead of caulk between the countertop and tiles. Reinstall any electrical fixtures you removed. After the grout has completely cured, apply grout sealer.

Embellishing a Tiled Wall

Many of us live with tile we don't particularly like. It's easy to see why: builders and remodelers often install simple, neutral tile in an effort not to put anyone off. Older homes sometimes have tile that's not quite vintage but certainly no longer stylish. Because tile is so long-lasting, new styles and trends often make it look dated. Here's a bit of good news: there's a choice beyond simply living with it or tearing out perfectly good tile to start over.

Removing a section of boring tile and replacing it with some decorative accent tile can transform a plain-Jane wall into one that makes a unique design statement. Because this project involves breaking the seal of the wall surface, it's a better choice for a tiled wall that gets little exposure to water (as opposed to a shower wall or tub deck).

Tools & Materials ▸

Tape measure	¼" notched trowel	Grease pencil	Thinset mortar
Grout saw	Grout float	Masking tape	Mosaic medallion or decorative tile
Grout scraper	Grout sponge	Safety glasses	Tile spacers
Flat head screwdriver	Buff rag	Drywall screws	Grout
Straightedge	Foam brush	Cementboard	Latex additive
Utility knife	Needlenose pliers	Construction adhesive	Grout sealer
Drill	Drop cloth	Drywall screws	Dust mask

How to Embellish a Tiled Wall

Measure the decorative tiles and draw a detailed plan for your project. Indicate a removal area at least one tile larger than the space required. If it will be necessary to cut tile, create a plan that will result in symmetrical tiles. Protect the floor with a drop cloth.

Using a grease pencil, mark the tiles to be removed according to the plan drawing. Remove a section of tile that's a minimum of one tile all around the project installation area. Put masking tape on the edges of the bordering tiles that will remain to keep them from being damaged by the grout saw.

Border tiles, set in a rather random fashion, create a focal point behind the counter and sink in this colorful bathroom. Don't limit your use of decorative tiles like these to conventional methods. Let your imagination run free—you may come up with your own unique take on their possibilities.

Decorative tiles can be mixed with plain to produce stunning designs like this one. Many manufacturers will customize tile with photographs that you choose or provide. Craft stores also offer kits that allow you to add your own photographs to tile.

Borders liven up walls and break up otherwise boring expanses of solid color.

Subway tile, simple rectangular tile, blends the shower into its surroundings. The room is brightened considerably by a backsplash of colorful mosaic tile. A niche, cleverly sized and placed, creates the appearance that the backsplash continues behind the shower, and the mosaic floor provides a visual anchor.

(continued)

3

Wearing eye protection and a dust mask, use a grout saw to cut grooves in all of the grout lines in the removal area. If the grout lines are soft this will only take one or two passes. If the grout's hard, it may take several. Using a grout scraper, remove any remaining material in the joint. Angle the tools toward the open area to protect the tile.

4

With a flathead screwdriver, pry up the edges of the tile at the center of the removal area. Wiggle the blade toward the center of the tile and pry up to pop it off.

5

Draw cutting lines on the drywall that are at least ½" inside the borders of the area where you removed tiles. Using a straightedge and utility knife, carefully cut out the old drywall. If the tile comes off very easily and the tile backer is not damaged, you may be able to scrape it clean and reuse it.

6

Cut and install cementboard backer strips that are slightly longer than the width of the opening. Align the strips so the ends are pressed against the back surface of the tile backer. Drive wallboard screws through the edges of the old tile backer and into the strips to hold them in place.

7

Cut a cementboard patch to fit the opening in the tile backer. Place the patch in the opening and drive drywall screws through the cementboard and into the backer strips. Also drive screws at any stud locations. Cover the edges with wallboard tape.

8

Apply thinset mortar using a notched trowel to spread it evenly.

Gently press the accent tiles into the adhesive, smoothing it from the center toward the edges. Let the mortar cure as directed.

Remove the protective sheets on the tiles. You may need to use a damp sponge to first soak the sheets. Once wet, slide the sheets off and throw them away.

Mix a batch of grout and fill the joints between tiles on the entire wall, one section at a time. Clean the tile with a damp sponge. Occasionally rinse the sponge in cool water (inset).

Design Suggestions ▶

Inserts add interest, texture, and color to tile designs. This piece combines tumbled stone with marble in a delicate floral motif.

This stone insert adds a contemporary flair to a simple tile design.

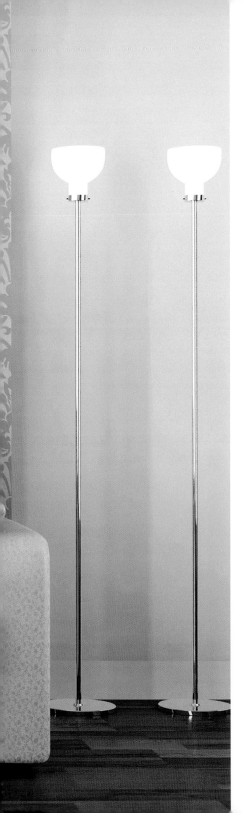

Wallcovering

Wallcovering today is so much more than coordinating floral prints. Whether you'd like to add fresh, clean stripes to your bathroom walls or turn a cool, spacious living room into a quiet hideaway with soft upholstered walls, wallcovering may be just what you need to perfect a room's style and ambience. A multitude of textures, prints, and colors are readily available to completely transform your space, or to perfectly highlight your existing design scheme. Wallcovering can also disguise imperfect walls, absorb or reflect sound and light, and help draw attention to the best features of your room or furnishings.

Choose wallcovering carefully, however. Each type and application method differs in its durability, maintenance, and ease of removal. Ask your salesperson plenty of questions when making decisions about what kind of wallcovering is best for your room, and always bring samples home to see how they look with the light in your room both during the day and at night. Each wallcovering application method also requires careful measurements and planning, but given the time up front, it can be one of the most rewarding ways to completely alter the look and feel of your space.

Be bold in your design choices and meticulous in your application, and you will not be disappointed in the outcome of any wallcovering project.

In this chapter:

- Stripping Wallcovering
- Hanging Wallcovering
- Wallcovering Panels
- Wall Upholstery

Stripping Wallcovering

Stripping wallcovering can be quick and easy or quite tedious, depending on the type of wallcovering to be stripped and how it was applied. Newer vinyl wallcoverings are designed to be strippable, which means they can be scraped off easily when dampened with water. Older wallcoverings, however, may require a fair amount of time and effort. The best way to find out what's lurking beneath your wallcovering is to grab an edge and gently pull!

If wallcovering is hung over unsealed drywall, it's nearly impossible to remove it without destroying the drywall. You may be able to paint or hang new wallcovering directly over the old, but always make sure the surface is smooth and prime it with an alkyd drywall primer.

Tools & Materials ▸

Putty knife
Hand pump sprayer
Wallpaper remover
Paint scraper

Rubber gloves
Sponge
Wallpaper
   perforating tool

Properly applied wallcovering—high-quality coverings that have been applied with good wallpaper adhesive over primed walls—can be stripped with a few simple materials and a little time and patience.

How to Strip Wallcoverings

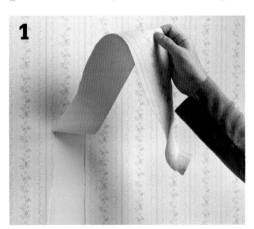

1

Begin to remove wallpaper by pulling upward. First, use a putty knife to pry a corner loose and then pull.

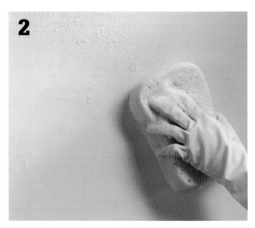

2

Wash the walls, working from the top down. Rinse walls with water and let them dry completely. Always dilute wallpaper remover according to the manufacturer's instructions.

How to Remove Stubborn Wallcoverings

Run a perforating tool over the surface of the wallcovering, creating holes that will enable the remover solution to penetrate the surface and loosen the adhesive.

Dilute wallpaper remover according to the manufacturer's instructions. Cover the floor with drop cloths and use a pressure sprayer to apply the remover solution. Let the solution soak into the covering according to the manufacturer's instructions

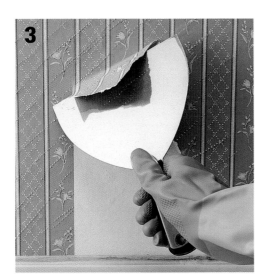

Scrape away loosened wallcovering with a wide paint scraper. Be careful not to damage the wall and be sure to remove any backing paper or other layers.

Rinse adhesive residue from the wall with the remaining remover solution. Rinse the wall with clear water and let walls dry completely. Inspect the walls carefully, making sure they are completely clean before painting or hanging new wallcoverings.

Hanging Wallcovering

Successful wallcovering projects start with careful planning. The materials can be expensive and mistakes are immediately obvious. Always measure the room and sketch out a hanging plan. Hanging should start at a focal point, such as a fireplace or large window. Bear in mind that every wallcovering project will likely have one mismatch: the point where a full strip meets a partial strip. Plan to place the mismatch in an inconspicuous area, such as behind a door.

Work during daylight hours whenever possible, as the light is better and the adhesive dries more evenly. Remember to turn off the power to the circuit in the room and remove covers on receptacles and switches before starting your project.

Hanging wallcovering requires careful planning and attention to detail. The work is not difficult, but the only way to avoid problems is to plan meticulously.

Tools & Materials ▸

Non-corrosive bucket
High-quality sponges
Bubble stick
Wallpaper paste
Smoothing brush
Razor knife
Smoothing tool
Wide drywall knife
Wallcovering scissors
Water tray
Seam roller

Other Considerations ▸

Removability: Strippable wallcoverings can be pulled away from the wall by hand, leaving very little residue. Peelable wallcoverings can be removed, but may leave a thin paper layer on the wall. Check the back of the sample for its strippability rating.

Washability: Washable wallcoverings can be cleaned with mild soap and water. Scrubbable wallcoverings are durable enough to be scrubbed with a soft brush.

Application Ease: Prepasted wallcoverings are factory coated with water-based adhesive that is activated when wetted in a water tray. Unpasted wallcoverings must be coated with adhesive before hanging.

Patterns: Large patterns are more difficult to match and will produce more waste. Covering a room with a large pattern or a pattern that repeats rarely can be more expensive and more time-consuming.

Applying the Rule of Scale ▸

You'll often hear that vertical prints add height to a room and large prints pull a room together, making it appear smaller (or cozier). This is only somewhat true. With all prints you must also consider the scale and depth of the print, the shade, the density (or repeat of the print), and the way that the light in the room will further advance (highly reflective prints, such as foil) or broaden (warm, dark, mute tones) the perceptual space.

Pastel verticals (left) typically broaden a room and make it seem larger both in height and width, but here the wide and large vertical repeat advances the pattern and pulls the room in. This disagreement adds energy to the space, which is also in opposition to the typical calming effect of pastels. A very small, dense vertical pattern (right) does elongate the wall, adding perceived height to the room. Sparse vertical prints with more white space maintain the illusion of height but also give a room an airy and bright feel, which perceptively adds overall space to the room.

Dark vertical prints typically add height to a room with low ceilings, but as seen here a very large-scale repeat vertical print with dark colors and large floras adds drama to a room and makes the room look more square.

Bold repeat prints visually take up a lot of space. This can become disorienting if used too much, so these prints have the best effect when used on accent walls and in moderation, as was done in this fun and inviting hallway.

Light shades of repeat prints, even when large (as shown here), visually recede. This makes a room appear larger while maintaining interest.

Types of Wallcovering ▸

Vinyls are made with a continuous flexible film applied over a fabric or paper backing. Some vinyls successfully duplicate the effect of grasscloth or fabric wallcoverings, but come with the advantage of pre-applied adhesives. Vinyls are easy to apply, clean, and remove.

Foils or mylars are coated with a thin, flexible metallic film. These highly reflective wallcoverings add brightness to a room, but they require careful handling during application. Foils also reflect all wall flaws, so surface preparation must be perfect.

Grasscloths are made of natural plant fibers. Grasscloths reflect very little light and soften the appearance of a room. They are also a good choice for floawed, irregular walls. Hang them with clear adhesive and be careful never to use water to rinse grasscloths.

Fabric wallcoverings are made of woven textiles. Fabrics soften the appearance of a room and absorb sound, but they may be difficult to clean.

Embossed wallcoverings are stamped with a relief pattern for an elegant, formal appearance. Remember not to use a seam roller if applying embossed wallcoverings, as they can easily be damaged.

Flocked paper has a raised fuzzy pattern that resembles velvet. It hides wall imperfections well. It is best used sparingly because it is very ornate.

Spot foils add brightness and interest to a room. A simple design like the one shown here will still take up a considerable amount of visual space in the room, so decorate to complement the wallpaper.

Creating a Hanging Plan ▸

Measure the room and create a sketch of the hanging plan. Center a plumb line on a focal point, such as a fireplace or window. If the room doesn't have an obvious focal point, start at the corner farthest from the entry. Measure a distance equal to the width of the wallcovering and mark a point. Work in both directions, marking the points where seams will fall.

Adjust the hanging plan for corners that fall exactly on seam lines. Wallcovering should overlap at least ½" on inside corners and 1" on outside corners. Similarly, adjust for seams that fall in difficult locations, such as near the edges of windows or doors. Always leave workable widths of wallcovering around obstacles.

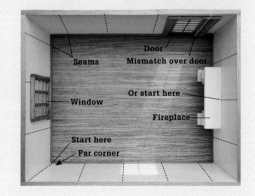

Door
Seams   Mismatch over door
Window   Or start here
Fireplace
Start here
Far corner

How to Prepare Wallcovering Strips

Hold the wallcovering against the wall so there is a full pattern at the ceiling line and the strip overlaps both the ceiling and the baseboard by at least 2". Cut the strip to length using scissors.

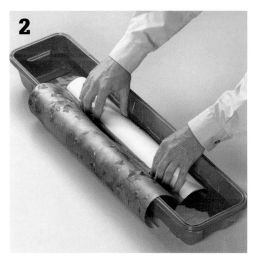

Fill a water tray half full of lukewarm water. Roll the cut strip loosely with the pattern side in. Soak the roll in the tray as directed by the manufacturer, usually about one minute, to activate the prepasted adhesive.

How to Apply Wallcoverings

From the starting point shown in your hanging plan, measure a distance equal to the width of the wallcovering minus ½" and mark a point. Draw a vertical plumb line from the ceiling to the floor using a bubblestick or level.

Position the top portion of the first prepared strip against the plumb line so the strip extends beyond the ceiling joint by about 2".

At the corner fold line, snip the top of the strip so the wallcovering wraps around the corner without wrinkling. Using your open palms, slide the strip into position with the edge butted against the plumb line. Smooth the strip with a smoothing brush.

(continued)

Position the bottom of the strip against the plumb line with your open palms. Smooth the strip with a smoothing brush, carefully pressing out any bubbles.

Trim the excess wallcovering at the ceiling and baseboard, using a drywall knife and a utility knife. With clean water and a sponge, rinse any adhesive from the surface of the wallcovering.

Hang additional strips, sliding strips into place so the pattern matches exactly. Let the strips stand for about half an hour, then roll the seams with a seam roller. (On embossed or fabric wallcoverings, set the seams with a smoothing brush.)

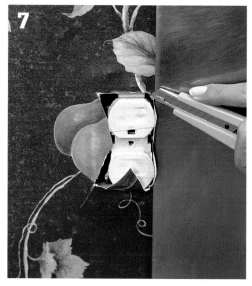

Where wallcovering covers receptacle or switch boxes, use a razor knife to make small diagonal cuts to expose the box. Finally, trim the paper to the edges of the box. *Note: Turn off power to the circuit and remove switch and receptacle covers before starting the project.*

How to Hang Wallcovering Around Doors & Windows

Position the strip on the wall, running the wallcovering over the window or door. Smooth, pressing the strip tightly against the molding.

Use scissors to make diagonal cuts at the corners of the casings. Trim away excess to about 1". Inset: Hold a drywall knife against the molding and use a razor knife to trim the strip.

Cut and position the next short strip to hang above (and below, if this is a window) the opening. Smooth it into place. Snip the corner diagonally and trim away excess as described in step 2. Continue around the opening.

Match the pattern at the seam on the bottom half of the next full strip. Trim the excess as you did in step 2. Rinse the wallcovering and casings using a damp sponge.

How to Hang Wallcovering Around a Wall-mounted Sink

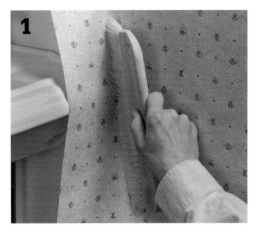

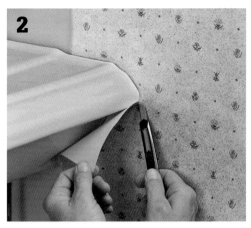

Cut and position the strip, brushing it up to the edge of the sink. Cut slits in the wallcovering, leaving a ¼" overlap around the edges of the sink.

Trim the wallcovering around the sink, leaving a slight overlap. Smooth the strip, tucking the overlap into a gap around the sink, if possible. Or, neatly trim the overlap.

How to Hang Wallcovering Around a Pipe

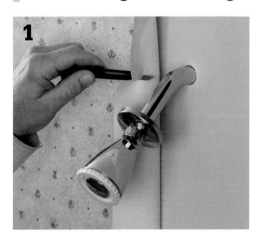

Pull the escutcheon plate out from the wall. Hold the strip against the wall so the pattern matches the previous strip. From the closest edge of the strip, cut the slit to reach the pipe. Press the strip flat up to the pipe with a smoothing brush.

Cut a hole at the end of the slit to fit around the pipe. Butt the edges of the slit together and brush them smooth.

Lot Numbers ▸

Make sure all of your wallpaper rolls have the same lot number. Color may vary between lots. Also, file away the lot number in case you need to purchase more later.

How to Hang Wallcover Borders

If you are positioning the border somewhere other than along the ceiling or baseboard, create a level line in the desired position using a laser level, or draw a light pencil line around the room using a carpenter's level. Cut and prepare the first border strip following the methods for preparing wallcovering (page 93).

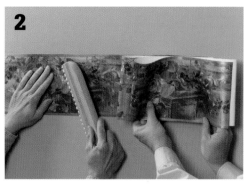

Begin at the least conspicuous corner, overlapping the border onto the adjacent wall by ½". Have a helper hold the border while you apply it against the line. Smooth with the smoothing brush as you go along. At inside corners, create a ¼" tuck from the overhang.

Apply the adjoining strip and trim it with a razor knife. Peel back the tucked strip and smooth the strip around the corner, overlapping the border on the adjacent wall. Press the border flat. Apply seam adhesive to the lapped seam, if necessary.

Where a seam falls in the middle of a wall, overlap strips so the patterns match. Cut through both layers, using a razor knife and a wide drywall knife. Peel back the strips and remove the cut ends. Press the strips flat. Roll the seam after 30 minutes and rinse with a sponge.

Mitering Corners ▶

Apply the horizontal border strip, extending it past the corner a distance greater than the width of the border. Apply the vertical strip over the horizontal one.

Then, hold a straightedge along points where the strips intersect and cut through both layers. Peel back the strips and remove the cut ends, then press the strips back into place. Roll the seams after 30 minutes and rinse any adhesive from the area with a damp sponge.

Wallcovering Panels

Combine wallcovering and coordinating borders to create decorative wall panels that add smart design elegance to painted walls. Panels can be identical in size, or alternate wide panels with narrow ones. Whatever your approach, carefully space the panels evenly on the wall to maintain the balance of the room, leaving slightly more space below the panel than above. To plan the placement of panels, it may help to sketch the room, taking into account the position of windows, doors, and furnishings.

Tools & Materials ▸

Butcher paper
Tape
Pencil
Carpenter's level

Framing square
Smoothing brush
Seam roller
Sponge

Wallcovering panels divide up walls in large rooms, and can add color and variety to accent your color scheme.

How to Make Wallcovering Panels

Determine the size and position of the wallcovering panels by cutting and taping butcher paper to the wall. Using a pencil and a carpenter's level, mark the outline of the panels on the wall. Measure and record the dimensions of each panel.

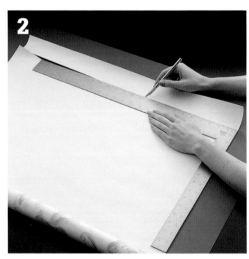

Cut a strip of wallcovering for the center of each panel to size, using a framing square to ensure 90° angles at the corners. Prepare the strip following the instructions on page 93.

3

Unfold and press the top portion of the booked strip lightly onto the wall, aligning the edges with the marked lines. Use flat palms to slide the strip into place. Press the top of the strip flat with a smoothing brush, and check for bubbles.

4

Unfold the bottom half of the strip. Use flat palms to position the strip against the marked lines. Press the strip flat with a smoothing brush, checking for bubbles.

5

Cut and apply any remaining strips, matching the pattern and butting the seams. Roll the seam after 30 minutes. Rinse any adhesive from the wallcovering and wall with a damp sponge. Prepare the border according to the instructions on page 93.

6

Apply the border strips in a clockwise direction, starting at the least conspicuous corner. Butt the inner edges of the border to the panel edges. Miter the corners (page 97). Smooth the first corner only lightly until the final strip is applied. Roll the outer edges of the border and seams after 30 minutes.

Wall Upholstery

Upholstered walls help create an inviting atmosphere. The fabric covers any imperfections on the walls, and the batting used as padding helps insulate the room and absorbs sound. Avoid using fabrics in plaids or strips, because they call attention to walls that are not squared. Stapling the fabric to drywall or paneled walls is easy; however, staples will not penetrate metal corner pieces. For plaster walls, check to see if staples will penetrate the wall and hold. Before starting, remove switch plates and outlet covers. Do not remove moldings or baseboards, because double welting will cover the fabric edges.

Cut fabric lengths as figured in the chart, next page; do not trim the selvages unless they show through the fabric. Measure around doors and windows and along the ceiling and baseboard; also measure from the floor to the ceiling at each corner. For the double welting, cut fabric strips, 3" wide, equal to the total of these measurements.

Upholstered walls add texture to a room. Soft fabrics are ideal for quiet rooms, such as a bedroom or an office. Coarse fabrics and vinyl are good for social spaces, such as a living room or a den.

Tools & Materials ▸

Decorator fabric	Single-edged
Polyester	razor blades
upholstery batting	Hot glue gun and
Staple gun	glue sticks
⅜ to ½" staples	Thick craft glue
Pushpins	Cording

Finishing Tip ▸

For an elegant finish, cover your outlet covers and switch plates with coordinating or matching fabric. Apply fabric, securing it well with diluted craft glue, and then clip and trim around openings. Turn raw edges to back of plate and glue in place.

Determine How Much Fabric to Purchase ▸

Before you get started, take measurements in your project room. Measure around all doors and windows, along the ceiling and baseboard, and from the floor to the ceiling at each corner. Then, use these measurements and the chart below to determine how much fabric you'll need to complete this project before you head to the store.

Worksheet for Calculating Fabric

Cut Length	in.
Measurement from floor to ceiling plus 3"*	=

Cut Width	
Width of fabric minus selvages	=

Number of Fabric Widths Needed for Each Wall	
Width of wall	=
Divided by cut width of fabric	÷
Number of fabric widths for wall**	=

Amount of Fabric Needed for Double Welting	
Total welting length (see cutting directions)	=
Divided by cut width of fabric	÷
Number of strips**	=
Multiplied by 3"	×
Fabric needed for double welting	=

Total Fabric Needed	
Cut length (figured above)	=
Number of fabric widths (figured above) for all walls	×
Fabric needed for all walls	=
Fabric needed for double welting	+
Total length needed	=
Divided by 36"	÷
Number of yd. needed	= yd.

* Allow extra for pattern repeat; do not subtract for windows and doors unless they cover most of the wall.
** Round up to the nearest whole number.

How to Upholster a Wall

Staple batting to the wall every 6", leaving a 1" gap between batting and the edge of the ceiling, corners, baseboards, and moldings. Butt edges between widths of batting. Cut out batting around switch and outlet openings.

Stitch the fabric panels together for each wall separately, matching the pattern, if necessary. Plan seam placement to avoid seams next to windows and doors. Make double welting (opposite).

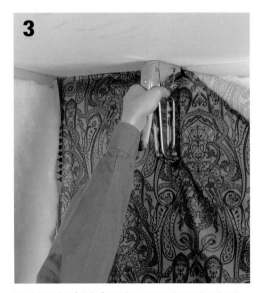

Start hanging fabric from the top, turning under ½" and stapling every 3 to 4". Begin at a corner where matching is not critical. Do not cut around the windows and doors.

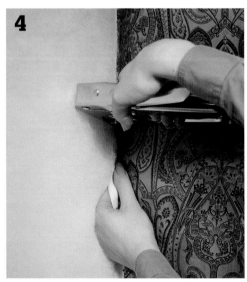

Anchor fabric in the corners, pulling taut and stapling close to the corner so the staples will be covered with double welting. Trim excess fabric. Start next panel at the corner.

Staple along the baseboard, pulling and smoothing fabric taut to remove any wrinkles. Trim the excess fabric along baseboard using a single-edged razor blade.

Mark outside corners of windows and doors with pushpins. Cut out openings with diagonal cuts into corners. Turn under the raw edges, and staple around the molding.

Apply hot glue to the back of the double welting, about 5" at a time; secure the double welting to the upper and lower edges of the wall and around window and door frames. Carefully push the double welting in place to cover the staples.

How to Make Double Welting

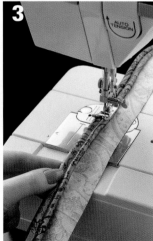

Place the cording on wrong side of the 3" fabric strip. Fold fabric over the cording, with an additional ½" seam allowance. Stitch with the zipper foot next to the cording.

Place the second cord next to the first cord. Bring the fabric over the second length of cording.

Stitch between the two cords on the previous stitching line. Trim off excess fabric next to the stitching; the raw edge is on the back of the finished double welting.

Wall & Window Trim

Decorative baseboards, moldings, and window casings are the best way to establish your rooms as refined, complete living spaces. Although beautiful trim is not usually the first thing many people notice about a room, it not only contributes to the entire aesthetic of a space, but also highlights the design choices that make your home stand apart.

Crown moldings, built-up baseboards, and artistic chair rails can add grace and elegance to flat walls without overwhelming the space. Framing a room-to-room transition or basement window can complete an element that you hadn't considered incomplete before. Stylistic trim can also serve a practical function, such as showcasing art and collectibles or protecting your walls from damage.

With a few common tools and an imaginative eye, transform your bare walls into unique, charming frames for day-to-day living with one of these projects.

In this chapter:

- Base Molding
- Picture Rail
- Chair Rail
- Built-up Chair Rail
- Wall Opening Trim
- Crown Molding
- Built-up Cornices
- Window Casing
- Arts & Crafts Window Casing
- Painting Window Casing
- Window Shelf
- Basement Window Trim

Base Molding

Baseboard trim is installed to conceal the joint between the finished floor and the wallcovering. It also serves to protect the wallboard at the floor. Installing plain, one-piece baseboard such as ranch-style base or cove base is a straightforward project. Outside corner joints are mitered, inside corners are coped, and long runs are joined with scarf cuts (see page 47 to 49).

The biggest challenge to installing base is dealing with out-of-plumb and nonsquare corners. However, a T-bevel makes these obstacles easy to overcome.

Plan the order of your installation prior to cutting any pieces and lay out a specific piece for each length of wall. It may be helpful to mark the type of cut on the back of each piece so you don't have any confusion during the install.

Locate all studs and mark them with painter's tape, 6 inches higher than your molding height. If you need to make a scarf joint along a wall, make sure it falls on the center of a stud. Before you begin nailing trim in place, take the time to pre-finish the moldings. Doing so will minimize the cleanup afterward.

Tools & Materials ▸

Pencil	Framing square
Tape measure	Table saw
Power miter saw	or circular saw
T-bevel	Base shoes
Coping saw	Cap rails
Metal file set	2" finish nails
Pneumatic finish	Wood glue
nail gun	1¼" brad nails
& compressor	Brad nailer
Moldings	18 gauge,
Pneumatic fasteners	⅝" brad nails
Carpenter's glue	Nail set
Finishing putty	Putty

How to Install One-piece Base Molding

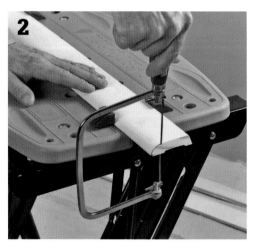

Measure, cut, and install the first piece of baseboard (1). Butt both ends into the corners tightly. For longer lengths, it is a good idea to cut the piece slightly oversized (up to ¹⁄₁₆" on strips over 10 ft. long) and "spring" it into place. Nail the molding in place with two nails at every stud location.

Cut the second piece (2) of molding oversized by 6 to 10" and cope cut the adjoining end to the first piece. Fine-tune the cope with a metal file and sandpaper. Dry-fit the joint, adjusting it as necessary to produce a tight-fitting joint.

3

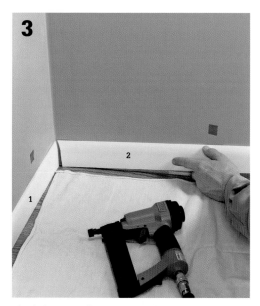

Check the corner for square with a framing square. If necessary, adjust the miter cut of your saw. Use a T-bevel to transfer the proper angle. Cut the second piece (coped) to length, and install it with two nails at each stud location.

4

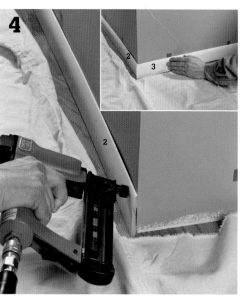

Adjust the miter angle of your saw to cut the adjoining outside corner piece (3, inset). Test fit the cut to ensure a tight joint (inset photo). Remove the mating piece of trim and fasten the first piece for the outside corner joint.

5

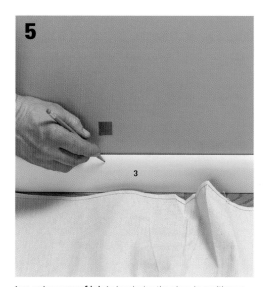

Lay out any scarf joints by placing the piece in position so that the previous joint is tight, and then marking the center of a stud location nearest the opposite end. Set your saw to a 30° angle and cut the molding at the marked location.

6

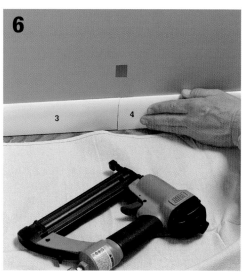

Nail the third piece in place, making sure the outside corner joint is tight. Cut the end of the fourth piece (4) to match the scarf joint angle and nail it in place with two nails at each stud location. Add the remaining pieces of molding, fill the nail holes with putty, and apply a final coat of finish.

How to Install Built-up Base Molding

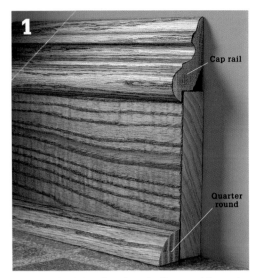

Cap rail

Quarter round

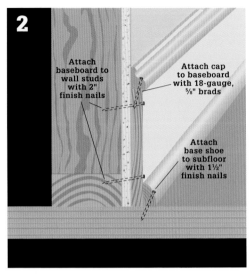

Attach baseboard to wall studs with 2" finish nails

Attach cap to baseboard with 18-gauge, 5/8" brads

Attach base shoe to subfloor with 1½" finish nails

Dress up simple baseboard stock with cap moldings and base shoes or quarter rounds. The baseboard can be made of solid wood, as shown above, or from strips of veneered plywood, as shown on the opposite page.

Built-up baseboard requires more attention to the nailing schedule than simple one-piece baseboards. The most important consideration (other than making sure your nails are all driven into studs or other solid wood) is that the base shoe must be attached to the floor, while the baseboard is attached to the wall. This way, as the gap between the wall and floor changes, the parts of the built-up molding can change with them.

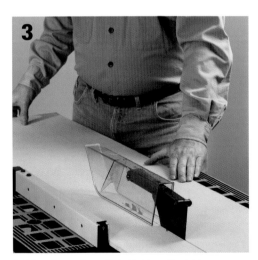

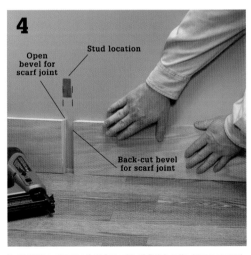

Open bevel for scarf joint

Stud location

Back-cut bevel for scarf joint

Cut the plywood panel into 6" strips with a table saw or a straightedge guide and a circular saw. Lightly sand the strips, removing any splinters left from the saw. Then, apply the finish of your choice to the moldings and the plywood strips.

Install the plywood strips with 2" finish nails driven at stud locations. Use scarf joints on continuous runs, driving pairs of fasteners into the joints. Cut and install moldings so that all scarf joints fall at stud locations.

5

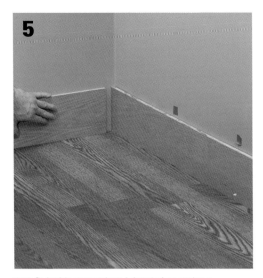

Test-fit inside corner butt joints before cutting a workpiece. If the walls are not square or straight, angle or bevel the end cut a few degrees to fit the profile of the adjoining piece. The cap molding will cover any gaps at the top of the joint.

6

Nail and glue 45° outside miter joint before attaching baseboard

Miter outside corners squarely at 45°. Use wood glue and 1¼" brad nails to pull the mitered pieces tight, and then nail the base to the wall at stud locations with 2" finish nails. Small gaps at the bottom or top of the base molding will be covered with cap or base shoe.

7

Use a brad nailer with 18-gauge, ⅝" brads to install the cap and base shoe moldings along the edges of the plywood base. Fit scarf joints on longer lengths, coped joints on inside corners, and miter joints on outside corners. Stagger the seams so that they do not line up with the base molding seams, following the suggested nailing pattern (previous page, top right). Set any protruding nails with a nail set and fill all nail holes with putty.

Finishing Baseboards ▸

Prepare the baseboards and wall for painting. Apply a light coat of paint starting at the top edge of the baseboard and working toward the floor. Hold a drywall knife or plastic shielding tool beneath the baseboard as you paint and wipe the tool each time it is moved.

Picture Rail

Picture rail molding is a specialty molding that was installed in many older homes so homeowners could hang artwork without making nail holes in the finished walls. Today, picture rail molding is still used as a clean, functional means to hang art—but it also provides its own decorative touch, breaking up the vertical lines from floor to ceiling. Many homeowners choose to install picture rails as a decorative accent alone.

Picture rail molding is easy to install but should be reinforced with screws, not brads or nails, especially if you will be hanging large, heavy items. Depending upon the style of your home, picture rails can be hung anywhere from 1 ft. to a few inches from the ceiling. If you already have cornices or crown molding, you may want to consider adding a picture rail just below to add an additional layer of depth. When applied this way, a picture rail is commonly referred to as a frieze board.

Tools & Materials ▸

Ladder
Pencil
Stud finder
Tape measure
Power miter saw
T-bevel
Pneumatic finish nail gun & compressor
4-ft. level or laser level
Drill with bits
Painter's tape
Moldings
Pneumatic fasteners
1⅝" wallboard screws
Wood filler

How to Install Picture Rail Molding

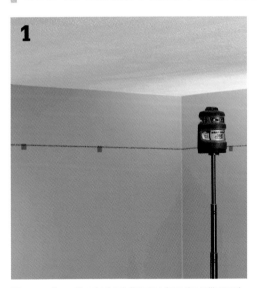

Measure down the desired distance from the ceiling and draw a level reference line around the room using a pencil and a 4-ft. level (or, take advantage of modern technology and use a laser level). While you are up there, use a stud finder to locate the framing members, and mark the locations on the walls with blue painter's tape.

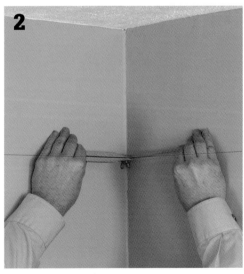

Most corners are close to 90°, but to cut a tight inside corner, the actual angle must be divided exactly in half. Use a T-bevel to measure the angle of the corner, tightening the lock nut with the blade and the handle on the reference line.

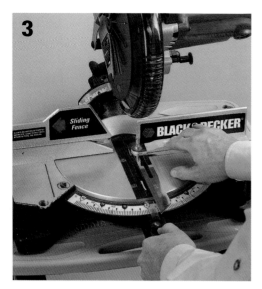

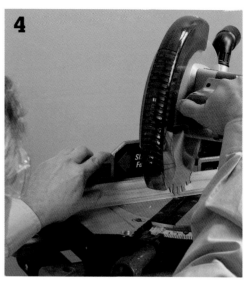

Place the T-bevel on the table of your power miter saw and adjust the miter blade so that it matches the angle. With the T-bevel tight to the fence, read the angle the saw is set to when it aligns with the T-bevel. If the blade is angled to the right of 0° the angle is larger than 90°; to the left, it's smaller.

Read the angle from the miter saw table, divide the number by 2, and add or subtract that number from 45° to find the proper cutting angle for each corner. Cut each molding slightly longer than the measured length.

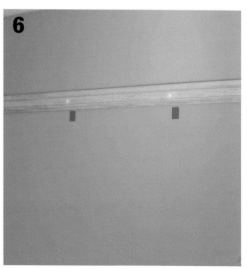

Nail the molding at the stud locations, covering the level line around the room (if you're using a laser level, you simply keep it in position and turned on to cast a reference line you can follow). After each molding is completely nailed in place, go back to each stud location and drive 1⅝" wallboard screws into the molding through counter-bored pilot holes.

Fill nail holes with wood filler. Let the filler dry and sand it smooth. Then apply a final coat of paint over the molding face.

Chair Rail

Chair rails were originally installed to protect walls from collisions with chair backs, but today, a chair rail is primarily a stylistic decorative element that helps to divide a wall visually. Chair rails may cap wainscoting, serve as a border for wallcoverings, or divide two different paint colors on a wall.

A chair rail typically runs horizontally along walls at a height of around 36" (the rule of thumb is to install it one-third of the way up the wall). When determining the height of your chair rail, keep in mind the height of your existing furnishings. It would be disappointing to discover that the new molding has a bad visual effect with your couch or chair backs when the project is completed.

Tools & Materials ▸

Pencil	Painter's tape
Stud finder	Carpenter's glue
Tape measure	Finishing putty
Power miter saw	Finishing materials
4-ft. level	Coping saw
Air compressor	180-grit sandpaper
Finish nail gun	
Metal file set	
Moldings	
Pneumatic fasteners	

How to Install a Chair Rail

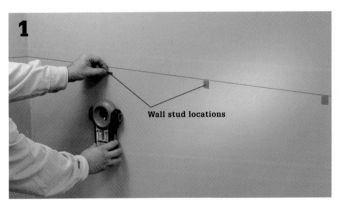

1

Wall stud locations

On the starting wall of your installation, measure up to the height at which you plan to install the chair rail, minus the width of the molding. Mark a level line at this height around the room. Locate all studs along the walls and mark their locations with painter's tape below the line.

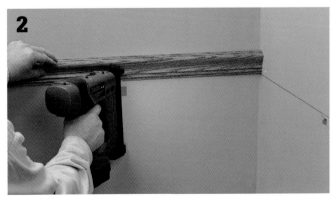

2

Measure, cut, and install the first piece of chair rail with the ends cut squarely, butting into both walls (in a wall run with two inside corners). Nail the molding in place with two 2" finish nails at each stud location.

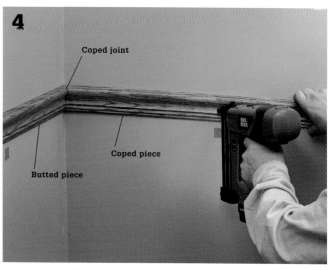

Miter-cut the second piece of molding with a power miter saw and then cope the end with a coping saw. Clean up the edge of the cope cut with a metal file to ensure a tight fit. Dry-fit the piece to check for any gaps in the joint.

Coped joint

Coped piece

Butted piece

When the coped joint fits tightly, measure, mark, and cut the opposing end of the second piece of trim squarely with a miter saw. Nail the second piece in place with two nails at each stud location. Follow the level line with the bottom edge of the molding.

Install the third piece of the chair rail with a cope cut at one end. Use a butt joint where the molding runs into door and window casings. Fill all nail holes with putty and apply a final coat of finish to the molding.

Option: Cut a mitered return for the chair rail in areas where it will end without joining into another molding. Cut the return with a miter saw and glue it in place using painter's tape to hold it until the glue dries.

Built-up Chair Rail

By combining stock chair rail moldings and multiple pieces of assorted trim that are available at most lumberyards and home centers, you can easily create intricate and elaborate chair rails on your own. When developing your design, bear in mind the style of your existing moldings so that the new chair rail will not look out of place. To maintain balance in the room, your chair rail should always be smaller than the crown molding and/or baseboards.

To accentuate your built-up chair rail, consider two-tone painted walls or adding a wainscot or wallcoverings to further emphasize the division of the wall.

A **built-up chair rail** is made up of several styles of moldings, so the design options are unlimited. Experiment with molding samples when finalizing your design. See inset for a cutaway view of the molding pictured here.

Tools & Materials ▸

Painter's tape	Coping saw
Moldings	Pneumatic finish
Pneumatic fasteners	nail gun
1⅝" wallboard screws	& compressor
Hole filler	4 ft. level
Pencil	or laser level
Stud finder	Combination square
Tape measure	2½" finish nails
Power miter saw	1⅝" brad nails

How to Install a Built-up Chair Rail

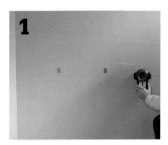

1

Mark the desired height of the 1 × 4 filler strip, or the first chair rail component you will install. Mark a level line around the room at this height, noting the location of studs with painter's tape.

2

Install the filler strip so that the top edge follows the level line around the room. Fasten with two 2½" finish nails at every stud location. Butt the ends of the filler strip together. Joints will be covered with additional moldings.

3

Install the upper piece of cove molding around the room, nailing it flush to the top edge of the filler strip. Drive one nail at every stud location and one nail between each stud into the filler strip. Install the lower piece of cove molding flush with the bottom edge of the filler strip.

4

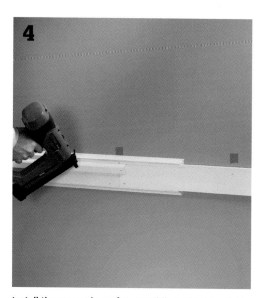

Install the upper piece of stop molding, driving two finish nails at each stud location. Install the lower piece of stop molding keeping the edge flush with the bottom edge of the filler strip. Stagger the seams of the stop molding so that they do not line up with the joints of the cove moldings.

5

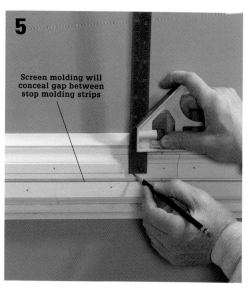

Screen molding will conceal gap between stop molding strips

Set a combination square to 1⅜". Rest the body of the square on the top edge of the upper stop molding and use the blade as a guide to mark a reference line for the top edge of the screen molding.

6

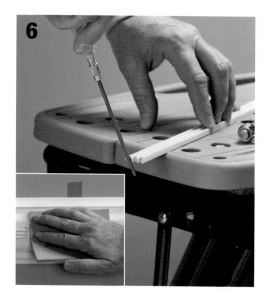

Fine-tune the cope cuts of the screen molding with a round metal file. Nail the molding in place with 1⅜" brad nails, keeping the top edge flush with the reference line. Set nail heads, fill nail holes and any gaps in the joinery. When dry, sand with 180-grit sandpaper and wipe clean with a dry cloth (inset).

Chair Rail Return ▸

Before you begin installing the molding pieces of the built-up chair rail, decide what type of return you will use. Returns are finish details that occur in areas where different moldings meet at perpendicular angles, or quit in the middle of a wall. A beveled return (below left) is a bit difficult to produce, but has a clean look. On some built-up chair rails, you can take advantage of the depth of molding by butting the back moldings up to the obstructions, but running the cap moldings onto the surface (below right).

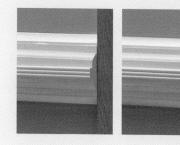

Wall Opening Trim

Transitions between rooms are an often-overlooked opportunity to add polished refinement to your home. Trimming out a wallboard opening frames the entrance for the room and protects the wallboard from damage. Choose either paint-grade materials, or utilize a clear finish, which showcases the wood grain and adds warm, natural detail to your interior. Trimming a wall opening draws attention to your home's structural detail, and invites old-world charm into contemporary spaces.

Bear in mind that finished wallboard corners are likely irregular, which will cause some minor differences in wall thickness along the jambs of the opening. When these irregularities are minute (less than ³⁄₁₆"), it is best to cut the jamb materials at the widest jamb measurement and let the casing bridge the difference. When wall thickness varies a lot (³⁄₁₆" or more), it is better to cut tapered jambs to cover the difference.

Storing Trim ▸

To avoid problems due to potential shrinkage after installation, stack the trim in the room where it will be installed and allow it to acclimate for several days. Apply a coat of primer or sealer to all sides of each piece and let it dry thoroughly before installing it. You may choose to paint or stain the trim before installing it, although this can be completed once installed as well.

Tools & Materials ▸

Jamb material (lumber or plywood)	Wood glue	Side cutters	Circular saw and straightedge guide
Case moldings	Shims	Pencil	Pneumatic finish nail gun
Base moldings	Scrap 2 × 4	Tape measure	Power miter saw
2½" finish nails	Pry bar	4 ft. level	Framing square

Before

Pass-through openings between rooms are often left naked by the builders, especially in modern homes. Give your living spaces a distinguished finish by adding trim and transforming openings into framed transitions between rooms.

How to Trim a Wall Opening

1

Remove the existing base molding with a pry bar and hammer. Be careful not to mar the surface of the moldings as you remove them. Pull the nails out of the moldings through the back face with an end nippers or side cutters.

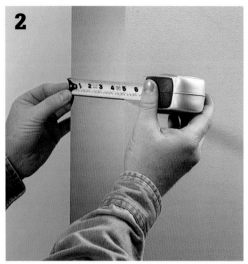

2

Measure the width and length of the head jamb and the width of each side jamb. Measure each jamb at both ends as well as in the middle of each run. Take note of the measurements. If a jamb differs in width by more than ³⁄₁₆", install a tapered length (see Tip, below).

Tip: Cutting Tapered Jambs ▶

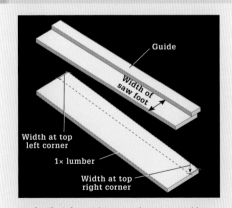

Guide

Width of saw foot

Width at top left corner

1× lumber

Width at top right corner

Jambs that do not taper can be cut on a table saw, but if you have enough variation in your jamb widths that a taper is called for, make a simple cutting jig and taper-cut the jambs to width with a circular saw. Then, lay out the dimensions on the head jamb using the measurements from step 2. The head jamb should run the full length of the opening.

3

Cutting guide

Jamb stock

Clamp a straightedge guide to the head jamb on the reference line from the measurements of step 2, and cut the piece to width with a circular saw. Keep the base plate tight against the fence and move the saw smoothly through the board. Reposition the clamp when you near the end of the board.

(continued)

Position the head jamb at the top of the opening, flush with the edges, and nail it in place starting in the middle. Before nailing the ends of the head jamb, check it for square with the walls of the opening, adjusting with shims if necessary. Drive a pair of 2" finish nails every 16".

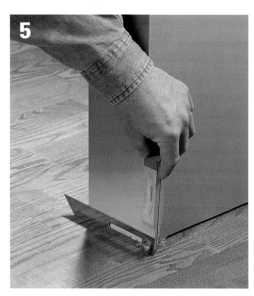

Place a T-bevel on the floor at the bottom of each side jamb to check for any angled cuts necessary to follow the pitch of the floor. The handle of the bevel should rest against the outer face of the wall, with the blade across the floor.

Transfer the angle from the T-bevel in step 5 to a power miter saw, and cut the side jambs to length. The top end of the jamb should be cut square (90°). Each jamb should butt against the head jamb and fit tightly to the finished flooring.

Nail the side jambs in place using pairs of 2" finish nails driven every 16" along the jamb. Check the edges of the jamb pieces as you go to make sure they are flush with the surface of the wall.

8

Install casing around the opening. Maintain a consistent ³⁄₁₆ to ¼" reveal around the opening.

9

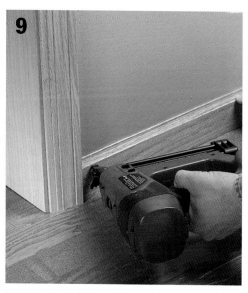

Measure, cut, and reinstall the existing baseboard so that the ends butt into the sides of the casing.

Tips for a Good Installation ▸

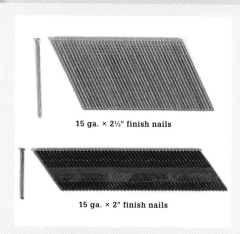

15 ga. × 2½" finish nails

15 ga. × 2" finish nails

Attach wood trim with finish nails, which have small nail heads that you drive below the surface using a nail set. Nails for most trim are size 6d or smaller, depending on the thickness of the trim and the wall surface. At a minimum, nails should be long enough to penetrate the framing by at least ¾"; heavier trim requires nails with more holding power. Use finish screws for securing trim to steel studs.

After the trim is installed and the nails are set, fill nail holes with wood putty and touch up areas with paint or stain.

Crown Molding

Crown molding is angled trim that bridges the joint between the ceiling and the wall and helps soften the transition between walls and ceilings. Crown molding comes in a variety of materials and finishes, from hardwood finished with a clear topcoat to paint-grade materials such as polymer.

If working with wood crown, inside corner joints of crown molding should be cope cut, not mitered, except in the case of very intricate profile crown that is impossible to cope (and therefore must be mitered). While mitering inside corners may appear to save time and produce adequate results, after a few changing seasons the joints will open up and be even more difficult to conceal.

Polymer crown, on the other hand, is just as easy to cut as wood, but won't shrink and can be repaired with vinyl spackling compound. Most polymers come in 12-ft. lengths and some have corner blocks that eliminate the need for corner cutting. If you'd like to apply crown to curved walls, flexible moldings are also available in polymer.

Tools & Materials ▸

Pencil
Tape measure
Circular saw
Straightedge guide
Drill with bits
Coping saw
Power miter saw
Pneumatic finish
  nail gun
Framing square
  or combination
  square
Nail set
Hammer
Metal files
3" wallboard screws

2 × 4 material
  for backing
Carpenter's glue
Crown molding
2", 1½" finish nails
Fine-grit sandpaper
Hole filler
Paint and brushes
Sandpaper
Mineral spirits
Polymer adhesive
Vinyl spackling
  compound
Paintable latex caulk
Caulk gun
Putty knife

How to Install Wood Crown Molding

Cut a piece of crown molding about 1 ft. long with square ends. Temporarily install the piece in the corner of the last installation wall with two screws driven into the blocking. This piece serves as a template for the first cope cut on the first piece of molding.

Place the first piece of molding upside down and sprung against the fence of the miter saw. Mark a reference line on the fence for placement of future moldings, and cut the first coped end with an inside miter cut to reveal the profile of the piece.

3

Cope cut the end of the first piece with a coping saw. Carefully cut along the profile, angling the saw as you cut to back-bevel the cope. Test-fit the coped cut against the temporary scrap from step 1. Fine-tune the cut with files and fine-grit sandpaper.

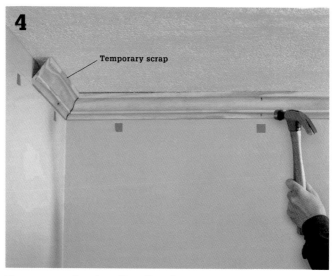

4

Temporary scrap

Measure, cut to length, and install the first piece of crown molding, leaving the end near the temporary scrap loose for final fitting of the last piece. Nail the molding at the top and bottom of each stud location.

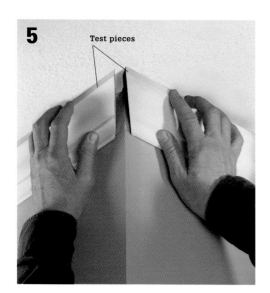

5

Test pieces

Cut two test pieces to check the fit of outside corners. Start with each molding cut at 45°, adjusting the angles larger or smaller until the joints are tight. Make sure the test moldings are properly aligned and are flush with the ceiling and walls. Make a note of your saw settings once the joint fits tightly.

6

Position the actual stock so a cut end is flush against the wall at one end. At the other end, mark the outside corner on the back edge of the molding. Miter cut the piece at the mark, according to the angles you noted on the test pieces.

(continued)

Measure and cut the third piece with an outside corner miter to match the angle of your test pieces. Cut the other end squarely, butting it into the corner. Install the piece with nails driven at stud locations. Install the subsequent pieces of crown molding, coping the front end and butting the other as you work around the room.

To fit the final piece, cope the end and cut it to length. Remove the temporary scrap piece from step 3 and slide the last molding into position. Nail the last piece at the stud locations when the joints fit well, and finish nailing the first piece.

Fill all nail holes. Use a putty knife or your finger to force spackling compound or tinted wood putty into loose joints. Caulk gaps ⅛" or smaller between the molding and the wall or ceiling with flexible, paintable latex caulk. Lightly sand the nail holes and joint gaps.

How to Install Polymer Crown Molding

Plan the layout of the molding pieces by measuring the walls of the room and making light pencil marks at the joint locations. For each piece that starts or ends at a corner, add 12" to 24" to compensate for waste. If possible, avoid pieces shorter than 36", because short pieces are more difficult to fit.

Hold a section of the molding in the finished position. Make a light pencil mark on the wall every 12" along the bottom edge. Remove the molding and tack a finish nail at each mark. The nails will hold the molding in place while the adhesive dries. To make the miter cuts for the first corner, position the molding in a miter box with the ceiling side against the table and the wall side against the fence (inset). Make the cut at 45°.

3

Check the uncut ends of each molding piece before installing it. Make sure mating pieces will butt together squarely in a tight joint. Cut all square ends at 90°. Lightly sand the backs of the molding where it will contact the wall and ceiling. Slightly dampen a rag with mineral spirits and wipe away the dust.

4

Run a small bead of polymer adhesive along the edges where the molding will contact the wall and ceiling. Set the molding in place with the mitered end tight to the corner and the bottom edge resting on the nails. Press to create a good bond.

5

Drive 2" drywall screws through countersunk pilot holes through the flats and into the ceiling and wall at each end of the piece.

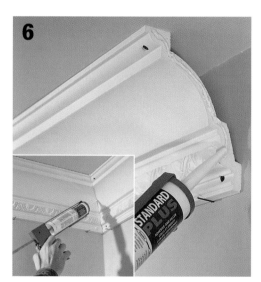

6

Apply a bead of adhesive to the end where the installed molding will meet the next piece. Prepare and install the remaining pieces, making sure the ends are joined properly. Allow adhesive to dry completely, and then carefully remove the finish nails. Fill nail holes with spackling compound and fill screw holes and any gaps in the joints with latex caulk (see inset). Wipe away excess and smooth the caulk over the holes.

Finishing Crown Molding ▸

Crown molding can be painted the same color as the ceiling or with highly elaborate details. Finish wood crown with a clear topcoat for an appealing natural look. For deeply patterned crown molding surfaces, use a stiff-bristled brush, such as a stenciling brush. Use small, circular strokes to penetrate recesses.

Built-up Cornices

Designing your own cornice molding is a creative and fun process that allows you to custom-design molding to fit the style of your room. A cornice is, by definition, an elaborate crown molding, bridging the space where the wall meets the ceiling. Although traditionally cornices have been made of one continuous plaster piece, built-up types are much cheaper to purchase and easier to install. And, they enable you to dictate every aspect of the cornice design.

First, go to the lumberyard and bring home samples of several types of moldings: baseboard, stop, crown, and bed moldings, as well as smaller trims like quarter rounds and coves. Bring the samples home and arrange them in different combinations and positions. As you design your cornice, be careful

Tools & Materials ▶

Molding	Chalk line
2" and 1¼" finish nails	Power miter saw
Carpenter's glue	Pneumatic
Construction adhesive	finish nailer
Pencil	Nail set
Tape measure	Hammer

not to overwhelm the room with a large, complicated molding. A good rule of thumb is to try to match the size of the cornice to the overall size of your baseboard for proportionate balance and an appealing finish.

Built-up cornices are made of smaller pieces of trim, installed in layers. Cornice design is 100 percent customizable, and can significantly add to the formal finish of any living space.

Cornice Variations ▸

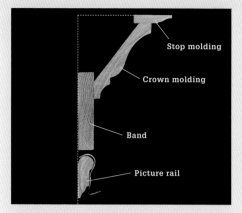

Stop molding

Crown molding

Band

Picture rail

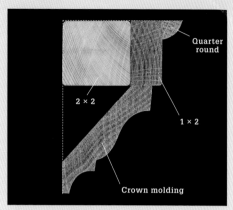

Quarter round

2 × 2

1 × 2

Crown molding

Use picture rail (page 110) to enhance a cornice molding. Standard height for picture rail is about 10 to 12" below the ceiling, but you can place it at any level. For a simple variation of the project shown, use a square-edged stock for the band (since the bottom edge will mostly be hidden), and add picture rail just below the band.

Install blocking to provide a nailing surface and added bulk to a built-up cornice. In this simple arrangement, a 2 × 2 block, or nailing strip, is screwed to the wall studs. A facing made from 1 × 2 finish lumber is nailed to the blocking and is trimmed along the ceiling with quarter-round. The crown molding is nailed to the wall studs along the bottom and to the nailer along the top.

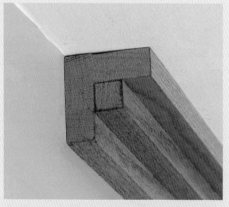

This highly detailed Victorian-style built-up cornice is made up of several pieces of stock trim and solid stock ripped down to different widths. The right-angle component of this cornice may be screwed directly to the wall to serve both as a decorative function as well as a nailer for the other trim elements. The screw holes are covered when the crown molding is installed.

This Arts and Crafts variation is made up of flat solid stock ripped down to specific dimensions. Two pieces of 1 × 2 stock are fastened together to form an L-shaped angle. The angle is then screwed to the wall at the stud locations. An additional piece of 1"-wide stock is nailed in place so the top edge is flush with the installed angle. This configuration creates a step cornice with a simpler appearance than the traditional sprung moldings. Notice that the L angle is nailed together with a slight gap at the back edge. This is done to compensate for irregularities in the corner joint.

How to Create a Built-up Cornice

Cut a 4- to 6"-long piece from each type of molding. Glue or nail the pieces together in the desired arrangement to create a marking template. Position the template flush with the wall and ceiling and mark along the outside edges of the ceiling and wall moldings. Mark at both ends of each wall.

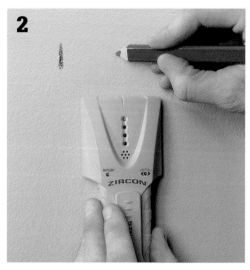

Locate and mark all of the wall studs and ceiling joists, marking in areas that will be hidden by the crown molding.

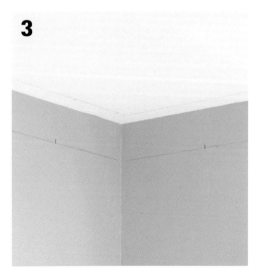

Snap chalk lines between the template marks you made in step 2 (you can also mark with a pencil and level). If the ceiling has a deep texture, scrape off the texture just behind the chalk lines, using a drywall taping knife.

Install the ceiling trim, aligning its outside edge with the ceiling pencil line. Nail into the joists with 2" (6d) finish nails, and miter the joints at the inside and outside corners. Wherever possible, place the nails where they'll be hidden by the crown molding.

5

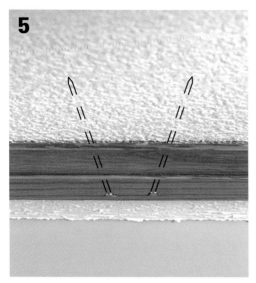

Where walls run parallel to the ceiling joists, and there are no joists to nail into, apply a bead of construction adhesive to the trim and nail it in place with pairs of nails driven at opposing angles. If you're hand nailing, drill oversized pilot holes and secure the trim with coarse-thread drywall screws. Let the adhesive dry before starting the next step.

6

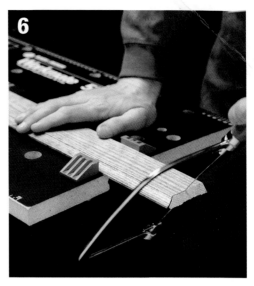

Cope the molding at inside corners by first cutting a 45° angle on the piece. Then cope cut the angle with a coping saw. Cut along the front edge of the molding, following the contour. Test-fit the cut and fine-tune it with a metal file if necessary. We chose to stain the pieces now, before installation.

7

Align and install the wall trim with the pencil lines, nailing into each stud with two 2" nails. Miter the band at outside corners.

8

Add the crown molding, fastening it to the ceiling trim and wall band with 1¼" (3d) nails. Miter the molding at outside corners, and miter or cope the inside corners. Use a nail set to set all nails that aren't countersunk.

Window Casing

Door and window casings provide an attractive border around doors and windows. They also cover the gaps between door or window jambs and the surfaces of surrounding walls.

Install door and window casings with a consistent reveal between the inside edges of the jambs and casings, making sure the casings are level and plumb.

In order to fit casings properly, the jambs and wallcoverings must lie in the same plane. If either one protrudes, the casings will not lie flush. To solve this problem, you'll need to remove some material from whichever surface is protruding.

Use a block plane to shave protruding jambs or a surface forming rasp to shave a protruding wallboard edge. Wallboard screws rely on the strength of untorn facing paper to support the wallboard. If the paper around the screws is damaged, drive additional screws nearby where the paper is still intact.

Tools & Materials ▸

Tape measure
Pencil
Combination square
Nail set
Level
Straightedge
Power miter saw

Hammer or
  pneumatic nailer
Casing material
Plinths and corner
  blocks (optional)
4d and 6d finish nails
Wood putty

Case molding is installed around windows and doors to conceal the gaps between jambs and the wall. Venturing beyond the very common ranch-style casing offers some high design payback.

How to Install Mitered Casing on Doors & Windows

On each jamb, mark a reveal line ⅛" from the inside edge. The casings will be installed flush with these lines. *Note: On double-hung windows, the casings are usually installed flush with the edge of the jambs, so no reveal line is needed.*

Place a length of casing along one side jamb, flush with the reveal line. At the top and bottom of the molding, mark the points where horizontal and vertical reveal lines meet. (When working with doors, mark the molding at the top only).

Make 45° miter cuts on the ends of the moldings. Measure and cut the other vertical molding piece, using the same method.

First drill pilot holes spaced every 12" to prevent splitting, and then attach the vertical casings with 4d finish nails driven through the casings and into the jambs. Drive 6d finish nails into framing members near the outside edge of the casings.

Measure the distance between the side casings, and cut top and bottom casings to fit, with ends mitered at 45°. If the window or door unit is not perfectly square, make test cuts on scrap pieces to find the correct angle of the joints. Drill pilot holes and attach the casings with 4d and 6d finish nails.

Locknail the corner joints by drilling pilot holes and driving 4d finish nails through each corner, as shown. Drive all nail heads below the wood surface, using a nail set, then fill the nail holes with wood putty.

Arts & Crafts Window Casing

Traditional Arts and Crafts casings are made of simple, flat materials with little to no decorative molding trimmed out of the stock. Add non-mitered corners and this casing becomes as sleek and stylized as intended. The back band installed on the perimeter of this project is optional, but it adds depth to the window treatment while maintaining simple style.

Traditionally, the wood used for this style of trim is quartersawn oak. The term *quartersawn* refers to the milling method of the material. Quartersawn oak is easily distinguishable from plainsawn oak by its tight grain pattern laced with rays of lighter color, known as rifts. Quartersawn oak is more expensive than plain oak, and may only be available at lumberyards or hardwood supply stores. Although quartersawn oak is the traditional material, plainsawn oak will finish nicely as well.

Tools & Materials ▸

1 × 4 finish lumber	Finishing putty	Hand saw	Pneumatic nailer
Back band trim	Tape measure	Circular saw or jigsaw	Combination square
Wood shims	Straightedge	Plane or rasp	Compass
4d, 6d, and 8d finish nails	Power miter saw	Drill hammer	Nail set

The Arts and Crafts style is similar to the overall look and feel of Mission furniture, as can be seen in this relatively simple oak window casing.

How to Install Arts & Crafts Casing

Install the stool and jamb extensions according to traditional stool and apron trim methods. Set a combination square to ³⁄₁₆" or ¼" and mark a reveal line on the top and side jambs.

To find the length of the head casing and apron, measure the distance between the reveal lines on the side jambs and add twice the width of the side casings. Cut the head casing and the apron to length. Install the head casing flush with the top reveal line. Use a scrap piece of trim to line up the head casing horizontally.

Measure and cut the side casings to length. Install them flush with the reveal lines. Make sure the joints at the top and bottom are tight. Measure the distance to the end of the stool from the outer edge of the side casing. Install the apron tight to the bottom of the stool at the same dimension from the end of the stool.

Back band

Measure, cut, and install the back band around the perimeter of the window casings, mitering the joints at the corners. Continue the back band around the edge of the apron, mitering the corners. Nail the back band in place with 4d finish nails.

Painting Window Casing

Windows are on the frontline of the daily bump and grind, and a fresh coat of paint can freshen their appearance and make your room décor bright and lasting. Always begin with the inside edges and work your way toward the walls. On windows, this means you should start with the sashes and finish with the case molding. To achieve a smooth, even finish, make sure all nail holes and dents are filled with latex wood filler and that the surface is sanded, primed, and sanded again before you begin.

Tools & Materials ▶

Primer and paint
Painter's tape
1½" tapered sash brush
Corner masks
Drill
Ladder or sawhorses
Sandpaper

A fresh coat of paint can both refresh the appearance and prolong the life of window casings.

How to Paint Window Casings

1

Prepare the window to be painted. Remove hardware, apply tape or corner masks to glass, and apply tape around the outside edges of the case molding.

2

Remove double-hung window sashes from their frames when possible. To release a spring-mounted, double-hung window sash, press against the frame and pull the sash toward you.

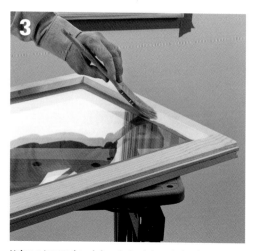

3

Using a tapered sash brush, begin by painting the wood next to the glass. Use the narrow edge of the brush. Then, paint the flat portions of the sash. Use slow brush strokes and smooth the paint carefully. Do not paint the sides or bottom of the window sash.

4

Paint the case moldings, sill, and apron. Let the paint dry completely. Sand lightly and apply a second coat. When dry, remove the tape and replace the sashes.

Casement Windows ▸

Remove the hardware and apply tape and corner masks. Paint the wood next to the glass, then the flat portions of the sash, followed by the case moldings and sills. Move the sash in and out to comfortably reach all areas. Do not paint the sides, top, or bottom of the sash.

Painting Sashes ▸

To paint sashes that have been removed, drill holes and drive 3" nails into the legs of a wooden stepladder. Set the window on the nails as though on an easel. Windows can also be placed flat on a bench or on sawhorses.

Window Shelf

Window shelves are a great place to showcase treasured decorative items and design your own decorative end pieces.

Shelves above windows are a delightful addition to bright rooms, and allow you to showcase plants, artistic collections, or dried flowers and herbs. They can be used alone or with brackets installed underneath for hanging items or window treatments.

Although the end pieces act as supports for the shelf, it's also a good idea to secure the shelf to a horizontal support piece. Then, attach the whole unit to the wall with wood screws. If you know what will be displayed on the shelf, plan your project around those objects. If you'd like to display heavy items, add strength by drilling more pilot holes for the wood screws to be closer together. If the objects are large, adjust the depth of the shelf to accommodate them.

Tools & Materials ▸

1 × 8 and 1 × 2 lumber	6d casing nails	Drill and bits	Router
2" wood screws	Paint or stain	Circular saw	Sander
	Hammer	Jigsaw	Nail set

Additional Shelf Ideas ▸

Window shelves are a great way to combine functionality with bold design choices. Add large, decorative supports to accommodate a dowel for hanging objects such as dried flowers or herbs. Add a coordinating backsplash to add to the presentation of items, or attach hooks to the underside for smart storage of essentials.

How to Build a Window Shelf

Attach the 1 × 8 shelf board and the 1 × 2 horizontal support piece at a 90° angle after you've cut them both to the same length as the total width of the window unit (including the outer casing). Use 2" wood screws, spaced every 6 to 10".

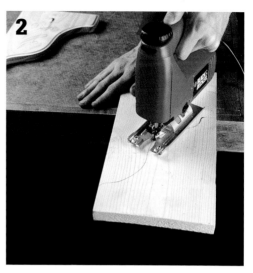

Cut out the two end pieces from 1 × 8 lumber. If the design has only straight lines, use a circular saw. If it includes curves, use a jigsaw. If desired, use a router to add a design to the end supports. Sand the faces and edges that will be exposed until smooth.

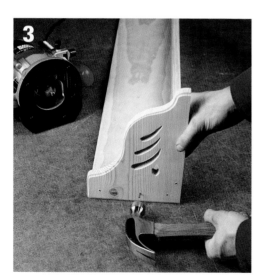

Attach end supports to the shelf unit using wood glue and 6d casing nails. Use a nail set to recess the nail heads. Finish the unit by staining or painting.

Drill pilot holes in the support piece every 6 to 10", avoiding the screws that attach the shelf to the horizontal support. Attach the shelf unit to the wall just above the window casing using 2" wood screws driven through the pilot holes. Plug and finish screw holes, if desired.

Basement Window Trim

Basement windows invite much-needed sunlight into dark areas, but they present multiple trimming challenges. Most basement foundation walls are at least 8" thick, in addition to a furred-out wall. In many cases the window starts to look more like a tunnel with a pane of glass at the end. But with some well-designed and well-executed trim carpentry, you can turn the depth disadvantage into an attractive trim shelf, great for potted plants, objects— even sunning cats.

Basement window openings may be finished with wallboard, but the easiest way to trim one is by making extra-wide custom jambs that extend from the inside face of the window frame to the interior wall surface. Because of the extra width, plywood stock is a good choice for the custom jambs.

Tools & Materials ▸

Finish-grade ¾" oak plywood	2-ft. level
Spray-foam insulation	Framing square
Shims	Utility knife
1¼" and 2" finish nails	Straightedge
1⅝" drywall screws	
Carpenter's glue	
Pencil	
Tape measure	
Table saw	
Drill with bits	

Set into thick foundation walls, basement windows present a bit of a trimming challenge but finish beautifully with creative trim work.

How to Trim a Basement Window

Check to make sure the window frame and surrounding area are dry and free of rot, mold, or damage. At all four corners of the basement window, measure from the inside edges of the window frame to the wall surface. Add 1" to the longest of these measurements.

Set your table saw to make a rip cut to the width arrived at in step 1. If you don't have a table saw, set up a circular saw and a straightedge cutting guide to cut strips to this length. With a fine-tooth panel-cutting blade, rip enough plywood strips to make the four jamb frame components.

Miter gauge

Cross-cut the plywood strips to correct lengths. In our case, we designed the jamb frame to be the exact same outside dimensions as the window frame, since there was some space between the jamb frame and the rough opening.

³⁄₈ × ³⁄₄" rabbet

Cut ³⁄₈"-deep × ³⁄₄"-wide rabbets at each end of the head jamb and the sill jamb. A router table is the best tool for this job, but you may use a table saw or hand saws and chisels. Inspect the jambs first and cut the rabbets in whichever face is in better condition. To ensure uniformity, we ganged the two jambs together (they're the same length). It's also a good idea to include backer boards to prevent tear-out.

(continued)

Glue and clamp the frame parts together, making sure to clamp near each end from both directions. Set a carpenter's square inside the frame and check it to make sure it's square.

Before the glue sets, drill carefully three perpendicular pilot holes countersunk through the rabbeted workpieces and into the side jambs at each corner. Space the pilot holes evenly, keeping the ones at the ends at least ¾" from the end. Drive a 1⅝" drywall screw into each pilot hole, taking care not to overdrive. Double check each corner for square as you work, adjusting the clamps if needed. Let the glue dry for at least one hour, overnight is best.

Remove the clamps and set the frame in the window opening. Adjust the frame so it is centered and level in the opening and the exterior-side edges fit flush against the window frame.

Taking care not to disturb the frame's position (rest a heavy tool on the sill to hold it in place if you wish), press a steel rule against the wall surface and use a pencil to mark trimming points at the point where the rule meets the jambs at each side of all four frame corners.

Scribe line

Remove the frame and clamp it on a flat work surface. Use a straightedge to connect the scribe marks at the ends of each jamb frame side. Set the cutting depth of your circular saw to just a small fraction over ¾". Clamp a straightedge guide to the frame so the saw blade will follow the cutting line and trim each frame side in succession. (The advantage to using a circular saw here is that any tear-out from the blade will be on the nonvisible faces of the frame).

Replace the frame in the window opening and install shims until it is level and centered in the opening. Drive a few finish nails (hand or pneumatic) through the side jambs into the rough frame. Also drive a few nails through the sill jamb.

Insulate between the jamb frame and the rough frame with spray-in polyurethane foam. Look for minimal-expanding foam for "windows and doors" and don't spray in too much. Let the foam dry for a half hour or so and then trim off the excess with a utility knife. *Tip: Protect the wood surfaces near the edges with wide strips of masking tape.*

Remove the masking tape, clean up the remaining foam, and install case molding. We used picture-frame techniques to install fairly simple oak casing.

Wall Paint

Arguably, no one element can have as large an immediate impact on your design scheme than the paint applied to your walls. However, too many decorators make the mistake of concentrating carefully on their color choice and then giving little or no thought to their technique and application method. As you will see in the following pages, painting techniques and faux finishes are a high-impact, low-commitment way to vastly improve your interior painting.

Each painting technique in this chapter has the potential to greatly affect the texture, tone, depth, and overall appeal of the colors you so carefully choose for your walls. Combine multiple colors using double-rolling or sponging techniques, carefully blend from one color to another, apply a flat geometric pattern or trowel classic veneer plaster to your wallboard. Use technique to cleverly highlight the rich boldness of your color choices or to blend in and accent your light, natural aesthetic.

In this chapter:

- Concrete Block Walls
- Double-Rolled Color
- Stripes
- Polka Dots
- Sponge Painting
- Rag-rolled Texture
- Terra-cotta Finish
- Blended Color Bands
- Color Wash Finish
- Stamped Mosaic
- Scumbled Wall Designs
- Faux Serpentine Finish
- Faux Grasscloth
- Caulk Designs
- Veneer Plaster

Concrete Block Walls

Painting a concrete block wall adds a long-lasting, durable finish to the porous block surface that will not only greatly improve the appearance of the blocks, but also increases their water resistance. All concrete walls must be cured for at least 30 days before being painted. They must also be free of mildew, dust, dirt, and efflorescence (a white, crystalline mineral deposit sometimes found on masonry surfaces). Keep in mind that the products used to prepare and paint concrete blocks will likely emit irritating fumes. Make sure your work area is well ventilated or wear a respirator when working with them.

Tools & Materials ▸

Masonry chisel
   or bottle opener
Wire brush
Hand vacuum
Hydraulic cement
Putty knife
Concrete cleaner
   and degreaser
Safety glasses

Etcher and
   rust remover
Heavy-duty
   rubber gloves
Sponge
Masking tape
Drill with paint-
   mixing bit

Concrete block walls need not look as industrial and dull as they often do—dress them up with bold colors or clean neutrals.

Prepare Your Concrete Block Walls for Painting ▸

Use a masonry chisel or a bottle opener and wire brush to remove any debris or dirt from holes and cracks. Clean all dust and debris from the surface with a hand vacuum.

To patch holes, apply hydraulic cement in layers no more than ½" thick until the patch is slightly higher than the surrounding area. Feather the patch until the edges are even with the surface. Let the patch dry according to the manufacturer's directions.

How to Paint a Concrete Block Wall

Press a piece of masking tape onto the blocks in several places, and then pull the tape away. If the tape doesn't pull concrete away from the surface, it can be painted. If loose concrete comes away with the tape, all loose bits need to be scraped away with a wire brush.

Wearing safety goggles and rubber gloves, clean the concrete blocks with a cleaner and degreaser (or etcher/rust remover). Thoroughly rinse the blocks with water and let them dry. Stir the paint using a variable-speed drill and paint-mixing bit.

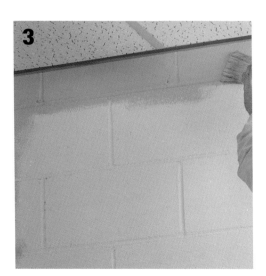

Working in roughly 2 × 4-ft. sections, start at the top and cut in with a paintbrush.

While the cut-in edges are still wet, roll paint onto the first section. Work the paint into the surface, making certain paint fills any pores. Repeat with the section immediately beneath the first. When you finish the room, let the paint dry according to the manufacturer's instructions, then apply a second coat of paint to the entire area.

Double-Rolled Color

Double rolling, also called color meshing, produces a complex texture with impressive color variations in only one step. Two-color meshing is perfect for beginners or anyone who wants to create a painted surface that has depth and variety without spending a lot of time.

This technique works best with satin-finish, standard latex paints and is not compatible with glazes. Choose your lightest color first and then find a second color that is three, four, or five shades darker. Colors that are three shades apart will produce muted variations, whereas colors that are five shades apart produce more dramatic textures. Choose colors that blend rather than contrast for best results.

If you're new to using creative painting techniques, experiment on a piece of scrap drywall or on an inconspicuous wall (behind the water heater is usually a good spot) until you've perfected your technique.

Tools & Materials ›

Dual roller
Two-compartment
    paint tray
1" brush
Accessory pad

Masking tape
Two colors of satin-
    finish latex paint
Drop cloths

Use a dual roller and two paint colors of varying shades to achieve a simple textured effect.

How to Apply Meshed Color

1

Select two colors of satin-finish latex paint, one color three-to-five shades darker than the other. Stir the paint well, then pour each color into one compartment of a divided paint tray.

2

Remove any lint from the paint roller by patting it with the sticky side of masking tape. Change the tape when it loses its stickiness, and continue patting until no more lint comes off the roller. Dampen the roller with water and thoroughly wring it out.

3

Roll the two-color roller into the paint and run it up and down the textured portion of the tray several times. Make sure the roller is loaded well, but not so full that it will drip.

4

Make a diagonal sweep about two feet long, rolling slowly enough to avoid splatters. Next, make a diagonal sweep in the opposite direction and then make a vertical sweep.

5

Draw the roller in a back-and-forth motion until the colors are blended to your satisfaction.

6

At the edges and in corners, apply ample splotches of each paint color using a 1" brush. Immediately pat the paint with the accessory pad to blend the colors to match the surrounding area.

Stripes

Painting stripes is a relatively simple painting project that can produce striking results. Stripes visually expand a small foyer or perk up a dull hallway or landing. In a kitchen, stripes can be an innovative treatment above upper cabinets. Wide stripes can relax formal furnishings in a living room or guest bedroom. If you're considering stripes, choose your colors and the size of your stripe carefully, as these elements will greatly impact the energy of your room when finished.

Begin by measuring the room and planning the width of your stripes so they work out evenly throughout the room. The challenges of this project are keeping your plumb lines straight and eliminating seepage under the painter's tape once you begin. A laser level greatly simplifies the line-drawing process, and every stripe painter should splurge on professional-quality painter's tape to avoid seepage.

Tools & Materials ▸

Paint
Roller
Professional-quality
   painter's tape
Pencil

Laser level or
   carpenter's level
Tape measure
Small roller or
   sponge applicator

Painted stripes can be subtle or dramatic—it's up to you! Coordinate with furniture and woodwork to ensure a classic, elegant final result.

How to Paint Stripes

1

Apply a base coat in your chosen color. Allow paint to dry.

2

Apply painter's tape against the plumb line shot with a laser level. Firmly press the edges of the tape to the wall to ensure a good bond.

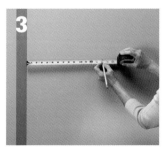

3

Measure from the inside edge of the painter's tape to the desired width of the stripe and make a pencil mark. Shoot a parallel boundary with the laser level and apply tape on the outside of the plumb line. Repeat until all stripes are taped off, checking for plumb from time to time.

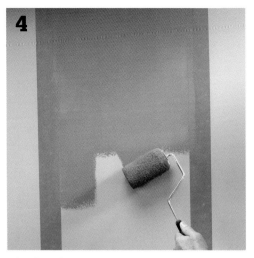

4

Paint the stripes, using a small roller or sponge applicator.

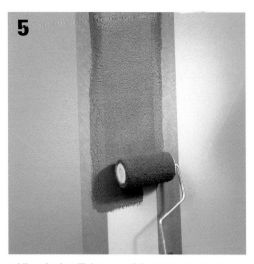

5

While paint is still damp, carefully remove the tape. Let paint dry completely.

Additional Stripe Ideas ▸

Stripes can be bold and energetic, subtle and elegant, or somewhere in between. Layer contrasting stripes of different widths for bold elegance. Or, add interest to a wall without expanding the color palette by adding evenly spaced stripes of similar colors. Paint glossy stripes over a flat background of the same color to create a quiet accent particularly suitable for formal spaces.

Polka Dots

A lively, lighthearted paint technique, polka dots are perfect for children's rooms, craft rooms, laundry rooms, bathrooms, and more. Part of the success of this technique depends on adjusting the spacing of the polka dots to suit the size of the room. Don't worry if the polka dots are imperfect, as randomness is part of what makes this technique appealing.

Color choice depends mostly on where the polka dots will be used in your home. Consider brighter colors for lively spaces like children's playrooms, bedrooms, and bathrooms. If you select complementary colors, use a lighter value for the background so the dots pop. Use subdued colors, perhaps two shades of the same hue, for an elegant, refined result. Colorwashing the walls after applying polka dots will soften the pattern even more for a subtle finished effect.

Tools & Materials ▸

Painter's tape
Drop cloths
Paint roller and tray

Latex paint for base coat
Latex paint in desired colors for dots

Paper plates
Styrofoam cups

Paper towels
Small foam applicator

Polka dots can be large or small—applied in small areas, such as within paneling frames, or on a large accent wall. If you're painting your entire room with polka dots, plan the spacing to appear consistent on all of the walls.

How to Paint Polka Dots

Prepare the room for painting—apply painter's tape and drop cloths. Apply the base coat and let it dry completely. Plan the spacing of the polka dots. Place a small piece of painter's tape wherever you would like the dots placed.

Pour a puddle of paint onto a paper plate. Dip the open end of a Styrofoam cup into the puddle, and then lightly press the cup onto several paper towels to remove excess paint.

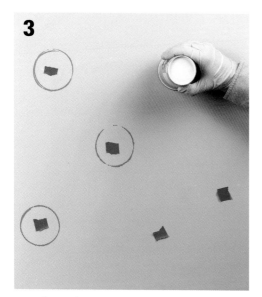

Press the cup firmly over the tape mark on the wall. Repeat to outline each polka dot.

Using a small foam applicator, fill in each polka dot with its paint color.

Sponge Painting

Applying paint with a sponge produces a pebbly, mottled finish. The technique is easy to master and the effect complements many décor styles beautifully. Today, sponging color choices are most often subtle and blended, unlike the high contrast color combinations that were a fad for a time. The sponge you choose will also greatly impact your final result. Use a natural sea sponge for small, condensed marks or sculpt a synthetic sponge for a larger, more defined pattern.

Semigloss, satin, and flat latex paints are all appropriate for sponge painting. For a translucent finish, mix a paint glaze by combining paint, paint conditioner, and water. Always practice your technique on a large piece of wallboard or an inconspicuous wall to experiment before you begin to perfect the application.

Tools & Materials ▸

Latex paint	Roller tray
Paint conditioner	Natural sea sponge

Sponge painting produces a soft texture; use varying hues of the same color for bold depth.

Additional Sponging Ideas ▸

Tape off stripes (see page 146) and apply sponge painted color to the unmasked areas for a textured pattern.

For a muted effect, use closely-related shades of the same hue. For bold texture, choose highly contrasting shades or similar shades of colors that are next to each other on the color wheel.

How to Sponge Paint a Wall

1

Mix together equal parts latex paint, latex paint conditioner, and water for the first sponged color, the darker color. Stir thoroughly.

2

Pour some of the paint into a roller tray, and press a natural sea sponge into the paint. Pat the sponge onto a paper towel to remove excess paint, then dab the paint onto the wall in a 2 × 4-ft. section.

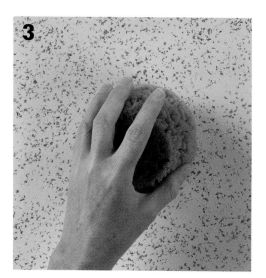

3

Continue sponging until the section is filled with sponged paint but the base coat is still visible. Wash out the sponge and let the paint dry. Mix the paint for the lighter color as described in step 1.

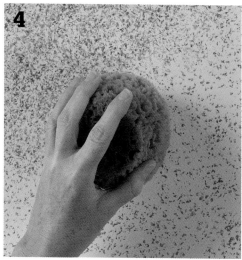

4

Dampen the sponge and wring it out. Press the sponge into the lighter color of paint and remove the excess by blotting it on a paper towel. Sponge the paint evenly over the wall. Don't cover the base coat or dark color. Stand back and evaluate the effect. Sponge more paint where necessary to even out the variations.

Rag-Rolled Texture

Ragging is a textural application technique that produces a soft, organic texture. Ragging is particularly effective in cottage- or country-styled spaces using soft colors that clearly reveal the rag imprints. In typical rag-rolled paint designs, a lighter color is used as the base coat with a darker color for the glaze. However, the reverse can also be quite lovely. Experiment with the technique as you test; apply the rag marks densely or sparsely, try ragging two different glaze colors over the base coat, or experiment with pulling color off with a rag rather than applying it.

Any clean, lint-free rags can be used, including gauze, burlap, chamois cloth, or jersey; your fabric

choice will affect the imprints, so test a few rags on a scrap before choosing your favorite. Though extremely versatile, ragging can be quite messy, so prepare your work area thoroughly before beginning.

Ragging can create rich texture and subtle interest when used with similar or complementary colors and consistent application.

How to Rag-Roll a Wall

In a clean bucket, mix together equal parts latex paint, latex paint conditioner, and water. Stir thoroughly.

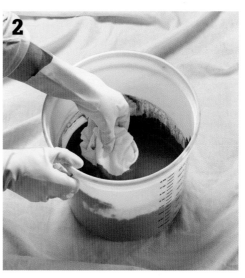

Put on rubber gloves, and then dip a lint-free rag into the glaze, saturating the entire rag. Wring out the rag thoroughly, and then wipe the excess glaze from your gloves onto an old towel.

Roll up the rag irregularly, then fold it to a length equal to the width of both your hands.

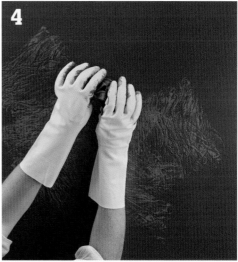

Roll the rag over the surface of a 2 × 4-ft. section of the wall, working upward at various angles. Rewet and wring the rag whenever necessary and continue application until you're satisfied with the effect. Move on to subsequent sections until the project is complete.

Terra-Cotta Finish

Introduce depth and warmth to a room by applying a terra-cotta finish to your walls. Although this finish has a sophisticated and refined appearance, it's quite easy to create. Unlike most other painting techniques included here, a terra-cotta finish does not require a preliminary base coat. Instead, use a wool pad to apply and blend several colors of paint to a primed surface. The more you blend the paints, the more muted the finish becomes.

The traditional terra-cotta finish consists of three colors of latex paint, usually shades of deep brown, dark clay, and apricot. For a rosier terra-cotta, choose colors with a red base; for an orange overtone, choose yellow-based colors. If you're not sure which colors will work best to achieve your desired effect, seek help from a salesperson to put together the right combination.

Tools & Materials ▸

Divided paint tray
Paint stirrer sticks

Wool paint pad
Wood finishing tool

Brown, clay and
   apricot latex paint

Paint glaze

The term terra-cotta originally referred to ancient unglazed ceramic clay used to make vessels and plumbing systems. Today, terra-cotta refers to a warm orange-brown, subtly textured color scheme.

How to Produce a Terra-cotta Finish with a Wool Pad

Pour each shade of paint into a separate section of a divided paint tray. Add a quarter cup of paint glaze to each color, blending it into the paint with a stir stick. Wet your hand with water and run it over the wool pad to remove lint and loose fibers.

Dip the wool pad into the brown paint and scrape the pad along the edge of the tray to remove excess paint. Working in 4 × 4-ft. sections, apply the paint by pressing the pad to the wall in a random pattern. Cover about 80 percent of the wall surface in each section, leaving some bare spots visible.

Scrape the pad to remove as much of the brown paint from the pad as possible. You do not need to wash the pad before applying the next paint color.

Dip the wool pad into the clay paint, and scrape off the excess. Using the same stamping technique you used to apply the brown paint, fill in the bare spots in the section with the clay paint. When you are finished, scrape the clay paint from the pad, as before.

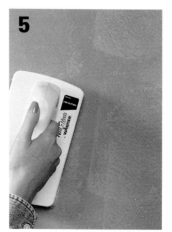

Dip the wool pad into the apricot paint, and remove the excess. Using the random stamping technique, lightly press the wool pad onto the painted section. You will begin to see the paint blend. The more you apply the apricot paint, the more the paint will blend and the lighter the final design will be.

Once you've finished the section, use a finishing tool to apply paint in the corners and at the edges of the section. First, remove lint and loose fibers from the tool (see step 1). Repeat steps 2 through 5, applying the brown, clay, and apricot paints, and blending until the design is complete. When the section is complete, move on to the next.

Blended Color Bands

This blending technique creates the illusion that the paint colors are fading into one another, a unique and striking effect that draws the eye around the room and highlights your artwork and furnishings. The success of this technique depends heavily upon careful color selection. Choose two paint colors that sit next to each other on the color wheel (see page 10). You'll create the third color by mixing together equal amounts of each. The resulting midtone will smooth the transition between the top and bottom bands and enhance the illusion of the blend.

The key to success with this application is that the paint must be wet in order to blend the bands properly, so it's best to work in small sections. If the paint gets too dry to blend well, add fresh paint to each band and blend it again.

Tools & Materials ▸

Carpenter's level or laser level
Tape measure
Straightedge
Pencil
Five 3" paintbrushes
Power drill and paint mixing bit
Three paint pails
Two colors of matte latex paint
Wallpaper paste

Blending color bands is a great solution for intimate spaces or very small rooms, as it creates the illusion of more space. Use this technique along with simple furnishings and decorations for the best effect.

How to Create Blended Color Bands

1

Measure the wall and divide it into three equal sections. Using a laser or carpenter's level, draw horizontal lines to act as guidelines for the bands of paint.

2

Pour equal amounts of each color into a pail and use a drill and paint-mixing bit to blend it thoroughly. In a second pail, mix equal amounts of the darkest paint and wallpaper paste. In a third, mix equal amounts of the lightest paint and wallpaper paste. Label the pails.

3

Paint a 2 to 3-ft. section of the darkest color at the bottom of the wall, spreading the paint roughly up to the first guideline.

4

Apply a coat of the blended midtone (created in step 2) to a 2 to 3-ft. section of the middle band. Leave an inch or so between this band and the first one.

5

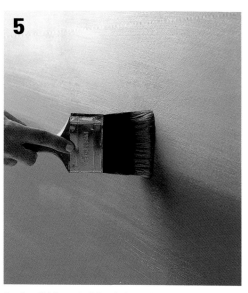

Apply a thick coat of the dark wash to the gap between the first and second bands. Dampen a clean paintbrush and run it along the line between the bands, blending the wash up and down into each band until the lines have disappeared into a subtle transition between colors.

6

Apply the lightest color to the top band, leaving a gap between it and the middle band. Apply a thick coat of the light wash between the bands, and then use a clean, damp paintbrush to blend the colors up and down as before.

7

Continue painting one section of the wall at a time, running over at the corners. Use the finished corner as a placement guide for the newly painted one, blending the edges to make sure the color shifts are consistent. Slight variations are inevitable, but try to keep the blends as consistent as possible.

Color Wash Finish

Color washing gives walls a translucent, watercolored appearance, adding the illusion of texture to flat surfaces and emphasizing the unique eccentricities of textured surfaces. Color wash glaze can be either lighter or darker than the base coat, but for best results, choose colors that are closely related or use a neutral color as one of your selections. Washing complementary or contrasting colors will result in a muddy, dull finish.

Color washing can be completed using either a sponge or a brush with varying results. The sponge application method requires a highly diluted glaze that is applied over a base coat of low-luster latex enamel, using a natural sea sponge. The result is a subtle texture with a soft blending of colors. Color washing with a paintbrush requires a heavier glaze to retain the fine lines of the brush strokes. As the glaze begins to dry, soften the appearance of brush stroke lines further by smudging the surface with a dry paintbrush.

A color wash creates a subtle decorative effect, highlighting the texture of your walls, or creating hints of depth on flat surfaces.

Tools & Materials ▸

Flat latex paint
Latex paint conditioner

Low-luster latex
enamel paint

Natural sea sponge or two 3 to 4"
natural bristle paintbrushes

Rubber gloves
Pail

Glaze Selection and Mixing ▸

Select colors for the base coat and glaze that are closely related or use at least one neutral color. A dark glaze over a lighter base coat (left) produces a mottled effect, whereas a light glaze over a darker base coat (right) produces a chalky or watercolored effect.

Sponge Color Wash Glaze
1 part latex or acrylic paint
8 parts water

Brush Color Wash Glaze
1 part flat latex paint
1 part latex paint conditioner
2 parts water

How to Color Wash with a Sponge

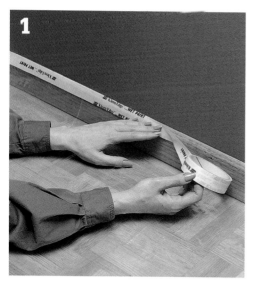

1

Mask off the surrounding area, using painter's masking tape, and cover the floor with waterproof drop cloths. Apply a base coat of low-luster latex enamel paint, using a paint roller. Allow the paint to dry.

Color Wash with a Brush ▶

After the base coat dries, mix the color-washing glaze as instructed on page 158. Dip a paintbrush into the glaze and apply to the wall in a cross-hatching manner, beginning in one corner. The more brushstrokes you create, the softer the texture will appear. Before the paint has dried completely, brush over the surface, with a dry natural bristle paintbrush to soften the look. Wipe excess glaze from the brush as necessary.

2

Mix the glaze as instructed on page 158 and immerse the sponge into the solution. Squeeze out excess liquid, but leave the sponge very wet.

3

Beginning in a low corner, wipe the color wash solution onto the wall in short, curving strokes. Overlap and change the direction of the strokes, quickly covering a 3 × 3-ft. section of wall.

4

Repeat steps 2 and 3, moving upward and outward until the entire wall has been color washed. Allow the paint to dry. Apply a second coat if additional color is desired.

Stamped Mosaic

Mosaic tile is a classic choice for walls, but tile can be expensive and time-consuming to install. A painted mosaic is inexpensive and easy to do, and it can be changed just as easily as it can be created.

The effect of a tile mosaic is too dramatic to use it in large spaces. Typically, it's best to choose a small area or the space below a chair rail for this finish. With its irregular coloration and varied pattern, a painted mosaic can cover many flaws, so the preparation steps for this project don't have to be quite as elaborate as for many other paint projects.

Tools & Materials ▸

Craft knife
Large paintbrush
Roller and roller tray
Three 1" paintbrushes
Small artist's brush
Ruler
Repositionable spray glue
High-density foam rubber
Low-tack masking tape or painter's tape
Three colors of latex paint

A stamped mosaic is a creative way to add color and texture to small spaces and works beautifully under a chair rail or wallcovering border.

How to Create a Stamped Mosaic

Place some of each paint color into the well of a clean roller tray. Using three clean paintbrushes, dab a generous amount of each color of paint onto the flat surface of the roller tray. It's fine for the colors to blend a little in a few places, but don't deliberately mix them.

To make a paper template for the stamp, draw a series of tiles divided by ¼" grout lines. Round the corners of the squares to resemble tile. Spray the back of the paper with repositionable spray glue and press the pattern onto the high-density foam. Cut around each tile, using a craft knife, and remove the excess pieces. (Try to consistently cut about halfway into the foam.) When the stamp is complete, press it into the paint until it's well coated but not dripping with paint.

Start at the top, left-hand corner and press the stamp squarely against the wall, being careful not to let it slip. After a moment, peel the stamp away from the wall from one side. Recoat the stamp and position it ¼" from the previous print, to create a grout line. Continue stamping in this manner. When you begin the next row, align the pattern lines before pressing the stamp to the wall. If the colors bleed together, reestablish the base color between "tiles" with a small artist's brush (inset).

Scumbled Wall Designs

Scumbling is a technique that creates textural geometric patterns that mimic the look of expensive wallcovering. To scumble, use a large stencil brush to dry-brush paint onto the wall in swirling motions over a base coat. Because very little paint is required for dry-brushing, pick up small jars of acrylic craft paints instead of more traditional latex buckets. Choose two or three related decorator colors, or use gold and silver metallic paints for a classy shimmer.

Scumbling can be a stunning finish over geometric shapes applied to an entire wall, a ceiling border, or as a faux wainscoting. Take care to measure each wall and sketch the geometric design on graph paper to help you determine the scale and placement of your design. Always experiment on a piece of cardboard or an inconspicuous wall, and remember to adequately prepare your work area before you begin.

Tools & Materials ▸

Ruler	Straightedge	Painter's tape	Latex or craft acrylic
Pencil	Putty knife	Latex paint	paints for scumbling
Paint roller	1" stencil brush	for base coat	Paper towels
Carpenter's level	Graph paper	Disposable plates	

Scumbling can recreate the classic, refined texture of expensive wallcovering or can be used to partition walls as a border or wainscot.

How to Paint a Taped-off Scumbled Design

Measure the wall and plan the design to scale on graph paper. Apply a base coat of paint using a paint roller.

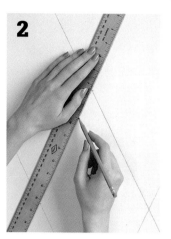

Allow the paint to dry. Draw the design on the wall with a pencil using a straightedge as a guide.

Mark the sections that will be masked off. Apply painter's masking tape to the marked sections using a putty knife to trim the tape diagonally at the corners. Press along all edges of the tape using a plastic credit card or your fingernail to create a tight seal.

Pour a small amount of each paint color onto a disposable plate. Dip the tip of the stencil brush into the first color. Using a circular motion, blot the brush onto a paper towel until the bristles are almost dry.

Brush the paint onto the wall with vigorous, wide, circular motions. Work in a small area at a time, and change the direction of the circular motions frequently. Overlap the paint onto the masking tape. Build up the color to the desired intensity, but allow the base coat to show through. Use all of the paint on bristles before applying more.

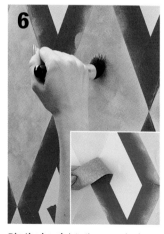

Dip the brush into the second color and blot. Apply the paint randomly over the same area, building up the color to varying intensities throughout the area. Repeat with a third color, if desired. Repeat this technique to complete the wall, working in one small area at a time. Remove the tape carefully when the paint is dry.

Faux Serpentine Finish

Serpentine is the name given to a variety of green marble that contains deposits of the mineral serpentine, speckles of black and white rock, and a conspicuous network of fine veining. Replicate this classic marble with paint to add sophistication and elegance to smaller portions of your living spaces, such as bathroom walls, beneath a wainscot in a kitchen or hallway, or to accent fireplaces and furnishings.

Because genuine marble is often cut into workable pieces for installation, a faux serpentine finish applied to a large surface is more realistic if applied in sections with narrow grout lines to mimic marble pieces. Mask off and complete application in sections, allowing each completed section to dry completely before masking it off and completing the next section. Always finish a faux serpentine project with a high gloss coat applied to the entire surface, imitating the lustrous appearance of genuine marble.

Faux serpentine adds sophisticated appeal to fireplaces, wainscot paneling, and furnishings.

Tools & Materials ▸

Low-napped paint roller (for base coat)
Sponge applicator or paintbrush
Stippler

Spray bottle
Turkey feather
Low-luster latex enamel paint
Newspaper

Craft acrylic paints in a darker shade than the latex enamel, black, and white
Cheesecloth

Water-based clear urethane
High-gloss clear finish or aerosol clear acrylic sealer

How to Apply a Faux Serpentine Finish

Apply a base coat of low-luster latex enamel. Mix equal parts clear urethane, paint, and water for each gloss color. Apply colored, black, and white gloss glazes separately in random broad, diagonal strokes with a sponge applicator or paintbrush. Cover most of the surface, allowing small patches of the base coat to show through.

Stipple the glazes in adjoining areas to blend them slightly, bouncing a stippler rapidly over the surface.

Fold a sheet of newspaper to several layers and lay it flat in the same diagonal direction as the original paint strokes. Press the newspaper into the glaze and then lift it off, removing some of the glaze. Repeat over the entire surface using the same newspaper. Occasionally turn the paper in opposite directions and add glazes as desired to develop the color.

Soften areas of high contrast by dabbing with wadded cheesecloth. Mist the surface with water if necessary, to keep the glazes workable.

Brush black glaze onto a piece of newspaper and touch it to the surface diagonally in scattered areas, adding drama and depth. Soften with cheesecloth, if necessary. Repeat the process using a white glaze in small, light areas.

Dilute a mixture of the white and colored glazes with water to the consistency of light cream. Run the edge and tip of the feather through the diluted glaze. Lightly drag the feather diagonally over the surface while fidgeting, turning it slightly, and varying the pressure to create an irregular, jagged vein. Begin and end veins off the edge of the surface. Repeat as necessary to create a veining pattern.

Connect adjacent vein lines occasionally to create narrow, oblong, irregular shapes. Dab veins lightly with wadded cheesecloth to soften if necessary. Allow the surface to dry.

Dilute glazes to the consistency of ink and apply randomly to the surface. Dab with wadded cheesecloth to soften the colors. Allow the glazes to dry. Apply several thin coats of high-gloss clear finish or aerosol clear acrylic sealer, allowing the surface to dry between coats.

Faux Grasscloth

Woven grass wallcoverings are a lovely, if a little expensive, way to bring a soft natural appeal to your décor. With paint, a squeegee, and a little hard work, however, you can create the same look with cleverly applied paint! A variation of combing, this technique manipulates the top coat of paint, removing fine lines of color to expose the base coat. Walls are taped of in sections similar in width to traditional wallcoverings, and the narrow lines of color where the sections overlap add to the illusion of traditional grasscloth seams.

For a realistic appearance, select paint colors that closely resemble natural grasses, such as sand and wheat. Because of the earthy nature of the technique, grasscloth walls work well in rooms that depend upon plants and natural textures for their design aesthetic.

Tools & Materials ▸

Painter's tape	Window squeegee
Drop cloths	Rubber gloves
Paint roller and tray	Latex paint
Latex paint for base coat	for top coat
Pencil	Sash brush
Long carpenter's level	Small paint comb
Scissors	Clean rags

Or, pair grasscloth with rich reds and classic black to replicate the luxurious elegance of Asian-inspired décor. Bear in mind, however, that this faux finish produces a pronounced texture. If you plan to repaint in the future, the walls will need to be sanded as well as primed.

Detail

Faux grasscloth is perfect for contemporary or natural décor—and blends beautifully with neutral or bold decór.

How to Create Faux Grasscloth Wallcoverings

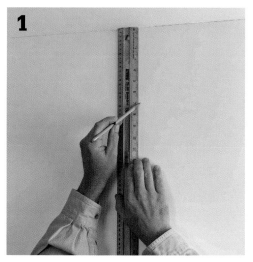

Prepare your work area and apply the base coat. Let it dry completely. Mark off 3 ft. vertical panels around the room with a pencil. Pencil in the edge lines with the level. Tape off every other panel.

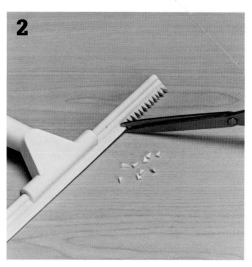

Using the scissors, cut the squeegee into a saw-toothed pattern, with pointed teeth about ¼" apart. Put on rubber gloves and cut in to the top and bottom of the panel with the top coat paint using a sash brush. Immediately fill in the rest of the panel with a paint roller.

Draw the squeegee across the painted panel horizontally, beginning at the top and working downward and overlapping the passes. After each pass, wipe excess paint from the squeegee with the rags. Use a small paint comb for hard-to-reach areas like corners and outlets and switches.

Remove the tape before the paint dries. Repeat step 3 for each alternating wall section. Allow each section to dry completely, and then mask off painted sections, positioning the tape ⅛" inside the painted edges. As the paint overlaps in these thin lines, it will imitate traditional grasscloth seams. Remove the tape and let the paint dry completely.

Caulk Designs

Caulk designs are drawn on the wall using tub and tile caulk. When the caulk designs are dry, the wall can be painted any color, and the shadows of the raised dots and lines produce patterns from beneath. The technique is simple, but the design options are unlimited! Create geometric patterns, swirls, flowers, words—whatever inspires you! Draw your designs freehand, or utilize an LCD or overhead project to enlarge patterns on the wall for you to trace.

The caulk adheres to the wall best if it is slightly cool when applied. The size of the dots and lines will depend on the size of the opening cut in the tip of the caulk tube. For tiny dots and thin lines, cut the tip close to the end; for more substantial strokes, cut the tip closer to the tube. To remove designs later, scrape them off with a paint scraper, patch and prime the walls for repainting.

Tools & Materials ▸

Painter's tape	Latex primer	Scissors	Satin latex paint
Drop cloths	Pencil	Paintbrush	for top coat
Paint roller and tray	Tub and tile caulk		

Caulked designs can add fanciful flair to children's bedrooms and other playful spaces, or they can dress up kitchens, bathrooms, or living spaces with subtle patterns and designs.

How to Apply Caulked Designs

1

2

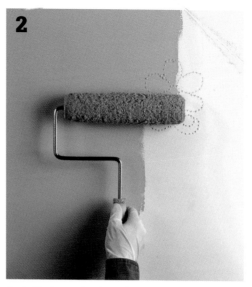

Lightly pencil in the design of your choice onto the wall surface. Apply dots and lines of caulk over the marked lines, squeezing the tube with even pressure. Stop squeezing and lift the top from the surface at the end of each line. Using a wet fingertip, smooth down any bumps and tails after 30 minutes. Allow 24 hours for the caulk to dry completely.

Apply the top coat to the entire wall.

Creating Your Design ▶

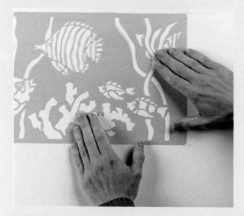

Use a stencil to trace dynamic designs onto your walls with a pencil. If your designs are complex or if you are applying words, tape a piece of graphite transfer paper to the wall, then place a photocopy or printout of the design over the transfer paper. Trace your design and remove the paper to reveal a penciled outline.

Veneer Plaster

Veneer plaster application recreates the classic look of homes from the 1940s and adds a solid, uniform surface that is highly resistant to nail pops, cracks, and surface damage. A skim coat of plaster is troweled onto a gypsum wallboard base that has a distinctive blue color, commonly called blueboard. Installed like standard wallboard, blueboard has highly absorptive face paper to which the wet-mix plaster bonds. Applying veneer plaster effectively does take some time to master. The key is to apply the plaster with a trowel in quick, short strokes, called scratching in, and then to immediately trowel it over with a steady, even stroke, smoothing the plaster to a consistent thickness (typically ¹⁄₁₆ to ⅛").

Finished plaster can be troweled smooth or tooled for an appealing texture. Sand and other additives can also be used to create coarser textures, which, when combined with sophisticated painting techniques, produce lovely, old-world decorative charm.

Veneer plaster adds character and depth to modern homes, evoking the classic look of homes from the early twentieth century.

Tools & Materials ▸

Stapler
Hammer
Heavy-duty ½" drill
  with mixing paddle
16-gal. drum

Mortar hawk
12" trowel
Fine-wire rake or broom
  (for base coat)
Spray water bottle

Metal corner bead with
  mesh flanges
1¼" wallboard screws
Non-adhesive fiberglass
  mesh tape
¼" staples

Clean potable water
Dry-mix veneer base
  coat plaster (for two-
  coat application)
Dry-mix veneer
  finish plaster

Textured Surface Options ▸

For textured surfaces, skip the final troweling and work the surface to create texture. Use a broom, paint-roller, paintbrush, or the trowel itself to achieve creative, eye-catching surfaces.

How to Apply a One-Coat Veneer Plaster System

Apply mesh flanges and a thin layer of plaster along all flat seams and corner bead at corners (inset). For inside corners, apply a thin bed of plaster and embed the loose tape, then cover with another thin layer. Allow all taped seams to set.

Variation: Blueboard joints can also be reinforced with paper tape. Embed the tape in a thin plaster bed, and then cover with another thin layer to conceal the tape fully. *Note: Some manufacturers recommend setting-type compound for embedding paper tape; always follow the manufacturer's directions for the products you use.*

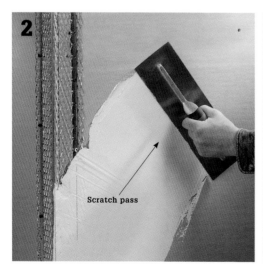

Scratch pass

Smooth pass

After the seams have set, begin plastering the surface beginning at one corner and moving to the opposite. Start with ceilings and then do the walls, completing one entire surface before moving on to the next. To apply the plaster, tightly scratch in the material up the wall (photo left), then immediately double-back over it, smoothing over the material to a thickness of $\frac{1}{16}$ to $\frac{3}{32}$", as specified by the manufacturer. Use tight, quick strokes to apply the plaster during the scratch pass and long, even strokes to achieve consistency during the smooth pass.

(continued)

Continue to apply plaster by scratching in and smoothing over the surface. Don't worry about uniformity and trowel ridges at this point. Rather, make sure the entire surface is completely concealed with a relatively even plaster coat ¹⁄₁₆ to ³⁄₃₂" thick.

Once the plaster begins to firm, trowel the surface to fill any voids and remove tooling marks and imperfections, integrating the surface into a uniform smoothness.

Prior to the plaster setting, make a final pass with the trowel to smooth the surface spraying water sparingly. Do not overtrowel; stop before the plaster begins to darken and set.

One- and Two-Coat Veneer Plaster Systems ▸

Finish

Gypsum plaster base

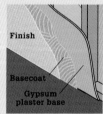

Finish

Basecoat

Gypsum plaster base

One-coat veneer plaster systems use a single ¹⁄₁₆ to ³⁄₃₂"-thick coat of finish plaster applied directly to a blueboard base. The coat can be troweled smooth or textured, resulting in a hard, monolithic surface.

Two-coat veneer plaster systems are composed of a ¹⁄₁₆ to ¹⁄₈" basecoat plaster applied to blueboard, followed by a ¹⁄₁₆ to ³⁄₃₂"-thick coat of finish plaster. The finish coat bonds with the scratched basecoat surface, forming a more uniform and monolithic surface than that of a one-coat system.

How to Apply Base Coat in a Two-Coat Veneer Plaster System

Apply a thin layer of basecoat along all flat seams and corner bead, feathering out the edges by 6". For inside corners, apply a thin bed of basecoat and embed the loose tape, then cover with another thin layer. Allow all taped seams to set.

Smooth pass

Scratch pass

After the seams have set, tightly scratch in basecoat, then immediately double-back over it, smoothing over the material to a thickness of 1/16 to 1/8", as specified by the manufacturer. Use tight, quick strokes to apply basecoat for the scratch pass and long, even strokes to achieve consistency for the smooth pass.

Once the plaster begins to firm, or take up, trowel the surface to fill any voids and remove tooling marks and imperfections, integrating the surface into a reasonably uniform surface—do not overtrowel to a smooth surface. Create keys for the final coat using a thin-wire rake to roughen the basecoat.

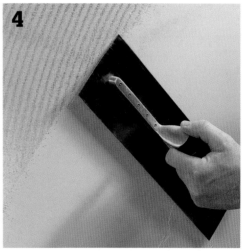

Approximately two hours after the basecoat has set, the finish coat can be applied using the same techniques used for a one-coat veneer plaster system (see pages 171 to 172).

Wall Décor

Wall decorations transform a beautifully decorated space into your beautifully decorated space. The collections, libraries, and artwork you display in your home are what make it uniquely your own; these elements tell the story of your family and are intimately tied to your decorative choices.

The wall décor projects in this chapter will help you display your personal belongings professionally and will provide ways to refresh and accent areas often neglected by decorators. Update your bathroom with new fixtures or a creatively tiled mirror—or accent your fireplace with a tiled surround. Apply a critical eye to your walls and then utilize these techniques to add style, polish, and personality to every area of your home.

In this chapter:

- Pictures & Mirrors
- Textiles
- Sticker Art
- Wood Shelving
- Glass Shelving

- Ceramic Tile Mirror Frame
- New Towel Bar
- Tile Fireplace Surround

Pictures & Mirrors

If you've ever made six holes in a wall to hang one picture, you know how frustrating the process can be. Most of us have done it, and none of us want to repeat the experience. Great news! By following the steps outlined here and using the right hardware, you can hang a picture without making a single unnecessary hole.

Before getting out your tools, study the size and shape of the room. Designers and decorators often suggest placing the center of a picture or mirror at eye level—57 to 60" above the floor—but that's a guideline, not a hard and fast rule. If you're placing a mirror behind a sideboard or a picture over a mantle, let the style of the room and a sense of balance guide its placement.

Tools & Materials ▸

D-rings or pictures hooks that will support the weight of your artwork	Tape measure Pencil Drill	Awl Screws Stud finder	Self-adhesive felt pads or silicone caulk Painter's tape

Hanging pictures and mirrors instantly personalizes a room, and it's easy to do when you approach it with the right tools and a good attitude. We'll show you how to position a piece properly and hang it securely—the first time.

Choosing Hardware ▸

Frames and mirrors remain level and secure when they're supported by wall studs and sturdy hardware. Before you choose hardware, find out what the piece weighs. While shopping, check the labels on the hardware you're considering to make sure it will support the weight of the piece you're going to hang.

If a stud is not available, then hardware selection is even more important. Take your specifications to a salesperson and find out which kind of self-tapping hollow wall anchor or heavy-duty wall hanger she/he recommends to both support your artwork sufficiently and protect the integrity of your walls.

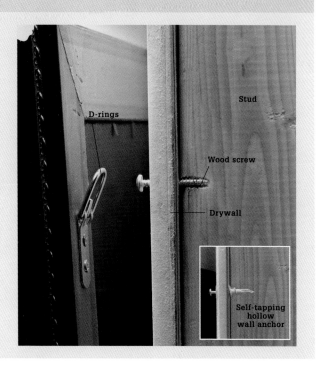

How to Hang a Picture

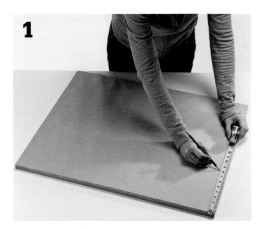

1

On each side of the frame, mark 8" down from the top. Purchase D-rings or picture hooks rated to support the approximate weight of the picture or mirror (package labels on the hardware give the suggested weight ranges).

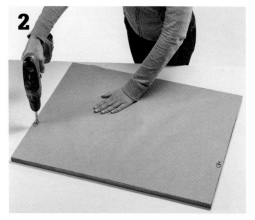

2

Set the D-rings aside, and then use an awl to punch a hole at each mark on the frame. Reposition the first D-ring and drive a screw into the mark, securely attaching the D-ring to the frame. Repeat on the other side.

(continued)

3

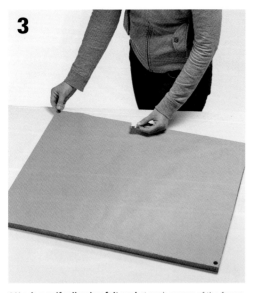

Attach a self-adhesive felt pad at each corner of the frame.

Variation: If you do not have felt pads available, put a dot of silicone caulk about the size of a pencil eraser on each corner instead. Continue to hang your artwork when the caulk is completely dry.

4

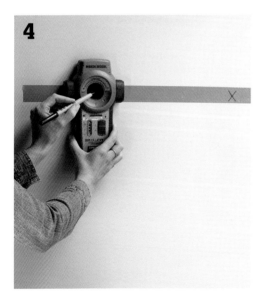

In the area where you want to hang the frame, place a piece of tape at the appropriate height, measured from the floor (usually 57 to 60", depending on the room's dimensions). Following manufacturer's directions, use a stud finder to locate the studs and mark the tape to indicate their positions.

5

Measure the width of the frame and divide that number by 2—this is the center of your frame. On the tape, mark the proposed center of the frame, and then mark the edge of the frame the calculated distance on each side. If possible, align the frame so that the three points are near your stud marks.

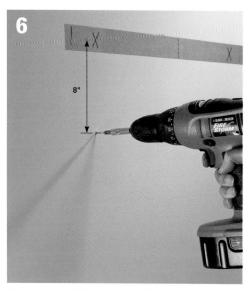

6

8"

Measure down 8" from the frame side marks for the D-ring placement. Drill wood screws into the studs.

7

Slip the D-rings or picture hooks over the screws on the wall. Your picture should now be straight and secure with nary an extra hole to repair.

Hanging a Picture When a Stud is Not Available ▸

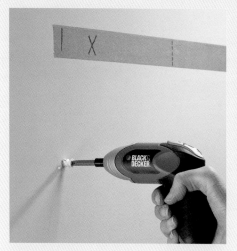

Use an awl to drill a small hole on your placement mark, then follow package instructions to drive self-tapping wall anchors into your wallboard. Drive a screw into each anchor as instructed.

Mels Enterprises, Inc. produces a heavy-duty wall hanger that is remarkably strong and easy to use, and is usable only where a stud is not available. To use, just push the chiseled anchor into the wall at your placement mark and twist until the hook is upright.

Textiles

Fabric wall hangings dress up walls and are easily replaceable as your décor changes. Quilts, tapestries, and other textiles make exquisite wall decorations, especially in bedrooms and living spaces, but are easily damaged when hung improperly.

Tools & Materials ▸

Cotton twill
  rug binding
Fabric-marking pen
Needle and thread
Level
Tape measure

Small hooks or screws
Dowel
Narrow board
Velcro strip
Drill

Hanging textiles is a creative way to add softness and warmth to your home—and to display family heirlooms and textile art.

How to Hang Textiles

Mark a straight line ½ to ¾" from the top edge of the textile. Cut a piece of cotton twill rug binding about 3" shorter than the width of the textile. Align the binding with the line and pin in place. Stitch the binding to the textile by hand, using a blind hem (page 31).

Mark a level line where you'd like to hang the piece about 1½" shorter than the width of the textile. Drive one small hook or screw eye into the wall at each end of the line. Insert a dowel or rod (cut 1½" wider than the rug binding piece) through the textile's casing and rest the dowel on the hooks or screws.

Variation: Position a narrow board along a level line at the desired height. Drive screws through the board into the studs in the wall. Cut a Velcro strip slightly less than the width of the textile and attach the "hook" side to the board. Hand-stitch the "loop" side along a line ½" from the top edge of the textile. Press the Velcro strips together to hold the textile in place.

Sticker Art

Wall stickers are an excellent decorative alternative to hung wall art—perfect for children's rooms or playful spaces. Stick-on wall art is even available as materials suitable to draw on with chalk. Today, manufacturers also make contemporary stickers in large, bold styles and patterns that are appropriate for any room in the home, including formal areas. Stickers are simple to use, apply professionally, and are available in a variety of styles and colors. Plus, they're easy to move and replace for those who change their décor frequently.

Tools & Materials ▸

Pencil   Wall stickers

Wall stickers can enhance decorative motifs in your room, or add a striking contrast to existing elements.

How to Hang Wall Stickers

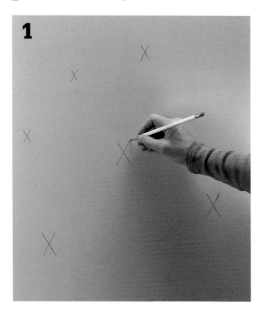

1

Clean walls then place light pencil marks where you plan to stick each item.

2

Peel the backing off each sticker and place it at your marked locations. Accurate placement is not necessary because wall stickers are easily removed and repositioned. However, bear in mind that continued removal and replacement will weaken the sticker's adhesive over time.

Wood Shelving

An attractive space to display collections, libraries, and mementos is a key element to every family's home décor, which explains why installing shelves is one of the first projects many decorators take on. Wood shelves fit invisibly into most design schemes, and are durable and easy to clean. By following a few basic guidelines, your shelves will be a sturdy and secure home for your belongings.

Before you purchase materials for this project, decide where you'd like your shelving placed and how wide you'd like it to be. It's also helpful to know the approximate weight of the items you'll be displaying—heavier collectibles will require more support than lighter items. Wood shelves are typically sold with all the hardware you'll need to install them, but always check the packaging to see if you will need to purchase hardware separately, and remember to purchase self-tapping hollow wall anchors if you cannot install your shelf into wall studs.

Indispensable to virtually every home, shelves provide storage and display space for everything from books to your favorite chachkas.

Tools & Materials ▸

Shelf and brackets
Pencil

Wood screws or self-tapping
hollow wall anchors

Laser level or
carpenter's level

Painter's tape

How to Install Wood Shelving

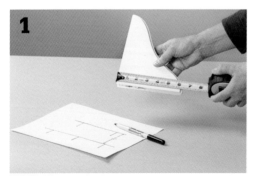

Measure the shelves and the brackets. Make a quick diagram of the shelves and their placement on the wall, including spacing between the shelves if there will be more than one. Be sure to consider the sizes of the items the shelf will hold as you decide how far apart to put the shelves.

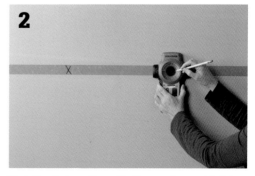

Mark the studs on the wall with easy-release painter's tape and plan to use them to support the shelf if possible.

3

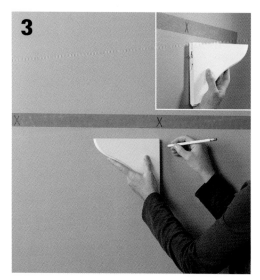

Position the first bracket and mark its screw holes on the wall. If there is a stud available to support the bracket, drive pilot holes at the marks and drive screws into the stud. If no stud is available, use an awl to make a small hole and then drive self-tapping hollow wall anchors into the holes and wood screws into the anchors. Attach the first bracket to the screws (see inset).

4

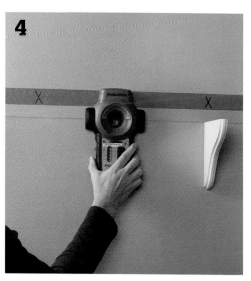

Use a level to create a line across the wall from the first bracket to the planned position of the next bracket. Attach the bracket to the wall as you did in step 3.

5

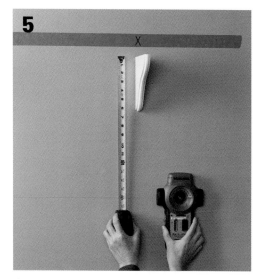

If the project includes more than one shelf, refer to the measurements from your diagram and use a level to draw a line for each of the remaining shelves.

6

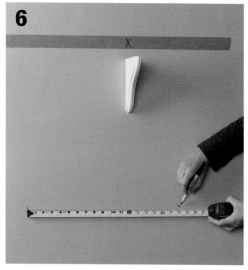

Remove the first bracket and use it to measure for the placement of all additional brackets. If shelves are more than 36" wide or will be supporting heavy items, install a bracket as a center support as well. Attach the remaining brackets and position the shelves upon them.

Glass Shelving

Glass shelving is sleek and unobtrusive, so it fits well into many rooms and décor styles. If you'd like to elegantly showcase items without drawing attention to the shelving as a structural statement, then glass shelves are the best choice for you.

Glass shelving is typically held in place with metal mounts, though the attachment method differs from shelf to shelf. The most basic models may have mounts that are screwed directly into the wall with exposed screws.

The directions here are for shelving that uses hidden brackets that attach to the wall. Mounts then slip over the brackets and are secured with setscrews.

Glass shelves are an excellent choice for bathrooms, kitchens, bedrooms, and living spaces.

How to Install Glass Shelves

Assemble the shelf and shelf holders (not the brackets). Hold the shelf against the wall in the desired location. On the wall, mark the center point of each holder, where the setscrew is. Remove the shelf from the holders and set aside.

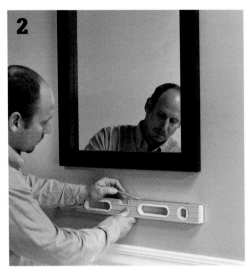

Remove the shelves and use the level to extend the mark into a 3" vertical line. Use the level to mark a horizontal line across the centers of these lines.

Center the middle round hole of the bracket over the intersection of the vertical and horizontal lines. Mark the center of each of the oblong holes. Put the bracket aside and drill a ¼" hole at each mark. Insert the included wall anchors in the holes. Replace the bracket, insert the screws into the wall anchors, and drive the screws. Repeat for the second bracket.

Slide a holder over a bracket, check that the shelf mount is level, and tighten the setscrew. Repeat with the other holder. Insert the shelf and fix in place. Check the shelf for level. If it's not level, remove one holder and loosen the bracket screws. Slide the bracket up or down to make the unit level. Replace the holder and shelf.

Ceramic Tile Mirror Frame

Framing a mirror with ceramic tile can transform the object from a flat, modern necessity to a beautiful decorative flourish. The process is extremely simple; in fact, choosing the tile can be the most difficult part of the project. If you're tiling the rest of the room, combine trim pieces that match or complement the field tile. If the room has no other tile, match your tile to the rest of your décor or create an elegant accent piece in bold, standout colors.

There are two ways to tile a mirror: apply the tile directly to the mirror, or tile around the mirror and butt up to the edges. We chose to remove the mirror and attach the tiles around the perimeter, and then rehang the mirror. Before you rehang the mirror, make sure the hanger and anchor are designed to support the mirror's new weight, as it will be considerably heavier with the addition of the tiled frame.

Our tile frame uses three types of trim tile: an outer chair rail tile, a thin band of mosaic tile, and a thin pencil tile as an inner ring.

Tools & Materials ▸

Tape measure	Putty knife	Heavy brown paper	Wide painter's tape
Permanent marker	Grout float	or cardboard	Grout with latex additive
Wet saw	Grout sponge	Trim tile	Grout sealer
Laser or carpenter's level	Foam paintbrush	Windshield adhesive	

How to Frame a Bathroom Mirror

Dry lay the tile around a mirror template made of heavy brown paper. Use spacers if the tiles are not self-spaced. Mark tiles that must be cut. Miter the one end of each corner tile at a 45° angle using a wet saw.

Dry lay the outermost row of chair rail tiles again—this time on the mirror. Check corner miters for proper alignment.

Dry lay the next couple of rows of field tile starting in the left-hand corner. For accurate placement, include spacers.

Dry lay the final row of pencil tiles. Cut tiles, as necessary, to fit onto mirror as planned. Once all tiles fit, remove all but the first row of chair tiles.

Apply adhesive to the back of the tile using a small putty knife. Set tiles on the mirror and twist to secure in place. Start at the top, left-hand corner and work around the entire mirror.

Repeat until all rows are secured to the mirror. Prepare a small batch of grout and fill all the tile joints. Clean and buff the tile.

Tiled Mirror Designs ▶

Tile has been added only to the mirror in this project. The mirror is framed by a mosaic of shards and small pieces of glass tile. Mosaic projects are incredibly easy to do and really add a lot to a small room like this one.

In new construction or major remodeling projects, place the mirror so the trim tile can be attached to the wall rather than to the mirror.

New Towel Bar

Replacing an out-of-date or damaged towel bar can spruce up your bathroom décor in a snap. If you're selecting new accessories, note the finish on the existing faucets and handles. Generally, bathroom décor looks best when faucets and accessories match, or at least coordinate.

It's also smart to measure the mounting plates on the existing towel bar before you purchase a new one. It will be easier to produce professional-looking results if the plates on the new bar are the same size or larger than the existing plates. In fact, sometimes your new accessories can be mounted on the existing plates if the hardware is the same size, greatly decreasing the time required for this project.

Most bathroom accessories are installed similarly, so these instructions could easily be applied to many different accessory installations.

Tools & Materials ▸

Towel bar with
  mounting plates
Pencil
Stud finder
Level
Drill
Screws
Screwdriver

New accessories can have a great impact on your bathroom décor without much time or expense.

Anatomy of a Towel Bar Mount ▸

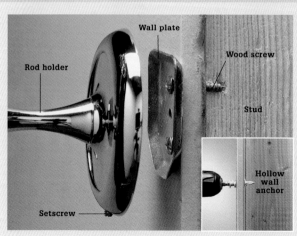

Wall plate
Wood screw
Rod holder
Stud
Hollow wall anchor
Setscrew

Towel bars and other bathroom accessories are supported by mounting plates attached to walls. The mounting plate must be securely supported by wall studs or self-tapping hollow wall anchors rated for the bar's weight.

How to Install a Towel Bar

Position the towel bar and make a mark along the outside of the mounting trim on each side. (Try to avoid positioning the bar so the new holes will fall directly over the old ones.) Repeat for the other side.

Center the mounting plate between the marks made in step 1, and then make marks for the screw locations. Repeat this process on the other side. Check the marks with a level, and adjust if necessary. Use a stud finder to check if the marks are located over studs.

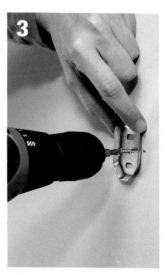

Drill pilot holes, and then hold the first mounting plate in place and drive screws to attach it to the wall. Repeat on the other side.

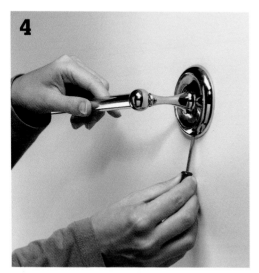

Settle the towel bar onto the mounting plates. Tighten the setscrews that hold the bar to the mounting plates. (These setscrews typically are found on the bottom of the trim.)

Ceramic Tile Walls ▸

Use a ceramic tile bit with a carbide tip to drill the pilot holes. Before beginning to drill, scratch a dimple into the tile with an awl or a sharp nail. Starting to drill beyond the tile's glaze helps keep the bit from dancing around on the tile.

Tile Fireplace Surround

Tile dresses a fireplace surround in style—any style you like. From simple ceramic to elegant cut stone to handmade art tile, anything goes. As long as it's sturdy enough to withstand significant swings in temperature, almost any tile will work.

Although the project shown here starts with unfinished wallboard, you can tile over any level surface that's not glossy. If you're tiling over old tile or brick, go over the surface with a grinder, then apply a thin coat of latex-reinforced thinset mortar to even out any irregularities. To rough up painted surfaces, sand them lightly before beginning the project.

The tile shown here is flush with the face of the firebox, which then supports it during installation. If necessary, tack battens in place to support the weight of your tile during installation. (Make sure the batten is level.)

You can finish the edges of the surround with wood cap rail trim, as shown here, bullnose tile, or other trim tile.

Tools & Materials ▸

Level	Tile spacers
Drill	Latex-reinforced
Hammer	thinset mortar
Nail set	Masking tape
Notched trowel	Grout
Grout float	Cap rail trim
2 × 4 lumber	6d and 4d finish nails
Mantel	Wood putty
Tile	Sponge

A tile surround can dress up home accents, like fireplaces. Choose tile that blends with or complements your other décor.

How to Tile a Fireplace Surround

1

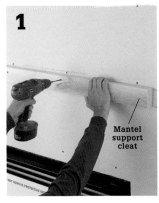

Mantel support cleat

To install the mantel, measure up from the floor and mark the height of the support cleat. Use a level to draw a level line through the mark. Mark the stud locations just above the level line. Position the cleat on the line, centered between the frame sides and drill a pilot hole at each stud location. Fasten the cleat to the studs with screws provided by the manufacturer.

2

Paint the areas of wallboard that won't be tiled. Finish the mantel as desired, then fit it over the support cleat and center it. Drill pilot holes for 6d finish nails through the top of the mantel about ¾" from the back edge. Secure the mantel to the cleat with four nails. Set the nails with a nail set, fill the holes with wood putty, then touch up the finish.

3

Dry-fit the tile around the front of the fireplace. You can lay tile over the black front face, but do not cover the glass or any portion of the grills. If you're using tile without spacer lugs, use spacers to set the gaps (at least ⅛" for floor tile). Mark the perimeter of the tile area and make any other layout marks that will help with the installation. Pre-cut tiles, if possible.

4

Mask off around the tile, then use a V-notched trowel to apply latex mastic tile adhesive to the wall, spreading it evenly just inside the perimeter lines. Set the tiles into the adhesive, aligning them with the layout marks, and press firmly to create a good bond. Install spacers as you work, and scrape out excess adhesive from the grout joints. Install all of the tile, then let the adhesive dry completely.

5

Mix a batch of grout and spread it over the tiles with a rubber grout float. Drag the float across the joints diagonally, tilting it at a 45° angle. Make another pass to remove excess grout. Wait 10 to 15 minutes, then wipe away excess grout with a damp sponge, rinsing frequently. Let the grout dry for one hour, then polish the tiles with a dry cloth. Let the grout dry completely.

6

Cap rail trim

Buildup strip

Cut pieces of cap rail trim to fit around the tile, mitering the ends. If the tile is thicker than the trim recesses, install buildup strips behind the trim, using finish nails. Finish the trim to match the mantel. Drill pilot holes and nail the trim in place with 4d finish nails. Set the nails with a nail set. Fill the holes with wood putty and touch up the finish.

Ceiling Décor

Though many decorators choose to focus their time and energy on wall detail, ceiling decoration can add considerably to the wholeness and energy of a room. Sometimes the best way to pull a newly decorated room together can be to paint, wallcover, panel, or tile a ceiling. These projects can also help to seal and protect your ceiling wallboard and insulate or reflect noise and light.

Careful preparation for ceiling projects will ease the process and cleanup, and most techniques will be vastly easier with the help of a partner. When planning your project, bear in mind that the ceiling edge closest to the entry of any room is the least visible, so always work from the farthest corner toward the entry. Also, always repair any ceiling damage before installing a decorative finish.

Before you decide on the technique that will best accent your room, consider how the ceiling treatment will complement or blend with your wall décor and make a plan for smoothing the transition between the ceiling and wall.

In this chapter:

- Ceiling Panels
- Acoustical Ceiling Tiles
- Metal Ceilings
- Painting a Ceiling
- Aluminum Leaf Gilding
- Ceiling Wallcovering

Ceiling Panels

Installing ceiling paneling in a den, bedroom, or attic adds balance and warmth, wrapping the room in the cozy natural glow of finished wood. Tongue-and-groove paneling made of pine is the most common type of paneling for this project, but any tongue-and-groove material can be used. These materials are typically ⅜ to ¾" thick and are attached directly to ceiling joists and rafters (over faced insulation, when required). If using a thin paneling, bear in mind that most codes require you to install ⅜" wallboard as a fire stop under ceiling material thinner than ¼"

Tongue-and-groove boards are attached with flooring nails driven through the shoulder of the tongue into each rafter. This technique is called blind-nailing because the nail heads will be covered by the next board. Nailing through the board face is only necessary on the first and last course and on scarf joints. Layout is very important to the success of a paneled surface because the lines clearly reveal

Tools & Materials ▸

Chalk line
Compound miter saw
Circular saw
Drill
Nail set

Tongue-and-groove
    paneling
1¾" spiral
    flooring nails
Trim molding

flaws such as pattern deviations, misaligned walls, and installation mistakes. Before beginning, measure to see how many boards will be installed. If the final board will be less than 2" wide, trim the long edge of the first board to allow more room.

If the angle of the ceiling peak is not parallel to the wall, compensate for the difference by ripping the starter piece at an angle so that the leading edge, and every piece thereafter, is parallel to the peak.

Tongue-and-groove paneling can be installed directly over rafters or joists or over wallboard. In attic installations, it's important to insulate first, adding a separate vapor barrier if required by building codes. Local code may also require that paper-faced insulation behind a kneewall be covered with drywall or other material.

How to Panel a Ceiling

To plan your layout, first measure the reveal of the boards. Fit two pieces together and measure from the bottom edge of the upper board to the bottom edge of the lower board. Calculate the number of boards needed to cover one side of the ceiling by dividing the reveal dimension into the overall distance between the top of the wall and the peak.

Use the calculation from step 1 to make a control line for the first row of panels—the starter boards. At both ends of the ceiling, measure down from the peak an equal distance, and make a mark to represent the top (tongue) edges of the starter boards. Snap a chalk line through the marks.

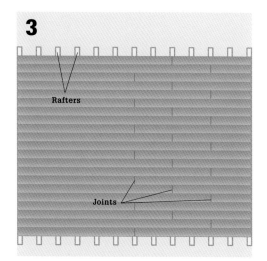

If the boards aren't long enough to span the entire ceiling, plan the locations of the joints. Staggering the joints in a three-step pattern will make them less conspicuous. Note that each joint must fall over the middle of a rafter. For best appearance, select boards of similar coloring and grain for each row.

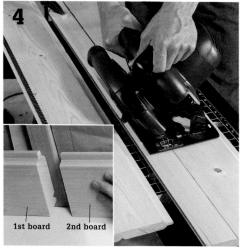

Rip the first starter board to width by bevel-cutting the bottom (grooved) edge. If the starter row will have joints, cut the board to length using a 30° bevel cut on the joint end only. Two beveled ends joined together form a scarf joint (inset), which is less noticeable than a butt joint. If the board spans the ceiling, square-cut both ends.

(continued)

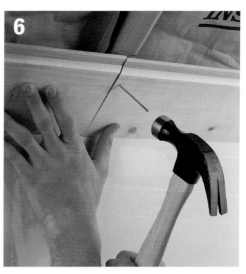

Position the first starter board so the tongue is on the control line. Leave a ⅛" gap between the square board end and the end wall. Fasten the board by nailing through its face about 1" from the grooved edge and into the rafters. Then, blind-nail through the base of the tongue into each rafter, angling the nail backward at 45°. Drive the nail heads beneath the wood surface, using a nail set.

Cut and install any remaining boards in the starter row one at a time, making sure the scarf joints fit together tightly. At each scarf joint, drive two nails through the face of the top board, angling the nail to capture the end of the board behind it. If necessary, predrill the nail holes to prevent splitting.

Cut the first board for the next row, then fit its grooved edge over the tongue of the board in the starter row. Use a hammer and a scrap piece of paneling to drive downward on the tongue edge, seating the grooved edge over the tongue of the starter board. Fasten the second row with blind-nails only.

As you install successive rows, measure down from the peak to make sure the rows remain parallel to the peak. Correct any misalignment by adjusting the tongue-and-groove joint slightly with each row. You can also snap additional control lines to help align the rows.

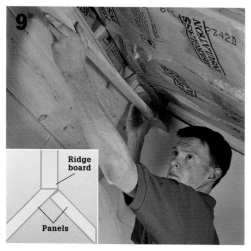

Rip the boards for the last row to width, beveling the top edges so they fit flush against the ridge board. Facenail the boards in place. Install paneling on the other side of the ceiling, then cut and install the final row of panels to form a closed joint under the ridge board (inset).

Install trim molding along walls, at joints around obstacles, and along inside and outside corners, if desired. (Select-grade 1 × 2 works well as trim along walls.) Where necessary, bevel the back edges of the trim or miter-cut the ends to accommodate the slope of the ceiling.

Tips for Paneling an Attic Ceiling ▸

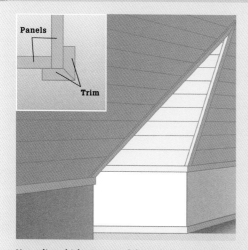

Use mitered trim to cover joints where panels meet at outside corners. Dormers and other roof elements create opposing ceiling angles that can be difficult to panel around. It may be easier to butt the panels together and hide the butt joints with custom-cut trim. The trim also makes a nice transition between angles.

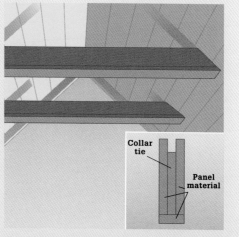

Wrap collar ties or exposed beams with custom-cut panels. Install the paneling on the ceiling first. Then, rip-cut panels to the desired width. You may want to include a tongue-and-groove joint as part of the trim detail. Angle-cut the ends of the trim so it fits tight to the ceiling panels.

Acoustical Ceiling Tiles

Easy-to-install ceiling tiles can lend character to a plain ceiling or help turn an unfinished basement or attic into beautiful living space. Made of pressed mineral and fiberboard, ceiling tiles are available in a variety of styles. They also provide moderate noise reduction.

Ceiling tiles typically can be attached directly to a drywall or plaster ceiling with adhesive. If your ceiling is damaged or uneven, or if you have an unfinished joist ceiling, install 1 × 2 furring strips as a base for the tiles, as shown in this project. Some systems include metal tracks for clip-on installation.

Unless your ceiling measures in even feet, you won't be able to install the 12" tiles without some cutting. To prevent an unattractive installation with small, irregular tiles along two sides, include a course of border tiles along the perimeter of the installation. Plan so that tiles at opposite ends of the room are cut

Tools & Materials ▸

4-ft. level	Stapler
Stepladder	1 × 2 furring strips
Chalk line	8d nails or 2" screws
Utility knife	String
Straightedge	Ceiling tiles
Hammer or drill	Staples
Handsaw	Trim molding

to the same width and are at least half the width of a full tile.

Most ceiling tiles come prefinished, but they can be painted to match any decor. For best results, apply two coats of paint using a roller with a ¼" nap. Wait 24 hours between coats.

Acoustic tile improves the sound quality inside a home theater and reduces the transmission of sound to the rooms surrounding it.

How to Install Ceiling Tile

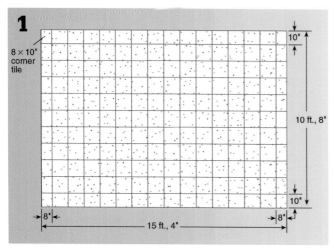

1

8 × 10" corner tile

10"

10 ft., 8"

10"

8"   8"

15 ft., 4"

Measure the ceiling and devise a layout. If the length (or width) doesn't measure in even feet, use this formula to determine the width of the border tiles: add 12 to the number of inches remaining and divide by 2. The result is the width of the border tile. (For example, if the room length is 15 ft., 4", add 12 to the 4, then divide 16 by 2, which results in an 8" border tile.)

2

Install the first furring strip flush with the wall and perpendicular to the joists, fastening with two 8d nails or 2" screws at each joist. Measure out from the wall a distance equal to the border tile width minus ¾", and snap a chalk line. Install the second furring strip with its wall-side edge on the chalk line.

3

Install the remaining strips 12" on-center from the second strip. Measure from the second strip and mark the joist nearest the wall every 12". Repeat along the joist on the opposite side of the room, then snap chalk lines between the marks. Install the furring strips along the lines. Install the last furring strip flush against the opposite side wall. Stagger the butted end joints of strips between rows so they aren't all on the same joist.

4

Check the strips with a 4-ft. level. Insert wood shims between the strips and joists as necessary to bring the strips into a level plane.

(continued)

5

Set up taut, perpendicular string lines along two adjacent walls to help guide the tile installation. Inset the strings from the wall by a distance that equals that wall's border tile width plus ½". Use a framing square to make sure the strings are square.

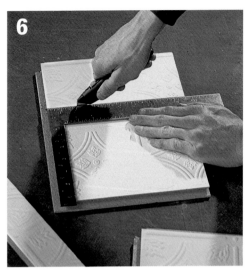

6

Cut the corner border tile to size with a utility knife and straightedge. Cutting the border tiles ¼" short will ease fitting them. The resulting gap between the tile and wall will be covered by trim. Cut only on the edges without the stapling flange.

7

Position the corner tile with the flange edges aligned with the two string lines and fasten it to the furring strips with four ½" staples. Cut and install two border tiles along each wall, making sure the tiles fit snugly together.

8

Fill in between the border tiles with full-size tiles. Continue working diagonally in this manner, toward the opposite corner. For the border tiles along the far wall, trim off the flange edges and staple through the faces of the tiles, close to the wall.

9

Install the final row of tiles, saving the far corner tile and its neighbor for last. Cut the last tile to size, then remove the tongue and nailing flange along the side edges. Finish the job by installing trim along the edges.

Metal Ceilings

Today's metal ceilings offer the distinctive elegance of 19th-century tin tile in a durable, washable ceiling finish. Available at home centers and specialty distributors, metal ceiling systems include field panels (in 2 × 2-, 2 × 4-, and 2 × 8-ft. sizes), border panels that can be cut to fit your layout, and cornice molding for finishing the edges. The panels come in a variety of materials and finishes ready for installation, or they can be painted.

To simplify installation, the panels have round catches called nailing buttons, that fit into one another to align the panels where they overlap. The buttons are also the nailing points for attaching the panels. Use 1" decorative conehead nails where nail heads will be exposed, and ½" wire nails where heads are hidden.

Install your metal ceiling over a smooth layer of ⅜" or ½" plywood, which can be fastened directly to the ceiling joists with drywall screws, or installed over an existing finish. The plywood provides a flat nailing surface for the panels. As an alternative, some manufacturers offer a track system for clip-on installation.

Begin your installation by carefully measuring the ceiling and snapping chalk lines to establish the panel layout. For most tile patterns, it looks best to cover the center of the space with full tiles only, then fill in along the perimeter with border panels, which are not patterned. Make sure your layout is square.

Tools & Materials ▸

Chalk line
Level
Tin snips
Drill with ⅛"
    metal bit
Compass
Metal file
⅜" or ½" plywood
2" drywall screws

Field panels
Border panels with
    molding edge
Cornice molding
Masking tape
½" wire nails
1" conehead nails
Wood block

Real metal ceilings have traditional embossed patterns with an unmistakable luxurious quality. But, they are expensive and a bit unwieldy to install. Acoustic panels with an embossed vinyl pattern layer are much cheaper and easier to install, but are also less authentic.

How to Install a Metal Tile Ceiling

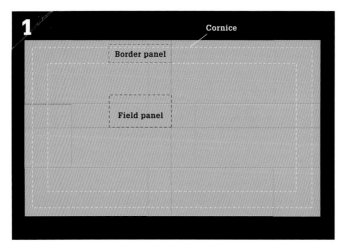

Cornice

Border panel

Field panel

Measure to find the center of the ceiling, then snap perpendicular chalk lines intersecting the center. On the walls, mark a level reference line representing the bottom edges of the cornice molding. Where possible, plan to install the panels so they overlap toward the room's entrance, to help conceal the seams.

Align the first field panel with the chalk lines at the ceiling's center, and attach it with ½" wire nails along the edges where another panel will overlap it. Drive the nails beside the nailing buttons—saving the buttons for nailing the overlapping panel.

Continue to install the field panels, working along the length of the area first, then overlapping the next row. Make sure the nailing buttons are aligned. Underlap panels by sliding the new panel into position beneath the installed panel, then fasten through both panels at the nailing buttons, using 1" conehead nails. Where field panels meet at corners, drill ⅛" pilot holes for the conehead nails.

Cut the border panels to width so they will underlap the cornice by at least 1". Use sharp tin snips, and cut from the edge without edge molding. Install the panels so the nailing buttons on the molding align with those on the field panels. Fasten through the buttons with conehead nails, and along the cut edge with wire nails. At corners, miter cut the panels, and drive conehead nails every 6" along the seam.

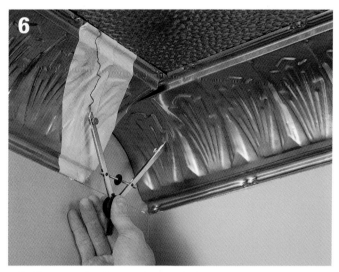

Install each cornice piece with its bottom edge on the level line. Drive 1" conehead nails through the nailing buttons and into the wall studs. Don't nail the ends until the succeeding piece is in place. Fasten the top edges to the ceiling.

At inside corners, install one cornice piece tightly into the corner, then scribe the mating piece to fit, using masking tape and a compass. Cut along the scribed line with tin snips, and make minor adjustments with a metal file. You may have to cut the mating piece several times, so start with plenty of length. If you have several corners, use this technique to cut templates for the corner pieces.

At outside corners, cut the ends of two scrap pieces at a 33° angle. Fit the pieces together at the corner, then trim and mark each piece in turn, making minor adjustments until they fit well. Use the scrap pieces as templates for marking the workpieces. Fasten near the corner only when both mating pieces are in place.

Using a hammer and a piece of wood, carefully tap any loose joints to tighten them. If the cornice will be left unpainted, file the joints for a perfect fit. If you're painting the ceiling, seal the seams with paintable silicone caulk, then apply two coats of paint using a roller with a ¼" nap. Allow the first coat to dry for 24 hours before applying the second coat.

Painting a Ceiling

Painting a ceiling can greatly enhance the stylistic rhythm of your room—whether you choose a clean neutral color, an extension of your wall color, or a bold accent color. Before painting a ceiling, make sure it is clean and that your room is prepared adequately. Although it's best to paint ceilings in sections, set aside time to complete the entire room in one sitting, which will ensure that the edges of each painted section are wet enough to blend seamlessly into one another.

A roller extension enables you to paint the ceiling with your feet firmly planted on the floor, but a ladder will still be necessary to cut in around the edges of the room. Also, eye protection is an absolute necessity when painting overhead. Before you begin, clean the ceiling and prime any stained areas.

Tools & Materials ▸

Paint roller and tray
Roller extension
Paint brush
Painter's tape
Ladder

Painting a ceiling a dark color can absorb light in large rooms, making them feel intimate and cozy. Painting a ceiling to match the color of your walls draws the room into a cohesive whole.

Preparing the Room ▸

If you have hanging light fixtures, shut off the power to the circuit, lower the plate cover and pull a trash bag up from the bottom of the fixture. Tie a knot at the top, neatly covering the entire piece.

Press painter's tape along the joint between the ceiling and the wall, leaving the bottom half of the tape loose. Then, slide sheet plastic under the masking tape and press the tape down just enough to hold it in place. Make sure the plastic is long enough to protect the baseboards as well as the walls.

How to Paint a Ceiling

Load your brush only about one-third of the length of the bristles, and tap the bristles against the side of the can. Do not drag the brush against the lap of the can as this tactic wears out the bristles.

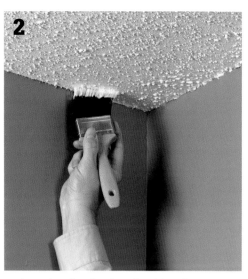

Cut in on the edge of a 3-ft. section of the ceiling starting in the corner furthest from the entry door. Press just hard enough to flex the bristles, use long, slow strokes, and paint from a dry area back into the wet paint.

Load the roller and begin rolling the section you just cut in. Roll across the area with diagonal strokes and lift the roller at the end of each sweep. For the final smoothing strokes, roll each section toward the wall with the entry door. Reposition your ladder under the next 3-ft. section and repeat steps 2 and 3 until the entire ceiling is painted.

Painting Large Areas ▸

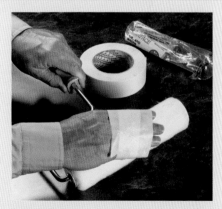

New roller covers sometimes have lint fibers that will stick in the paint unless they're removed. To clean out lint, wrap masking tape around your hand and blot the surface of the cover. When no more lint comes off the roller cover, wet it, using water for latex paint or solvent for alkyd. Squeeze out as much liquid as possible and slide the cover onto the roller frame.

Aluminum Leaf Gilding

An aluminum-leafed ceiling is a spectacular accent and looks wonderful in large dining rooms where the lights from the chandelier can dance across the shiny surface or in intimate spaces that need a little kick. If you do not want to apply many single sheets of aluminum leaf to a ceiling over your head in the traditional manner, however, there is an easier way: aluminum leaf comes on a roll! It is made just for this type of large, continuous surface application.

As with any gilding process, the final look is only as good as your prep, so make sure that your ceiling surface is smooth and free of any blemishes and cracks. The leaf will expose all flaws in your surface texture. Basecoat the ceiling to be leafed in a pale warm gray, eggshell-sheen latex paint applied with a foam roller to keep roller stipple to a minimum. The eggshell texture will ensure proper sealing of the surface.

Tools & Materials ▸

Water-based gold-leaf size	7" roller handles	6" spreading knife	Denatured alcohol
4" paintbrush	Aluminum leaf on a roll	Wallpaper blade	Lint-free rag
		Lamb's wool pad	Satin acrylic varnish

An aluminum leaf ceiling can transport a modern dining room back in time 100 years, evoking the elegance and sophistication of formal parlors and dining spaces.

How to Apply Aluminum Leaf Gilding

1

Gilding products include adhesive, the leaf roll, top coat, sealer, and brushes. Brush the size to an area of ceiling that you can comfortably gild in one day. Do not leave any skips. Follow the instructions on the size bottle to know how long to wait before applying the leaf. Start along the edge where the ceiling meets the wall. Tuck the side of the roll into the edge with the spreading knife, allowing ½" excess to fall onto wall.

2

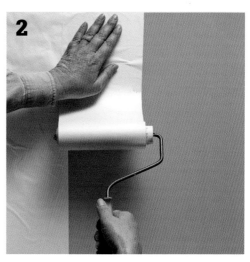

With mild tension, pull the roll of leaf at a 45° angle to the opposite side of the ceiling, using your free hand to lightly press leaf to ceiling as you go. When you get to the opposite wall, cut the leaf with a sharp wallpaper knife into the corner. Repeat until the ceiling is covered, overlapping each previous row by ¼".

3

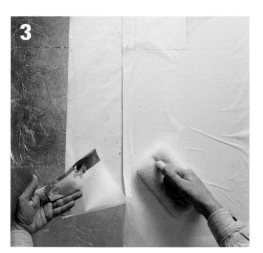

With a lamb's wool pad, softly brush over the paper and the leaf. This will adhere the leaf to the ceiling. The paper will fall off at this time.

4

Continue softly cleaning until all excess leaf is removed. Dampen a rag with denatured alcohol and gently wipe the entire gilded surface down. This removes the wax on the surface of the leaf and allows your topcoat to be applied. Topcoat cannot be applied over the wax film. Apply a coat of satin acrylic varnish to the entire gilded surface with a latex brush.

Ceiling Wallcovering

Applying wallcovering to a ceiling is a tidy way to add detail and panache to a room. It works particularly well in kitchens and bathrooms. Similar to most wallcovering projects, applying wallcovering to a ceiling is a two-person project. When planning a ceiling project, remember that the pattern on the last strip may be broken by the ceiling line. Since the least visible edge is usually on the entry wall, begin hanging ceiling strips at the far end of the room and work back toward the entryway.

If you plan to cover the walls in addition to the ceiling, bear in mind that the ceiling pattern can blend perfectly into only one wall. Select your "match" wall, and plan the ceiling project so the strips will blend into it easily. Always cover the ceiling first, and then cover walls.

Tools & Materials ▸

Wallcovering
Pencil
Straightedge

Water tray
Scissors

Smoothing brush
Razor knife

Wallboard knife
Seam roller

Wallcovering a ceiling in a room with wallcovered walls draws the entire decorating scheme into a cohesive whole, and creates an intimate, comfortable space.

How to Wallcover a Ceiling

1

Measure the width of the wallcovering strip and subtract ½". Near a corner, measure this distance away from the wall at several points, marking points on the ceiling with a pencil. Using the marks as guides, draw a line along the length of the ceiling with a pencil and straightedge. Cut and prepare the first wallcovering strip (page 92).

2

Working in small sections, position the strip against the line. Overlap the side wall by ½" and the end wall by 2". Flatten the strip with the smoothing brush as you work.

3

Cut out a small wedge of wallcovering in the corner so that the strip will lay flat. Press the wallcovering into the corner with a wallboard knife.

4

Trim the overlap to ½" on all walls that will be covered with wallcovering, using a razor knife and wallboard knife. On walls that will not be covered, trim the excess to the ceiling by holding a wallboard knife against the corner and cutting with a sharp razor knife (see inset). Repeat steps 2 through 4, butting edges of the wallcovering so the pattern matches.

5

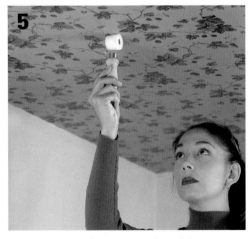

Let the strips stand for 30 minutes, then roll the seams lightly with a seam roller.

Cabinets & Doors

Adding a decorative stain, creative molding, or new hardware to doors, cabinets, and drawers is a quick and easy way to vastly improve the overall appearance of these home essentials. Kitchen cabinets contribute massively to kitchen décor, and with a little creativity, standard cabinets can be transformed with a luxurious, custom-built appearance. Interior and closet doors can also easily be renewed—improving both their appearance and functionality—with many of the projects in this chapter.

Try applying a faux mahogany finish to cabinets or repainting doors in an accent color for a dramatic change. Or, simply replace the knobs on your drawers or cabinets or install a wineglass rack for a subtle decorative shift. Consider how your decorative choices will contribute to the overall tempo of your home and spend time in preparations and planning, and any of these projects will complete your overall home décor with accented detail.

In this chapter:

- Painting Wood Cabinets
- Faux Mahogany
- Antique Stained Finish
- Faux Stainless Steel
- Cabinet Molding
- Decorative Brackets
- Wineglass Rack
- Knobs & Pulls
- Prehung Interior Door
- Bifold Doors
- Painting Wood Doors
- Decorative Door Headers
- Door Mirror

Painting Wood Cabinets

Painting cabinetry can drastically alter the final appearance of a kitchen. Update an outdated color scheme or add a clean shine to a new kitchen. Painted cabinets are attractive, easy to clean, and durable, especially if you use heavy-duty enamel paint.

Although painting cabinetry isn't difficult, it is a time-consuming process. Most cabinets require two coats of paint on both sides and all surfaces must be lightly sanded between coats. Plan to spend about two hours per foot of cabinetry to complete this project.

Tools & Materials ▸

Screwdriver	3" paintbrush, trim
Pliers	brush, tapered
Sponge and bucket	sash brush
Latex wood filler	Paint roller and tray
Putty knife	Primer
Sander and sandpaper	Paint

Painting wood cabinets is an inexpensive way to give your kitchen an instant face-lift.

How to Paint Wood Cabinets

First, empty the cabinets, and then remove the shelf pins, shelves, and all hardware. Sand the cabinet frames and use a damp cloth to remove dust.

Brush paint onto the interior of the cabinet frames, starting with the back wall, then the top, sides, and bottom. Roll the paint on the outside surfaces, working from top to bottom.

Fill scratches, dents, or cracks with latex wood filler using a putty knife as necessary. Let the wood filler dry completely. Sand all surfaces with an orbital sander and 150-grit sandpaper.

Using a trim brush, paint the inside of each door. Once dry, paint the other side using a tapered sash brush. Allow the paint to dry and then add a second coat of paint, if needed. Let the doors dry for several days, then replace the hardware and rehang the doors.

Faux Mahogany

Mahogany is an elegant wood, and this finishing technique can replicate the grace and luxury of real mahogany on wood surfaces throughout your home. Using wood graining, a deep basecoat color, and the addition of rich reds to the graining varnish, this finish is simple and believable—perfect for tabletops, inset side panels, and cabinets.

Mahogany grain is fine, fairly straight, and without knots and whirls. Apply this technique carefully and consistently for the best finish. Before you stain, apply a coat of a dark, rosy brown latex eggshell paint as your base coat, and allow to dry completely.

A **mahogany finish** adds depth and sophistication to a kitchen.

Tools & Materials ▸

Eggshell latex paint for base coat
3" latex paintbrush
One pint measuring cup
Satin oil-based varnish, clear
Paint pail
UTC, Burnt Umber
UTC, Raw Umber
UTC, Venetian Red
3" and 1½" chip brush
T-shirt rags
Flogger brush
Steel wood-graining combs

How to Apply a Wood-Grain Finish

1

Repetitive raking creates a realistic wood grain. After the basecoat has dried, apply tinted varnish in the direction of the grain using a chip brush. Rake a comb back and forth quickly, multiple times, from top to bottom until a grain pattern emerges.

2

Pull a soft T-shirt rag from top to bottom, jittering the motion slightly to create a vaguely rippled linear pattern.

3

Hold the flogger brush parallel to the surface, bristles downward. Slap the surface with quick snaps, working from the top down. Flog the entire surface a couple of times until you are satisfied with the look, then allow to dry for 24 hours. Top coat with one or two coats of varnish.

How to Create a Faux Mahogany Finish

Mix the graining medium. Pour one pint of varnish into the jar, then drip the UTC colors into the varnish slowly: start with three parts Burnt Umber, two parts Raw Umber, and one-part Venetian Red. Continue to add/mix colors until you create a varnish color you're happy with. You may need to add more colorant to make enough solution for large pieces, but continue slowly; if too much colorant is added, it will not mix and the varnish will never dry. Also, colorant will not dry, so wipe up spills immediately. Apply graining varnish with a large chip brush using a straight top-to-bottom stroke, then rake gently with the wood grain combs (see step 1, opposite page).

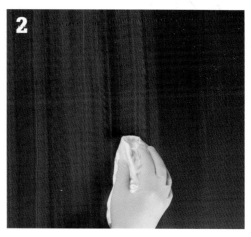

Texture the varnish by lightly pulling a soft T-shirt rag over the surface from top to bottom. Jitter the motion slightly to create a vaguely rippled linear pattern. Repeat over the entire surface.

Hold the flogger brush parallel to the surface, bristles downward. Slap the surface with quick snaps, working from the top down. Flog the entire surface.

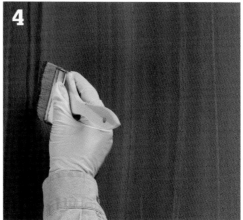

Dip the tip of the chip brush into the graining varnish. Hold it at a 45° angle to the grain and lay in a dark accent by dragging the chisel-edge down the length of the grain. Use this accent sparingly, perhaps once per side. Allow to dry for 24 hours, and then top coat with one or two coats of varnish.

Antique Stained Finish

A dd extra punch to your cabinets' stain with this easy-to-accomplish antique finish. Use antiqueing over a freshly stained surface or enhance previously stained cabinetry. When working with an older or already stained piece, wash the surface well and allow to dry thoroughly before you begin.

Tools & Materials ▶

Gel stain: golden oak and dark walnut
1" flat oil paintbrush
T-shirt rags

The soft beauty of an aged finish can add spark and character to a modern kitchen.

How to Apply an Antique Stain Finish

Dip a rag into the oak stain and apply using a circular motion. Use the small paintbrush to reach into corners or crevices. Wipe the excess stain off with a clean rag. Allow to dry completely.

Apply the walnut stain to the edges and corners of the project surface; leave a clear oval area in the center. Wipe the stain into the center with a clean rag until the entire surface is antiqued. Top coat with one or two coats of varnish.

Faux Stainless Steel

Applying a faux stainless steel finish is a great way to modernize old appliances—such as dishwashers, refrigerators, and trash compactors. This technique also works well on metal cabinet doors and frames. The finish will only successfully replicate stainless when used on flat surfaces, however. The technique is not effective over pebbly, textured appliance fronts or wood grain.

Paint color choice is crucial to this technique's success. Choose a latex-based metallic paint close to the color of the existing stainless in your kitchen. You may need to add a few drops of UTC to tweak the color, or you might find that a warm champagne metallic mixed with a silver metallic will match the coloration. Prime the surface with a high-quality latex bonding primer tinted to a color close to your metallic. The primer should be applied using the same technique as your final, metallic coat to help replicate the slight grain in real stainless steel. Use a slight, linear pattern to your brushwork to aid in this effect.

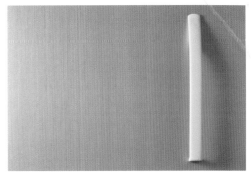

A faux stainless paint finish is a great way to modernize old appliances.

Tools & Materials ▸

High-quality latex bonding primer, tinted to a color close to the metallic final coat	Metallic latex paint
	3 or 4" paintbrush
	Metal straightedge
	Satin latex polyurethane

How to Create a Faux Stainless Steel Paint Finish

1

Apply the metallic paint in a very straight up-and-down manner with the paintbrush, after the surface has been primed. To keep your strokes straight, place a straightedge onto the surface and use as a guide for your brush.

2

After the first coat of metallic paint has completely dried, apply a second coat in the same manner. Finish the project with a clearcoat of durable latex polyurethane.

Cabinet Molding

If you love the color or finish of your cabinets, but feel like something is missing, try applying ornamental molding to your cabinet panels. This raised molding can be stained or painted in a similar or complementary color and can greatly enhance the detail and drama of your kitchen. Use the molding as an accent on flat cabinets, or apply around recessed areas for added definition. To further the effect, build moldings in layers, or lay one within another.

Use wood glue sparingly for a clean application; wood glue holds securely, even when a very small amount is used. Also, if your moldings will be attached to cabinets with beveled or routed edges, it will be necessary to adjust the angle of the mitered cuts somewhat by sanding the edges of the mitered molding strips. You may also need to fill in small gaps

between the strips with wood putty. Bear in mind that there will likely be minute measurement differences from one cabinet door to another, so always measure the panels on each side before cutting the molding to ensure an accurate fit.

Tools & Materials ▸

Miter box
   and backsaw
Pencil
220-grit sandpaper
Wood glue
Clamps

Paint or stain, clear
   acrylic finish,
   and matching
   wood putty
Lumber scraps
Wool fabric

Applying molding to kitchen cabinetry adds depth and character to a contemporary kitchen.

How to Apply Cabinet Moldings

Using a miter box and backsaw, cut molding strips at each end according to your measurements and the marked angle of your cuts. Repeat to cut remaining strips.

Check the fit of the molding strips and sand the corners, using 220-grit sandpaper, as necessary for proper fit.

Paint or stain the moldings and allow to dry completely. Apply wood glue sparingly to the underside of the molding.

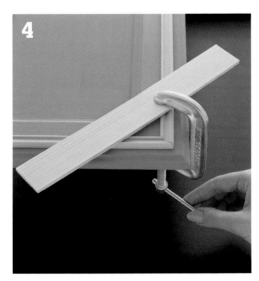

Position the molding on the cabinet and clamp it in place. Use a scrap of lumber to protect the trim from the clamps. If there is any excess glue, remove it immediately using a scrap of wool fabric.

Remove the clamps when the glue has dried thoroughly. Fill any gaps between the molding strips at the corners, using wood filler if trim is painted; touch up paint. If trim is stained, fill gaps with putty that matches the stain.

Decorative Brackets

Transform your cabinetry from plain to custom-fabulous with the easy addition of decorative shelf brackets underneath wall cabinets. Shelf brackets are affordable, and are available in a multitude of shapes and styles—stain or paint them to match your cabinetry for nostalgic, old-world appeal. Always paint or stain your brackets before you install them.

Tools & Materials ▸

Decorative brackets
Paint or stain and clear acrylic finish,
    wood putty to match stain
4d finish nails
Nail set
Drill
$\frac{3}{32}$" drill bit
Countersink bit

Installing decorative shelf brackets beneath kitchen cabinetry gives your kitchen custom-built detail.

How to Install Decorative Brackets

Determine the location of the brackets; they may be flush to the cabinet, protrude slightly beyond the cabinet, or be recessed inboard.

Cut end strips. Mark the placement for screws on all the molding strips; predrill screw holes through molding strips using a countersink bit.

Mark the placement for screws on the bottom of the cabinet using molding strips as guides; predrill screw holes using a $\frac{3}{32}$" bit. Secure the molding strips with screws.

Wineglass Rack

Bring your stemware out of the cabinet and display it proudly on a wineglass rack beneath your cabinets, easing storage space within your cabinetry and adding to the elegance of your kitchen. Molding designed just for this purpose is sold through specialty woodworking stores in predetermined lengths that can be cut to fit beneath your cabinetry.

If the bottom shelf of your cabinets is recessed, add layers of plywood to fill this space before installing the molding to ensure that glasses can slide easily in and out of the rack without breakage. Position the moldings so that the center of one molding is about 4" from the center of the next to accommodate a wide variety of stemware.

Tools & Materials ▸

Molding for wineglass rack	8-gauge flathead wood screws
Plywood (if bottom of cabinet is recessed)	Drill
	³⁄₃₂" drill bit
Screwdriver	Countersink bit

Add wineglass moldings to display your stemware and add to the beauty of your kitchen.

How to Install a Wineglass Rack

1

Plan and mark the placement of molding strips, including the end strips. Cut the end strips to span the distance from the wall to the front of the cabinet.

2

Mark screw hole locations on the molding strips and predrill holes using a countersink bit. Mark the position for screws on the cabinet bottom, using the molding strips as a guide. Predrill holes using a ³⁄₃₂" bit.

3

Attach the moldings to the cabinet with screws.

Knobs & Pulls

Switching out old drawer or cabinet knobs and pulls with updated hardware is a small, inexpensive decorating project that can significantly update a room, or convert an insignificant piece of furniture into a one-of-a-kind conversation piece. Like the perfect piece of jewelry or an exquisite accent color, attractive knobs and pulls can truly transform the conventional into the exceptional with a touch of sparkle, elegance, and class.

Before you select new hardware (especially if shopping for pulls instead of knobs), always measure your existing pulls. If you can avoid filling old holes and drilling new ones, you will save a significant amount of time needed to complete this project. Also, for kitchen or bathroom cabinetry, carefully note the color of the existing hardware in the room and select knobs or pulls that will match or accent your décor, faucets, and knobs.

Tools & Materials ▸

Pulls or knobs	Pencil	WD-40	Sandpaper
Measuring tape	Cardboard	Masking tape	Paint or stain
Screws	Scissors	Wood filler	Escutcheons (optional)
Screwdriver	Drill	Small putty knife	

Drawer pulls and cabinet knobs serve an important function, but also add a decorative flair to furniture and cabinetry.

Hardware Selection Considerations ▸

- **Finish:** Before you select a finish, consider both the existing faucets and metal work nearby your cabinetry or furniture — and the overall decorative style of the room. If your style is traditional, then brushed finishes, shiny brass, or pewter may be a good choice for you. If more contemporary, look for enameled or high-gloss metals. If you prefer extremely unique hardware, shop around at a local antique store, or scavenge hardware off of second-hand furniture.

- **Style:** Knobs are available in varying shapes, sizes, and with drop-loops or colorful enameled accents. Drawer pulls do not only vary in length; choose sleek, contemporary D-rings or classic antique bails or drops in a variety of shapes and colors.

- **Escutcheon:** An escutcheon, or baseplate, may be used behind knobs or pulls to conceal previous holes or to highlight and frame hardware.

- **Functionality:** If your knob or pull is uncomfortable to use or doesn't adequately support the weight and/or size of your door or drawer, then it won't matter how beautiful or unique it is. It's usually best to gauge the general size required for your project based upon the previous hardware. If selecting hardware for a heavy drawer on a new piece, consult your salesperson for advice on the size, style, and placement that will work best for your piece.

How to Install Cabinet or Drawer Hardware

1

Measure the thickness of doors or drawer fronts and count the number of total knobs or pulls needed to finish your project before you buy hardware. Drawers over 24" wide should have two pulls to prevent the drawer from twisting when opened.

2

Compare the length of the screws provided with your new hardware to the thickness of the doors or drawer fronts. The screws should be between ⅛ and ½" longer than the thickness of the front. If necessary, purchase screws separately.

3

Experiment with the placement of knobs or pulls. Generally, pulls are centered side-to-side and top-to-bottom on drawer fronts. If your drawer requires two pulls, divide the length of the drawer front by 6 and mark this distance from the outside of your drawer front on both sides. Center your pull upon this mark.

(continued)

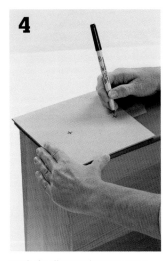

Mark the distance between screw holes on a piece of cardboard, then cut these holes out to make a template. Hold the template against doors or drawers and mark the screw hole placements.

One at a time, drill holes as marked on the doors and drawer fronts. Doors can remain in place, but it's easiest to remove drawers and place them on a table or workbench.

Align the new pull with the holes and drive a screw through the first hole and into the pull. Drive the second screw, and then test the pull to make sure it's secure.

How to Replace Cabinet or Drawer Hardware

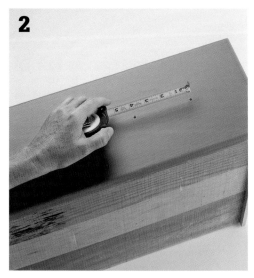

Remove the screws holding the old hardware in place. If screws are stubborn, spray a little WD-40 and let it sit for a few minutes before removing. Clean the front and back of the drawer or door thoroughly.

Measure the distance between holes, center to center. If your measurement matches the width of your new pulls, install the new pulls as on page 223.

Variation: If the filled holes are too obvious to cover, attach escutcheons to camouflage them.

Mark and drill screw holes and install hardware as instructed on page 224 (top).

Covering Holes ▸

If your new pulls measure differently than the old, place masking tape securely across the front of the drawer or door, covering the holes. From the backside of the drawer or door, fill the holes with wood filler using a small putty knife. When the holes are filled evenly and completely, remove the tape and allow the filler to dry.

Sand the filler and touch up the paint, if necessary. If you intend to repaint the drawer, sand or strip now and repaint.

Prehung Interior Door

Replacing an old door with a clean, new one can instantly update a room's décor and can help coordinate your paint selections with the woodwork in the room. When adding a new door, always match the finish to any existing trim. If working in new construction, install after the framing work is complete and the wallboard has been installed. If the rough opening for the door has been framed accurately, installing a door should take no more than an hour.

Standard prehung doors have 4½"-wide jambs and are sized to fit walls with 2 × 4 construction and ½" wallboard. If you have 2 × 6 construction or thicker wall surface material, you can special-order a door to match or add jamb extensions to a standard-sized door.

Tools & Materials ›

Level
Hammer
Handsaw

Prehung interior door
Wood shims
8d casing nails

Tool Tip ›

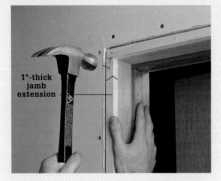

1"-thick jamb extension

If your walls are built with 2 × 6 studs, you'll need to extend the jambs by attaching 1"-thick wood strips to the edges of the jamb after the door is installed. Use glue and 4d casing nails when attaching jamb extensions. Make the strips from the same wood as the jamb.

Prehung doors are shipped as single units with the door already hung on hinges attached to pre-installed jambs.

How to Install a Prehung Interior Door

Slide the door unit into the framed opening so the edges of the jambs are flush with the wall surface and the hinge-side jamb is plumb.

Insert pairs of wood shims driven from opposite directions into the gap between the framing members and the hinge-side jamb, spaced every 12". Check the hinge-side jamb to make sure it is still plumb and does not bow.

Anchor the hinge-side jamb with 8d casing nails driven through the jamb and shims and into the jack stud.

Insert pairs of shims in the gap between the framing members and the latch-side jamb and top jamb, spaced every 12". With the door closed, adjust the shims so the gap between door edge and jamb is ⅛" wide. Drive 8d casing nails through the jambs and shims, into the framing members.

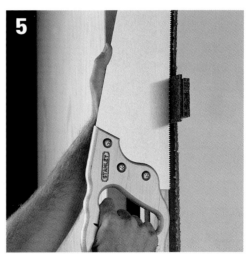

Cut the shims flush with the wall surface using a handsaw. Hold the saw vertically to prevent damage to the door jamb or wall. Finish the door and install the lockset as directed by the manufacturer. See page 129 to install trim around the door.

Bifold Doors

Bifold doors are available in many colors and styles, and they provide easy access to a closet without requiring much clearance for opening. Most home centers stock kits that include two pairs of prehinged doors, a head track, and all the necessary hardware and fasteners. Typically, the doors in these kits have predrilled holes for the pivot and guide posts. Hardware kits are also sold separately for custom projects. There are many types of bifold door styles, so be sure to read and follow the manufacturer's instructions for the product you use.

Tools & Materials ▸

Tape measure	Screwdriver
Level	Hacksaw
Circular saw	Prehinged bifold doors
Straightedge	Head track
(optional)	Mounting hardware
Drill	Panhead screws
Plane	Flathead screws

A variety of designer bifold doors are available for installation between rooms and closets. They provide the same attractive appearance as French doors but require much less floor space.

How to Install Bifold Doors

Cut the head track to the width of the opening using a hacksaw. Insert the roller mounts into the track, then position the track in the opening. Fasten it to the header using panhead screws.

Measure and mark each side jamb at the floor for the anchor bracket so the center of the bracket aligns exactly with the center of the head track. Fasten the brackets in place with flathead screws.

Check the height of the doors in the opening, and trim if necessary. Insert pivot posts into predrilled holes at the bottoms and tops of the doors. Insert guide posts at the tops of the leading doors. Make sure all posts fit snugly.

Fold one pair of doors closed and lift it into position, inserting the pivot and guide posts into the head track. Slip the bottom pivot post into the anchor bracket. Repeat for the other pair of doors. Close the doors and check alignment along the side jambs and down the center. If necessary, adjust the top and bottom pivots following the manufacturer's instructions.

Painting Wood Doors

Painting wood doors can add an extra splash of color to a new space or help older doors blend with updated décor. If you're working on a raw wood door or repainting an old piece, always take the time to prepare the wood adequately before painting for the best, most lasting result.

Tools & Materials ▶

Screwdriver
Hammer
Wood filler
Putty knife

Fine-grit and extra fine-grit sandpaper
Lead-testing kit (optional)
Sawhorses

3" paintbrush
Paint
Tack cloth

Clear wood sealer
Latex wood patch (optional)
Drill

Painting interior doors can help old doors blend with updated décor or add a punch of accent color.

How to Paint a Wood Door

Remove the door by driving out the lower hinge pin with a screwdriver and hammer. Next, have a helper hold the door in place while you drive out the middle and then the upper hinge pins.

Prepare the door for painting. Apply wood filler to any dents or damaged areas, then sand the surface of the woodwork thoroughly. Start with a fine-grit sandpaper and progress to an extra fine-grit sandpaper, sanding with the grain of the wood. If painting a door that may have been painted before 1978, take a sample of the paint and test the paint for lead with a lead-testing kit before you proceed. If the test indicates the presence of lead, consult a lead-abatement specialist.

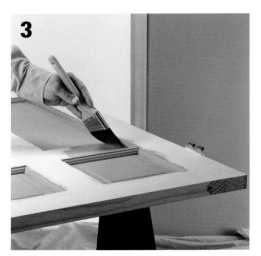

Place the door flat on a pair of sawhorses. On paneled doors, use a paintbrush to paint in the following order: 1) recessed panels, 2) horizontal rails, and 3) vertical stiles. Let the paint dry thoroughly. If a second coat is required, sand the door lightly and wipe it with a tack cloth before applying it.

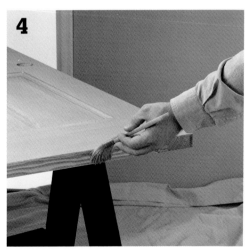

Seal the unpainted edges of the door with clear wood sealer. Allow the sealer and paint to completely dry. Rehang the door, using the old screw locations. If the screw holes in the wall no longer support the screws firmly, fill them with latex wood patch and drill pilot holes before hanging.

Decorative Door Headers

Adding a decorative head casing to a door is a tasteful way to dress up your existing trim. Although head treatments like this are more common over doors, you can use this technique over windows as well. Designing your own decorative molding can be creative and fun, but try not to overwhelm the room with trim that will detract from the décor.

Standard door casings have an outer-edge thickness of approximately ¹¹⁄₁₆". Build your custom header around this thickness. Use it to create a reveal line to a thinner piece of trim, or build out from the edge for a bolder, more substantial appearance.

Tools & Materials ▸

Moldings
Wood glue
Pencil
Tape measure
Power miter saw
Finish nail gun
Brad nail gun

Replacing plain head casing on a door or window with a decorative built-up version is a quick and easy way to add sophistication to these standard home features.

How to Install a Decorative Door Header

Measure the width of your door casing and rough cut a piece of bed or crown molding 6" longer. Use the casing width dimension to layout cut marks on the bottom edge of the molding. Start the marks 2" from the end to allow space for cutting the mitered ends.

With the molding upside down and sprung against the fence, cut a 45° outside corner miter angle at each end on the casing reference marks from step 1. See pages 120 and 122 for more information on miter-cutting crown molding.

Cut mitered returns for the molding using the leftover piece. Set the angle of the power miter saw to the opposing 45° angle and cut the returns with the molding upside down and sprung against the fence. Dry fit the pieces, recutting them if necessary. Apply glue to the return pieces and nail them to the ends of the head molding with 1" brad nails.

Nail the new header in place with 2½" finish nails driven at an angle through the bed molding and into the framing members of the wall.

Cut lattice molding 1" longer than the length of the bed molding and nail it in place with ⅝" brad nails so that it has a uniform overhang of ½". Fill all nail holes with spackle and sand them with fine-grit sandpaper. Apply the final coat of finish.

Door Mirror

Mirrors create the illusion of extra space in a room, and help move light easily around a space. Installing mirrors on the back of bedroom or closet doors is not only an efficient use of the extra space, it also adds detail and a smart finished appearance to an area otherwise left neglected by decorators.

Most mirrors will come with all the necessary hardware, but if you are purchasing your own, consult the weight loads suitable for the product and ensure that the screws will support the weight of your mirror. Also, measure the door to ensure that it is

Tools & Materials ▶

Tape measure   Drill
Pencil   Mirror
Adhesive-backed hooks

deep enough for the screws you've chosen, or that came with the mirror. Some toggle bolts, for example, require a radius to flip open that is too large for most prehung doors.

Installing mirrors on doors is both a functional and an aesthetically pleasing use of space.

How to Attach a Mirror to a Door

Measure up from the floor to the desired heights at which you want the top and the bottom of the mirror to rest on the door. Draw a level line.

Fasten adhesive-backed hooks (or hooks provided by the manufacturer) along level lines. Here a plastic anchor was drilled into the wall and then the screw with plastic fastener was drilled into the anchor. For detailed instructions on self-tapping wall anchor use, see page 179.

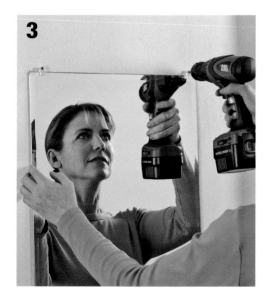

Place mirror into the hooks and make sure each screw is thoroughly and securely driven into the wall.

Creative Mirror Decoration ▸

Spraying a stenciled frost to a mirror can add to its decorative flair. Purchase a can of "frosted glass" and apply it to the mirror using a stencil for this contemporary, whimsical effect. When dry, correct any stencil mistakes or oversprays with a safety razor. See page 134.

Flooring

Floors are one of the largest surface area elements in each room of your home, and your selection of a flooring surface is a high-impact decorating decision. If you're considering a new decorative finish for your existing floors or installing new flooring, consider both the decorative appeal and the durability of any finish you choose. Floors that are not sealed or maintained properly will reveal wear more quickly than other design elements; conversely, some of the most durable floor surfaces will outlive their design statement and will become a force to be dealt with in updated or remodeled homes.

Regardless of the technique you choose, prepare your existing floor surface completely before beginning and be bold in your design choices. Use your floors as an outlet for your creativity—the color or design you choose can set the tone for any room in your home, so be confident and get ready to transform your space.

In this chapter:

- Resilient Tile
- Glass Mosaic Tile
- Carpet Squares
- Concrete Floors
- Wood Floors
- Custom Floor Mats
- Sheet Vinyl
- Stencils

Resilient Tile

Resilient tile comes in thousands of colors and styles and is a dynamic flooring choice for kitchens, hallways, and other high-traffic areas. Because tiles are inlayed with a pattern, you can create a design with the tiles that will have a large impact on your overall decor. One way to create a design is the quarter-turn method in which each tile is placed so its pattern grain runs perpendicular to that of adjacent tiles. Or combine complementary tiles in different patterns and styles into a pleasing design.

As with any tile installation, resilient tile requires carefully positioned layout lines. Before committing to any layout and applying tile with adhesive, conduct a dry run to identify potential problems. Also, keep in mind the difference between reference lines and layout lines. Reference lines mark the center of the room and divide it into quadrants. If the tiles don't lay out symmetrically along these lines, you'll need to adjust them slightly, creating layout lines. Once layout lines are established, installing the tile is a fairly quick process. Be sure to keep joints between the tiles tight and lay the tiles square.

Resilient tiles have a pattern layer that is bonded to a vinyl base and coated with a transparent wear layer. Some come with adhesive preapplied and covered by a paper backing, others have dry backs and are designed to be set into flooring adhesive.

Tools & Materials ▸

Tape measure
Chalk line
Framing square
Utility knife
1/16" notched trowel
Heat gun
Resilient tile
Flooring adhesive
 (for dry-back tile)

Tips for Laying Out Your Tile ▸

Check for noticeable directional features, like the grain of the vinyl particles, to help determine your layout. Set the tiles in a running pattern, placing them so the directional grain runs in the same direction (left), or in a checkerboard pattern using the quarter-turn method (right). Always plan the layout of the room thoroughly before you begin.

How to Make Reference Lines for Tile Installation

Position a reference line (X) by measuring along opposite sides of the room and marking the center of each side. Snap a chalk line between these marks.

Measure and mark the centerpoint of the chalk line. From this point, use a framing square to establish a second reference line perpendicular to the first one. Snap the second line (Y) across the room.

Check the reference lines for squareness using the 3-4-5 triangle method. Measure along reference line X and make a mark 3 ft. from the centerpoint. Measure from the centerpoint along reference line Y and make a mark at 4 ft.

Measure the distance between the marks. If the reference lines are perpendicular, the distance will measure exactly 5 ft. If not, adjust the reference lines until they're exactly perpendicular to each other.

How to Install Dry-back Resilient Tile

Snap perpendicular reference lines with a chalk line. Dry-fit tiles along layout line Y so a joint falls along reference line X. If necessary, shift the layout to make the layout symmetrical or to reduce the number of tiles that need to be cut.

If you shift the tile layout, create a new line that is parallel to reference line X and runs through a tile joint near line X. The new line, X1, is the line you'll use when installing the tile. Use a different colored chalk to distinguish between lines.

Dry-fit tiles along the new line, X1. If necessary, adjust the layout line as in steps 1 and 2.

If you adjusted the layout along X1, measure and make a new layout line Y1 that's parallel to reference line Y and runs through a tile joint. Y1 will form the second layout line you'll use during installation.

Apply adhesive around the intersection of the layout lines using a trowel with 1/16" V-shaped notches. Hold the trowel at a 45° angle and spread adhesive evenly over the surface.

Spread adhesive over most of the installation area, covering three quadrants. Allow the adhesive to set according to the manufacturer's instructions, then begin to install the tile at the intersection of the layout lines. You can kneel on installed tiles to lay additional tiles.

When the first three quadrants are completely tiled, spread adhesive over the remaining quadrant, then finish setting the tile.

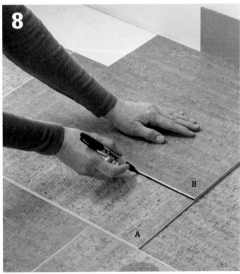

To cut tiles to fit along the walls, place the tile to be cut (A) face up on top of the last full tile you installed. Position a 1/8"-thick spacer against the wall, then set a marker tile (B) on top of the tile to be cut. Trace along the edge of the marker tile to draw a cutting line.

(continued)

Tool Tip ▸

To mark tiles for cutting around outside corners, make a cardboard template to match the space, keeping a ⅛" gap along the walls. After cutting the template, check to make sure it fits. Place the template on a tile and trace its outline.

9

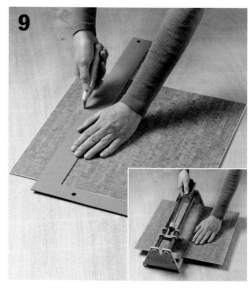

Cut the tile to fit using a utility knife and straightedge. Hold the straightedge securely against the cutting line to ensure a straight cut. *Option: You can use a ceramic-tile cutter to make straight cuts in thick vinyl tiles (see inset).*

10

Install cut tiles next to the walls. If you're precutting all tiles before installing them, measure the distance between the walls and install tiles at various points in case the distance changes.

11

Continue installing the tile in the remaining quadrants until the room is completely covered. Check the entire floor. If you find loose areas, press down on the tiles to bond them to the underlayment. Install metal threshold bars at room borders, where the new floor joins another floor covering.

How to Install Self-adhesive Resilient Tile

Once your reference lines are established, peel off the paper backing and install the first tile in one of the corners formed by the intersecting layout lines. Lay three or more tiles along each layout lines in the quadrant. Rub the entire surface of each tile to bond the adhesive to the floor underlayment.

Begin installing tiles in the interior area of the quadrant. Keep the joints tight between tiles..

Finish setting full tiles in the first quadrant, then set the full tiles in an adjacent quadrant. Set the tiles along the layout lines first, then fill in the interior tiles.

Continue installing the tile in the remaining quadrants until the room is completely covered. Check the entire floor. If you find loose areas, press down on the tiles to bond them to the underlayment. Install metal threshold bars at room borders, where the new floor joins another floor covering.

Glass Mosaic Tile

Mosaic tile is an excellent choice for smaller areas and is available in many different colors to accent or blend with your décor. Variations in color and texture are likely when working with tile, so always buy all tile for one project from the same lot and batch to ensure a good match. Also, mortar or mastic intended for ceramic tile may not work with glass mosaic tile—check with your salesperson to determine what product will best suit your project.

Sheets of mosaic tile are held together by a fabric mesh backing. This makes them more difficult to hold, place, and move. They may not be square with your guidelines when you first lay them down. Mosaic tiles also require more temporary spacers and much more grout, so calculate the materials you'll need carefully before beginning this project.

Tools & Materials ▸

Carpenter's square	Notched trowel
Chalk line	Recommended
Cleaning supplies	adhesive
Coarse sponge	Rubber mallet
Craft/utility knife	Sanded grout
Grout sealer	Scrap lumber
Marking pen	Straightedge
or pencil	Tile nippers
Measuring tape	Tile spacers

Mosaic tiles come in sheets (usually 12 × 12") and can be made from ceramic, porcelain, glass, or any number of designer materials. Normally installed for their appearance, mosaics are relatively high maintenance and prone to cracks because of all of the grout lines.

How to Install Mosaic Tile

Clean and prepare the area and then draw reference lines (see page 239). Beginning at the center intersection, apply the recommended adhesive to one quadrant. Spread it outward evenly with a notched trowel. Lay down only as much adhesive as you can cover in 10 to 15 minutes.

Select a sheet of mosaic tile. Place several plastic spacers within the grid so that the sheet remains square. Pick up the sheet of tiles by diagonally opposite corners. This will help you hold the edges up so that you don't trap empty space in the middle of the sheet.

Gently press one corner into place on the adhesive. Slowly lower the opposite corner, making sure the sides remain square with your reference lines. Massage the sheet into the adhesive, being careful not to press too hard or twist the sheet out of position. Insert a few spacers in the outside edges of the sheet you have just placed. This will help keep the grout lines consistent.

When you have placed two or three sheets, lay a scrap piece of flat lumber across the tops and tap the wood with a rubber mallet to set the fabric mesh in the adhesive and to force out any trapped air.

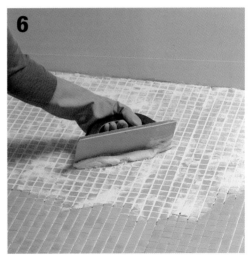

At the outer edges of your work area, you will probably need to trim one or more rows from the last sheet. If the space left at the edge is more than the width of a regular grout line, use tile nippers to trim the last row that will fit. Save these leftover tiles for repairs.

After the adhesive has cured, usually 24 to 48 hours, apply grout. With many more spaces, mosaic tile will require more grout than usual. Follow the manufacturer's instructions for spreading and floating the grout. Wipe a damp grout sponge diagonally over about 2 sq. ft. of the floor at a time and rinse the sponge between wipes. Wipe each area only once, to avoid pulling grout out of the joints. Allow to dry for 4 hours, then buff with a soft cloth.

Carpet Squares

Most carpeting has a single design and is stretched from wall to wall. It covers more square feet of American homes than any other material. But if you want a soft floor covering that gives you more options, carpet squares are an excellent choice.

Manufacturers have found ways to create attractive new carpet using recycled fibers. This not only reuses material that would otherwise become landfill, it reduces waste in manufacturing as well. So, instead of adding to problems of resource consumption and pollution, carpet squares made from recycled materials help reduce them.

The squares are attached to each other and to the floor with adhesive dots. They can be installed on most clean, level, dry underlayment or existing floor. If the surface underneath is waxed or varnished, check with the manufacturer before you use any adhesives on it.

Tools & Materials ▸

Adhesive
Aviator's snips
Carpenter's square
Chalk line
Cleaning supplies
Craft/utility knife

Flat-edged trowel
Marking pen
  or pencil
Measuring tape
Notched trowel
Straightedge

Carpet tiles combine the warmth and comfort of carpet with do-it-yourself installation, custom designs, and easy replacement. They can be laid wall-to-wall or in an area rug style, as shown above.

How to Install Carpet Squares

1

Take the squares out of the package. Be sure the room is well ventilated. Carpet squares should be at room temperature for at least 12 hours before you lay them down.

2

Check the requirements for the recommended adhesive. You can install carpet squares over many other flooring materials, including hardwood, laminates, and resilient sheets or tiles. The carpet squares shown here are fastened with adhesive dots, so almost any existing floor provides a usable surface.

3

Make sure the existing floor is clean, smooth, stable, and dry. Use floor leveler if necessary to eliminate any hills or valleys. If any part of the floor is loose, secure it to the subfloor or underlayment before you install the carpet squares. Vacuum the surface and wipe it with a damp cloth.

4

Snap chalk lines between diagonally opposite corners to find the center point for the room. In rooms with unusual shapes, determine the visual center and mark it. Next, snap chalk lines across the center and perpendicular to the walls. This set of guidelines will show you where to start.

(continued)

Lay a base row of carpet squares on each side of the two guidelines. When you reach the walls, make note of how much you will need to cut. You should have the same amount to cut on each side. If not, adjust the center point and realign the squares.

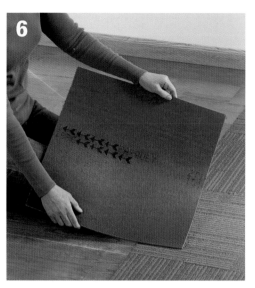

Check the backs of the squares before you apply any adhesive. They should indicate a direction using arrows or other marks so that the finished pile has a consistent appearance. If you plan to mix colors, this is the time to establish your pattern.

Fasten the base rows in place using the manufacturer's recommended adhesive. This installation calls for two adhesive dots per square. As you place each square, make sure it is aligned with the guidelines and fits tightly against the next square.

When you reach a wall, flip the last square over. Push it against the wall until it is snug. If you are planning a continuous pattern, align the arrows with the existing squares. If you are creating a parquet pattern, turn the new square 90° before marking it.

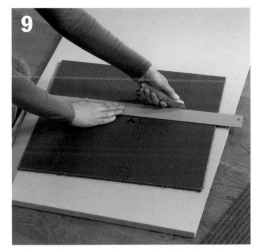

9

Mark notches or draw a line across the back where the new square overlaps the next-to-last one. Using a sharp carpet knife, a carpenter's square, and a tough work surface, cut along this line. The cut square should fit neatly in the remaining space.

10

At a door jamb, place a square face up where it will go. Lean the square against the jamb and mark the point where they meet. Move the square to find the other cutline, and mark that as well. Flip the square over, mark the two lines using a carpenter's square, and cut out the corner.

11

Finish all four base rows before you fill in the rest of the room. As you work, check the alignment of each row. If you notice a row going out of line, find the point where the direction changed, then remove squares back to that point and start again.

12

Work outward from the center so that you have a known reference for keeping rows straight. Save the cut pieces from the ends. They may be useful for patching odd spaces around doorways, heat registers, radiator pipes, and when you reach the corners.

Concrete Floors

Concrete is a versatile building material. Most people are accustomed to thinking of concrete primarily as a utilitarian substance, but it can also mimic a variety of flooring types and be a colorful and beautiful addition to any room.

Whether your concrete floor is a practical surface for the garage or an artistic statement of personal style in your dining room, it should be sealed. Concrete is a hard and durable building material, but it is also porous. Consequently, concrete floors are susceptible to staining. Many stains can be removed with the proper cleaner, but sealing and painting prevents oil, grease, and other stains from penetrating the surface in the first place, thus cleanup is a whole lot easier.

Tools & Materials ▸

Acid-tolerant pump sprayer
Rubber boots
Alkaline-base neutralizer
Acid etcher

Acid-tolerant bucket
Sealant
Garden hose
Broom

Paintbrush
Extension pole
Respirator
Paint roller and tray

High-pressure washer
Wet vacuum
Rubber gloves

Although concrete is most common in garages and basements, it is not limited to these parts of the house, especially in contemporary design. Pair concrete floors with elegant furnishings for modern industrial sophistication.

Acid Etching Safety ▸

WARNING: Risk of serious injury. Always read manufacturer's instructions.

Acid etching is the process used to open the pores in concrete surfaces, allowing sealers to bond with it. All smooth or dense concrete surfaces should be etched before applying stain or sealant. An etched surface should feel gritty and be easily penetrated by water. A variety of acid-etching products are available, including citric acid, sulfamic acid, phosphoric acid, and muriatic acid.

All of these acids are dangerous, so use caution while handling them. It is critical that your room is well ventilated, and that you wear protective clothing, including long sleeves and pants, rubber boots and gloves, a respirator, and safety goggles.
Also, never add water to acid—only add acid to water.

How to Seal a Concrete Floor

Clean and prepare the surface by first sweeping up all debris. Next, remove all surface muck: mud, wax, and grease. Finally, remove existing paints or coatings.

Saturate the surface with clean water—the surface must be wet before acid etching. Check for any areas where water beads up; this indicates that contaminants still need to be cleaned off. Test your acid-tolerant pump sprayer with water to make sure it releases a wide, even mist. Check the manufacturer's instructions for the etching solution and fill the pump sprayer with the recommended amount of water.

Add the acid etching contents to the water in the acid-tolerant pump sprayer. Follow the directions (and mixing proportions) specified by the manufacturer. Use extreme caution when using these materials.

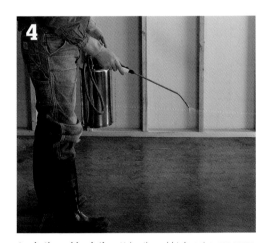

Apply the acid solution. Using the acid-tolerant pump spray unit, evenly apply the diluted acid solution over the concrete floor. Do not allow the acid solution to dry at any time during the etching and cleaning process. Etch small areas at a time, 10 × 10 ft. or smaller. If there is a slope, begin on the low side of the slope and work upward.

Use a stiff-bristle broom or scrubber to work the acid solution into the concrete. Let the acid sit for 5 to 10 minutes, or as indicated by the manufacturer's directions. A mild foaming action indicates that the product is working. If no bubbling or fizzing occurs, it means there is still grease, oil, or a concrete treatment on the surface that is interfering with the etching product.

(continued)

Once the fizzing has stopped, the acid has finished reacting with the alkaline concrete surface and has formed pH-neutral salts. Neutralize any remaining acid with an alkaline-base solution. Put a gallon of water in a 5-gallon bucket and then stir in an alkaline-base neutralizer. Using a stiff-bristle broom, make sure the concrete surface is completely covered with the solution. Continue to sweep until the fizzing stops.

Use a garden hose with a pressure nozzle or, ideally, a pressure washer in conjunction with a stiff-bristle broom to thoroughly rinse the concrete surface. Rinse two to three times. Reapply the acid and repeat steps 4, 5, 6, and 7.

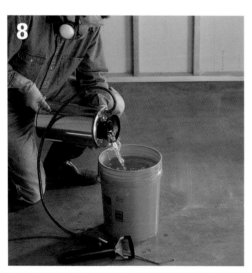

If you have any leftover acid you can make it safe for your septic system by mixing more alkaline solution in the 5-gallon bucket and carefully pouring the acid from the spray unit into the bucket until all of the fizzing stops.

Use a wet vacuum to clean up the mess. Check your local disposal regulations for proper disposal of the neutralized spent acid, which may be hazardous to local vegetation or your drainage system. Check for residue by rubbing a dark cloth over a small area of concrete. If white residue appears (inset), continue the rinsing process.

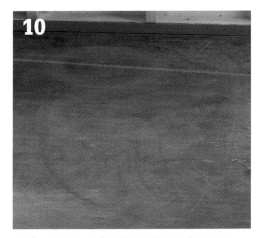

Let the concrete dry for at least 24 hours and sweep up dust, dirt, and particles leftover from the etching process. Mix the sealer in a bucket with a stir stick.

Create a testing patch with painter's tape and apply sealer to this area to ensure desired appearance. Add an antiskid additive to aid with traction, especially on stairs.

Use wide painter's tape to protect walls, and then using a good-quality 4"-wide synthetic bristle paintbrush, coat the perimeter with sealer.

Use a long-handled paint roller with at least a ½" nap to apply an even coat. Work in small sections at a time (about 2 × 3 ft.) and work in one orientation. Always maintain a wet edge to avoid lap marks and do not rework partially dry areas. Allow the surface to dry according to the manufacturer's instructions, usually 8 to 12 hours. Then apply a second coat in the opposite direction to the first coat.

Tip for Painting a Concrete Floor ▸

If you decide to paint instead of apply clear or stained sealant, check to make sure that the paint is designed for use on concrete floors. Also, once the paint has dried for a few days, apply two to three coats of water-based polyurethane.

Wood Floors

If your wood floors need a lot of work and your room is desperate for color, warmth, or a clean finish, then painting your floors may be the best decorating solution for your space. Both formal and informal spaces can benefit from this technique. Unify a space by extending a painted floor through a hallway to a staircase, or add a faux antique finish to edges to make a large room feel cozy and inviting. Or lay out and paint a checkerboard pattern, which will draw the eye around the room quickly as well as disguise worn spots under darker paint colors. When purchasing supplies, always purchase paints and sealers that are designed specifically for floors to improve the durability of your finish.

Tools & Materials ▸

Paint scraper
Pole sander
Medium- or fine-grit
   sandpaper
Damp cloth
Lacquer thinner
Hammer
Nail set
Painter's tape

Primer
4" paintbrush
Roller, extension
   pole, and tray
Semigloss paint
Polyurethane sealer
Painting pad
   and pole
Tack cloth

Rev up a worn-out floor with a bright paint color. Paint can not only disguise flaws, but it can also add warmth and character to a room.

How to Paint Wood Floors

1

Use a paint scraper to smooth rough spots. Use a pole sander to sand with the grain of the wood. For coarse wood, use medium-grit sandpaper. Scuff glossy hardwoods with fine sandpaper (#120) for good adhesion.

2

When finished sanding, sweep or vacuum. Use a damp cloth to remove fine dust. Use a cloth dampened with lacquer thinner for a final cleaning. If you see any nails sticking up, tap them down with a hammer and nail set.

3

Protect the baseboards with wide painter's tape. Press the tape edges down so paint doesn't seep underneath.

4

Mix primer well. Use a 4"-wide brush to apply the primer around the perimeter of the room. Then paint the remaining floor with a roller on an extension pole. Allow the primer to dry.

5

Cut in with a 4" brush, then paint the rest of the floor using a roller on an extension pole. Always roll from a dry area to a wet area to minimize lap lines. Wait to dry, then apply a second coat.

6

When the paint is dry, apply two or three coats of a matte-finish, water-based polyurethane sealer, using a painting pad on a pole. Allow the sealer to dry. Sand with a pole sander, using fine sandpaper. Clean up the dust with a tack cloth.

Custom Floor Mats

Painting a stenciled design onto your indoor/outdoor floor mats is a quick project that adds instant custom detail to your home. Showcase your family monogram, stencil a pattern or image, or share a friendly message with visitors. Add fun and creativity, sophistication, or unify a décor scheme with a painted motif found elsewhere in the room.

To complete this project effectively, select a nonheat-sensitive fabric paint (nonheat-sensitive paint does not require heat to set). Explore your craft store for a fuller-bodied paint as opposed to a paint that is very thin. Full-bodied paint will bond to the rug fibers, resulting in a lasting design. Apply this technique to jute, cotton, or sisal rugs. Always make a mock-up of your design to check placement, measurements and spacing to spare any surprises once you get started.

Tools & Materials ▸

Rug
Stencil
Ruler
Triangle
¾" medium stiff
   stencil paintbrush
Green tape (will
   stick to hard-to-
   stick surfaces)
Nonheat-sensitive
   full-bodied
   fabric paint

Add a traditional monogram to indoor/outdoor floor mats – or stencil a creative overall design, image or message.

How to Stencil a Floor Mat

Make a mock-up of your design and position it on the mat. Set a level line beneath your stencil with green tape. Use a triangle to set a side line, creating a 90° angle where your design will begin. If your design will cover the entire mat, skip this step.

Begin to apply the design one stencil piece at a time. Use green tape to hold the stencil in place along your guidelines and softly pounce the paint on with the stencil brush, starting in the center and off-loading a bit before moving to the edges. Stencil in all the pieces of your design, one stencil at a time.

Inspect your design, then reposition stencils to add detail or correct forms, if necessary. Allow paint to fully dry before use.

Stencil Selection ▶

A wide variety of stencils—letters, numbers, and images—are available at your local craft store. If you're a new stenciler, select stencils that are fairly simple, without many small spaces or intricate details. If you will be using a stencil with intricate detail, select a stencil brush in a size that will accommodate your project. For a truly one-of-a-kind piece, make your own design on your home computer, print on heavy cardstock and cut out your stencil with a sharp razor knife.

Sheet Vinyl

If your sheet vinyl flooring is outdated, replacing it isn't your only option. Paint selected areas of the floor with updated colors to freshen up the look of your room and add detail to a tired, dated floor. Remember, always strip off any wax buildup and dirt before applying paint.

Tools & Materials ▸

1" artist acrylic paintbrush
White latex bonding primer
Darkly tinted latex bonding primer
White semigloss latex paint
Black semigloss latex paint
Semigloss latex floor polyurethane

Paint selected squares of a floor to update the entire surface.

How to Paint Sheet Vinyl

Prime selected squares with the appropriately tinted primer. The embossing on the linoleum will not be straight—so simply hold the brush flat to the surface and follow the edge around the squares.

After the primer dries, apply the semigloss paint over the tinted primer, white over white and black over black. When dry, coat the painted squares with polyurethane primer to seal and protect your work.

Floor Stencils

A beautiful way to dress up a large slab of cement flooring or other flat surface is with an overall stenciled pattern. For the best effect, choose a design that is airy and appealing underfoot. Always use the same side and directional orientation throughout your application, especially with complex stencils like the one shown. If you are stenciling over raw cement, always seal your floor before adding decorative painting (page xx).

Tools & Materials ▶

Chalk line
Triangle
Spray adhesive or
     painter's tape
Large floor stencil
4" foam roller brush
Latex enamel
     floor paint
Hair dryer

A stenciled pattern can transform a dull surface into a masterful design statement.

How to Stencil a Floor

1

Use chalk lines, snapped from the room's corners, to determine the center of the room. Use a triangle to make a square off the center point. Align your first stencil within this square and affix to the floor with spray adhesive or painter's tape.

2

Apply paint to the stencil with the roller, working from the center out. Force the paint dry with a hair dryer, then reposition your stencil and repeat. For best results, apply a clear topcoat when finished. Be careful with the fresh stencil for the first week, until the paint cures completely.

Slipcovers
& Upholstery

Upholstery projects can be very rewarding; consider
the creative satisfaction of returning a tattered
castoff to its like-new state, or transforming an
extremely well-loved chair to the beauty of its better
years. Similarly, slipcovers can make the old new
again, with careful measurements and a few simple
sewing techniques.

Whether you're merely adding seat covers to dress
up your dining room or reupholstering an entire garage
sale sofa complete with welting and new cushions, the
projects in this chapter will challenge and inspire you.
Start to imagine your furniture dressed in updated
prints, colorful stripes, or classic florals—and get
started on one of these creative projects, suitable for
all skill and experience levels.

In this chapter:

- Upholstery Basics
- Stripping Furniture
- Repairing a Frame
- New Cushions
- Button-tufted Cushions
- Re-upholstering a
  Drop-in Seat
- Re-upholstering a Chair
- Upholstered Ottoman
- Upholstered Headboard
- Reversible Seat Covers
- Ottoman Slipcover
- Chair Slipcover
- Futon Slipcover

Upholstery Basics

Completing a high-quality upholstery project will require a few specialized tools and fabrics. Before beginning your first project, familiarize yourself with the materials you'll need to be successful. If you can, speak with a salesperson at an upholstery supply store or an experienced upholsterer in your area about your project's specific needs.

Stripping & Upholstering Tools

Tack and Staple Removers (A)
Small screwdriver (B): Can be used for removing staples during the stripping process.
Upholsterer's Tack Hammer (C): Has one magnetized tip to hold a tack, leaving your other hand free to hold fabric.
Electric Staple Gun (D): Choose a model that will accommodate both ⅜" and ½" staples.
Webbing Stretcher (E): Pulls webbing taut with one hand while tacking or stapling with the other.
Mallet (F): Chose rubber or rawhide for best results.
Stretching Pliers (G): Made for webbing and leather, these can also be used to grasp and stretch fabric for stapling.
Upholstery Regulators (H): One end of these 8" or 10" metal skewers is used for pleating or forcing padding into tight corners. The other is used to make holes in fabric by gently separating yarns in the weave, which can be closed by coaxing them back into position.

Measuring, Marking & Cutting Tools

Yardstick (I)
Cloth Tape Measure (J)
Dustless Chalk Sticks (K): Used for marking cutting lines on fabric and tailoring patterns. If you already have a fabric-marking pencil or marker, this will work as well.
Cutting Mat & Rotary Cutter (L)
Heavy-duty Shears (M)

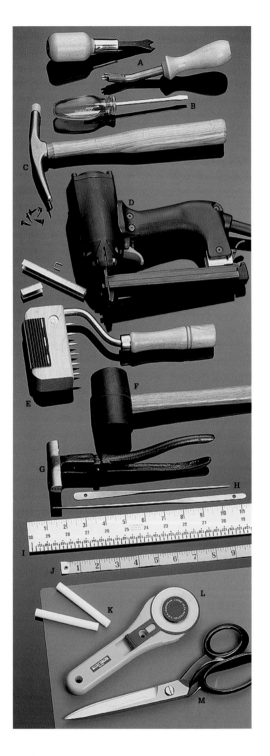

Pins & Needles

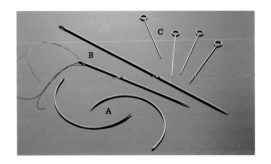

Curved Needles (A): Used for blind-stitching fabric where stapling or tacking are not possible. Round-point curved needles are used for fabrics, while wedge-point needles are used for leather or vinyl.

Button Needles (B): Available in a variety of lengths from 6 to 18", these are used to secure buttons and stitch through padding.

Upholstery Pins (C): Hold fabric in place temporarily before tacking or sewing.

Nails, Tacks, Staples & Zippers

Webbing Nails (A): Narrow, with sharp points, these nails can hold webbing securely without damaging the frame.

Upholstery Tacks (B): The most commonly used sizes are #3 and #6. Most upholstery tacks will be sold in sterile packaging, as many upholsterers hold them in the mouth while working.

Staples (C)

Decorative Tacks (D): Available in many sizes, designs, and finishes to complement fabric and furniture style.

Tack Strip (E): ½" cardboard stripping used to maintain a straight, sharp line between upholstered fabric pieces.

Tacking Strip (F): Tacks are spaced evenly for securing fabric panels invisibly when tacking is not possible.

Flexible Metal Tacking Strip (G): For curved areas.

Metal-toothed Heavy-duty Zipper (H): Length determined by cushion size.

Nylon-toothed Heavy-duty Zipper Tape (I): Can be cut to size and fitted with a zipper pull.

Extra zipper pulls (J)

Foundation Fabrics

Cambric (A): Black fabric used to cover the bottom of a furniture piece as a dustcover, and to finish the piece.

Burlap (B): Used as a covering over springs or webbing to form a support base.

Denim (C): Strong, thin fabric used to cover the deck area of a chair.

Synthetic Webbing (D): Stronger than jute webbing, synthetic webbing will not rot over time due to moisture.

Jute Webbing (E): Used when working with antiques to maintain the authenticity of the piece.

Edge Roll (F): Long, firmly stuffed tube used to cushion a wood or wire edge, keep padding from shifting, and reduce wear on fabric.

Threads, Twines & Cords

Polyester Thread (G): Strong and thin, used for machine sewing.

Nylon Thread (H): Fits the eyes of curved needles, used for hand sewing.

Nylon Button Twine (I): Used to fasten buttons, hand-stitch edge rolls and nosing seams, and secure springs to webbing and burlap.

Spring Twine (J): Used for tying springs.

Welt Cording (K)

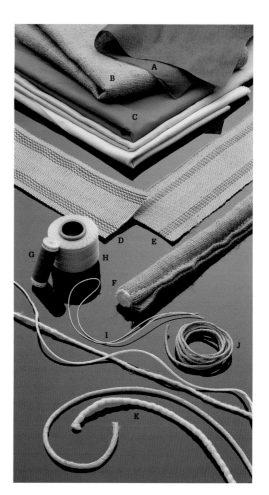

Sewing Machine Equipment

16/100 Needle (A): For lightweight to medium-weight fabrics.

18/110 Needle (B): For heavyweight fabrics.

Leather/Vinyl Needles (C): Specially designed with a wedge-shaped point.

Welting or Piping Foot (D): Designed to accommodate welting and trim up to ¼" thick.

Zipper Foot (E)

General Purpose Foot (F)

Straight-stitch Foot (G)

Walking Foot (H): Prevents layers from shifting when sewing unwelted seams upon difficult fabrics, such as velvet or satin.

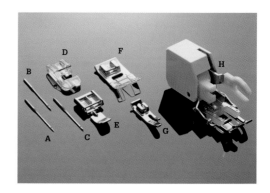

Padding Materials

Foam (A): Used for seat cushions, foam is available in many thicknesses and degrees of firmness. Cut foam with an electric foam saw knife or electric kitchen knife. Thin foam (less than 1" thick) can be cut with shears.

Spray Foam Adhesive (B): Used to secure foam to webbing or batting.

Bonded Polyester Batting (C)

Cotton Batting (D): Available in different grades of purity, cotton batting is often torn to size rather than cut.

Deck Pad (E): Stiff padding material, suitable for areas that require minimal foundation padding, such as chair decks or thinly padded chair backs or arms.

Rubberized Hair (F): Used when a thicker or fuller appearance is required.

Upholstery Fabric Considerations

Color and Texture: Carefully select a color and pattern that will coordinate with or complement your existing décor.

Fiber Content: Consider the durability, color brilliance, ease of stitching and manipulation, and stability of a fabric's fibers.

Weave Structure: Some fabrics are woven so the pattern or design is railroaded, meaning that the pattern runs the lengthwise grain horizontally on the piece rather than vertically.

Surface Treatment: Most upholstery fabrics are treated with a stain-resistant or crease-resistant finish, which greatly increases the durability of the fabric.

Measuring & Calculating Fabric

Before beginning to strip a piece, take careful measurements of every section of your project. This will help determine how much upholstery fabric to purchase and help you plan your cutting layout. Note the measurement of each piece (length times width), then add the necessary allowances. Remember that the total length of many pieces must include several inches of fabric that cannot be seen before stripping. Include the approximate amount of hidden fabric in your measurements as well. Most pieces will be cut out as rectangles and trimmed to shape as they are attached, so measure each piece at its longest and widest points.

Last, measure the total length of all welting. Use the chart below to help you calculate the amount of fabric you'll need to purchase. Your measurement chart may differ, and may include pieces not listed on the example chart, such as a skirt, arm boxing, or back boxing.

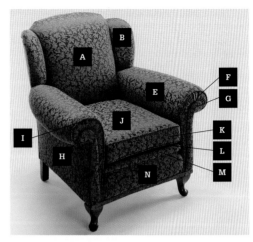

Sample Measurement Chart ▸

	Piece	Actual Size (includes hidden fabric)	Allowances ½" seam, 2" pulling	Cut Size
A	Inside Back (IB)	36 × 32"	+ 4 × 4"	= 40 × 36"
B	Inside Wing (IW)	17 × 9"	+ 4 × 4"	= 21 × 13"
C	Outside Back (OB)	30 × 23"	+ 4 × 4"	= 34 × 27"
D	Outside Wing (OW)	15 × 7"	+ 4 × 4"	= 19 × 11"
E	Inside Arm (IA)	27 × 27"	+ 4 × 4"	= 31" × 31"
F	Front Arm Band (FAB)	18 × 8"	+ 4 × 2½"	= 22 × 10½"
G	Arm Panel (AP)	15½ × 4"	+ 4 × 4"	= 19½ × 8"
H	Outside Arm (OA)	14 × 26"	+ 4 × 4"	= 18 × 30"
I	Welting (W)	250 × 1⅝"	+ 16" (for seaming and waste)	= 266 × 1⅝"
J	Cushion (C)*	22 × 19"		= 22 × 19"
K	Cushion Boxing (CB)*	4 × 63"		= 4 × 63"
L	Deck (under cushion)**			
M	Nosing (N)	6 × 21"	+ 1 × 4"	= 7 × 25"
N	Front Band (FB)	5½ × 21"	+ 2½ × 4"	= 8 × 25"

*The cut size of cushion pieces and cushion boxing are determined after tailoring a pattern for the cushion (page 272).
**Deck will be covered with other fabrics. Do not include these measurements to calculate amount of upholstery fabric needed.

Cutting Fabric

Use measurements from the chart to diagram a layout of all the pieces on graph paper, as in the examples below. The amount of fabric needed can be determined from this diagram. If your fabric has a large pattern, plan to center the large motifs on the exposed areas of prominent pieces, such as cushion tops and bottoms, inside and outside backs, and inside and outside arms. You will need to purchase considerably more fabric to lay out your pieces this way.

Cut the end of the fabric squarely, either by following a thread in the weave, using a carpenter's square, or aligning a straightedge to the pattern repeat markings on the selvages. Transfer the diagram to the right side of the fabric, marking the cutting lines with chalk and measuring from the squared end. Label the wrong side of every piece with its location as it is cut. It's also a good idea to draw a chalk line near the lower edge to indicate the downward direction.

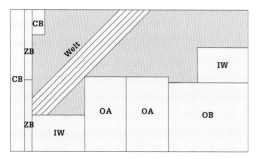

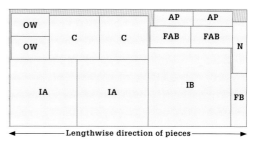

Sample Layout (fabric with no pattern, or small pattern). Most upholstery fabrics are 54" wide. Because the pieces are cut as rectangles, this layout is suitable for fabric with or without a nap.

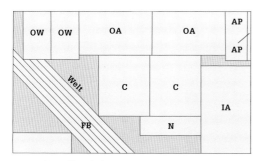

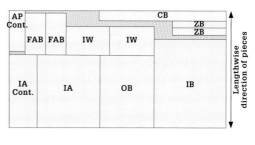

Layout for Railroaded Fabric. If the fabric can be railroaded, lay out the pieces so that their length runs on the crosswise grain. This is often a more efficient layout.

Stripping Furniture

Removing the old cover from a furniture piece is an educational experience—in fact, the detailed notes you take during this process will become your re-upholstery instructions. Before you begin, sketch or photograph any unique details you would like to recreate in the new cover, such as the pleating arrangement on an arm front or a series of tucks at a nosing corner, and make a note of any areas that will need more padding.

Before you remove any pieces, label each fabric piece with its name and direction; after the pieces are removed, they will only be puzzling shapes, so good labeling is key to a successful project. Document the seams and joints that have welting and measure the total amount of welting used after it has been removed.

Loosen or remove pieces in the reverse order from that in which they were attached to the frame. For example, in reupholstering a wing chair, remove pieces in the following order:

1. Remove the skirt, dustcover, and any welting around the lower edge.
2. Remove the outside back, outside arms, and outside wings.
3. Loosen the inside back, inside arms, and inside wings, leaving them staple-basted in position to keep the padding in place.
4. Remove the deck and nosing.

As each piece is loosened or removed, record the method used to attach it to adjoining pieces or to the frame in your notes: machine sewn, hand sewn, stapled, or attached with a tacking strip. Set the pieces aside for reference throughout the upholstery project.

Strip the padding and foundation only as far as necessary. Check to see if the frame is sturdy, if the webbing and springs are secure, and if the padding needs to be replaced or replenished.

Tools & Materials ▸

Camera
Pliers

Tack hammer

Pencil and paper for note taking

Tack lifter or staple remover

Stripping upholstery is messy and dusty; cover your work area with a tarp. Discard used tacks, nails, staples, tack strips, tacking strips, and any musty-smelling foundation materials.

How to Remove Tacks, Nails & Staples

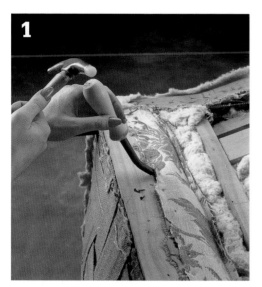

Hold the tack lifter or staple remover at a sharp angle, with the tip touching the wood at the edge of the tack nail, or staple. Strike the end of the handle with the side of the tack hammer, wedging the tip under the tack, nail, or staple.

Pry the tack, nail, or staple up from the wood.

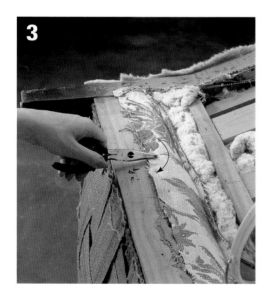

Grasp the tack, nail, or staple with the pliers; roll the pliers in the direction of the wood grain, extracting the tack, nail, or staple. (Extracting against the wood grain damages and weakens the wood.) Remove all tacks, nails, and staples. Pound in any broken points that cannot be removed.

Tip ▶

Avoid back strain and sore knees by standing the project on a raised platform or padded sawhorses during the stripping process. You can then do the upholstery work while standing or sitting at a comfortable height, without repeatedly bending over or kneeling.

Repairing a Frame

Before you can beautify your old furniture with new upholstery, spend some time making sure your frame is structurally sound. After you remove the outer cover, check to see if there are any loose joints or cracked rails or posts. Minor repair work can be done with minimal carpentry skills. This is also a great time to completely refinish any exposed wood, if that is a part of your project. However, shallow scratches and general dullness can be corrected with a few simple techniques.

Tools & Materials ▸

Touch-up markers
Wood polish and
   cleaner with
   lemon oil
Extra fine steel wool
Wood glue
Wood screws

Screwdriver
Hot vinegar
File
Clamps
Glue syringe
Chisel

Repair minor scratches using touch-up markers in the same color as the stained and finished woodwork.

Frame Maintenance ▸

Clean a dull finish by applying wood polish and cleaner and gently rubbing with extra-fine steel wool.

Tighten loose corner blocks by first applying wood glue and then inserting wood screws.

How to Repair Loose Joints

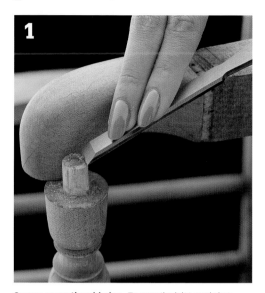

Scrape away the old glue. To open the joint, apply hot vinegar to the old glue to soften.

Apply an ample amount of wood glue to the joint. Close the joint; clamp or tie (as shown here) tightly. Allow to dry, following the glue manufacturer's directions.

How to Repair a Cracked Rail or Post

Inject wood glue into the crack, using a glue syringe.

Clamp the rail or post securely. Allow to dry, following the glue manufacturer's directions.

New Cushions

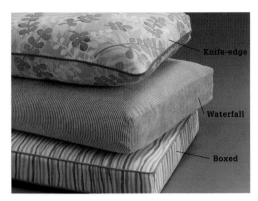

The three most common cushion styles are boxed, waterfall, and knife-edge, each of which offers a distinct decorative flair to a finished piece. All three styles can be fitted flush to the front of the chair or T-shaped, wrapping around the front of the chair arms. Boxed cushions are sturdy and classic, and can be sewn with or without welting at the top and bottom seams. Knife-edge cushions fit nicely on older furniture and usually have a welted seam around the center seam, where the cushion is exposed; hidden sides are then constructed with a boxing strip. Waterfall cushions are a beautiful contemporary style, sewn with one continuous piece of fabric wrapping over the front from top to bottom. Waterfall cushions have a boxing strip around the sides and back and are usually constructed without welting.

As a general rule, the finished width of the boxing strip should be ¾" narrower than the height of the foam. Many waterfall cushions, however, are made with narrower boxing strips. The fabric wraps over the sides from the top and bottom and forms small pleats around the curved front of the boxing strip. To copy this type of cushion cover, it is best to make a pattern from the original cushion.

Chair and sofa cushions are generally constructed with a zipper closure around the back corners of the cushion, which makes it easy to remove covers for cleaning, if necessary.

Tools & Materials ▸

Muslin	Electric knife
Upholstery fabric	Marker
Welt cording and fabric	Polyester batting
Upholstery zipper or	and spray foam
continuous zipper	adhesive, or
tape and pull	button needle
Foam	and heavy thread

How to Tailor a Pattern for a Boxed Cushion

Measure the seat opening in both directions at the widest point and add 2" to each measurement. Cut muslin to this size and mark a centerline from front to back. Center muslin over the chair deck, turning excess muslin up along the arms and back. For a T-cushion, clip muslin around the curves, allowing it to lie flat.

Mark an outline of the cushion, holding a sharpened stick of chalk perpendicular to the deck and following the shape of the inside arms and back of the chair. The chalk should brush against but not push into the chair padding. Mark the cushion front along the crown of the nosing.

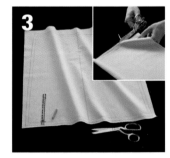

Remove the muslin and draw a ½" seam allowance outside the marked line; cut out the pattern. Fold the pattern in half on the centerline, checking to see that the pattern is symmetrical. If edges are off by less than 1", trim uneven edges and unfold the pattern (inset). If edges are off by more than 1", adjust the chair padding and draw a new pattern.

Boxed Cushion Cover Cutting Guide ▸

	Length	Width
Top/Bottom Pattern (2)	See pattern	See pattern.
Fabric Strips for Welting	Cushion Circumference × 2 + 8 to 10"	Cording circumference × 2 + 1"
Boxing Strip	Front + sides of cushion. Add 1" for each seam, if necessary	Cushion foam + ¼" or width of original strip + 1"
Zipper Tape & Pull	Back cushion measurement + 8"	
Zipper Closure Strips (2)	Length of zipper tape	Boxing strip width ÷ 2 + ¾"

How to Sew a Boxed Cushion Cover

Prepare welting and sew around the outer edges of the cushion top and bottom pieces.

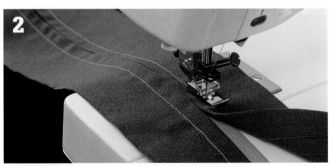

Press under a ¾" seam allowance on one long edge of the zipper strip. Position the pressed edge along the center of the zipper teeth, right sides up. Use a zipper foot to topstitch ¾" from the fold. Repeat on the opposite side, making sure folds meet at the center of the zipper. Attach a pull to the tape if necessary.

Center the zipper strip over the back of the cushion top and stitch, beginning and ending on sides about 1½" beyond the corners. Clip once into the zipper strip seam allowance at each corner and pivot.

(continued)

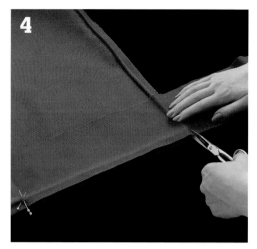

Align the center of the boxing strip to the front center of the cushion top, matching print, if necessary; pin-mark the pieces separately. Smooth strip to the right front corner; mark with a ⅜" clip into the seam allowance. Smooth strip along the right side of the cushion top and pin about 6" from the back corner.

Stitch boxing strip to cushion top ½" from the seam, beginning at the side pin. Match the clip mark to the front corner and pivot stitching. Continue stitching the strip, matching center marks. Clip once into the seam allowance at the left front corner; pivot. Stop stitching about 6" from the back left corner.

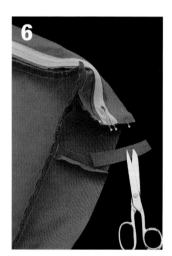

Cut the boxing strip 4" beyond the point where it overlaps the zipper pull end of the zipper strip. Pin the end of the boxing strip to the end of the zipper strip, right sides together, matching all cut edges.

Stitch together 2" from the end; pivot at the zipper tape. Stitch along the outer edge of the zipper tape to within ½" of the end; pivot. Place a small scrap of fabric over the zipper teeth and stitch slowly across the teeth to the opposite side of the zipper tape; pivot. Stitch along the opposite side of the zipper tape until 1" from the end; pivot and stitch to the edge.

Finger-press the seam allowance toward the boxing strip; finish sewing the zipper strip and boxing strip to the cushion top. A small pocket will form to hide the zipper pull when closed.

Cut the opposite end of the boxing strip 1" beyond the point where it overlaps the end of the zipper strip. Pin the ends together. Stitch ½" from the ends, placing a scrap of fabric over the zipper teeth. Turn the seam allowance toward the boxing strip; finish sewing the zipper strip and boxing strip to the cushion top.

Fold the boxing strip straight across at the corner; mark the opposite side of the strip with a ⅜" clip into the seam allowance. Repeat for all corners, then open the zipper partially.

Pin the boxing strip to the cushion bottom, matching clip marks to the corners. Stitch. Turn right side out through the zipper opening.

How to Tailor a Pattern for a Waterfall Cushion

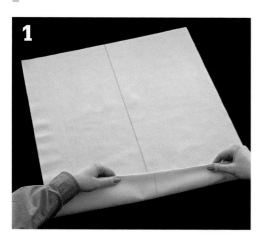

Measure the seat opening in both directions at the widest points. Multiply the depth by 2 and add the cushion height. Add 4" to the depth and 2" to the width; cut muslin to this size. Mark a centerline through the entire length. Fold fabric in half, perpendicular to the centerline; crease. Draw a line across the muslin a distance above the fold equal to half the cushion height.

Unfold and center one end over the chair deck, aligning the line to the crown of the nosing and turning excess muslin up along the arms and back. For a T-cushion, clip muslin around the curves, allowing it to lie flat. Follow steps 2 to 3 on page 272. Fold under the uncut end of the pattern along the crease; cut the lower layer to match the cutting line of the upper layer. Mark the lower layer even with the nosing line (inset); unfold.

Waterfall Cushion Cover Cutting Guide ▶

	Length	Width
Tom/Bottom Piece	See pattern	See pattern
Side Boxing Strips (2)	Side of cushion + 1"	Cushion foam + ¼" or width of original strip + 1"
Zipper Tape & Pull	Back of cushion + 8"	
Zipper Closure Strips (2)	Length of zipper tape	Boxing strip width ÷ 2 + ¾"

How to Sew a Waterfall Cushion Cover

Follow steps 2 and 3 on page 273. Fold the zipper strip straight across at the corner; mark the opposite edge with a ⅜" clip into the seam allowance. Repeat for opposite corner. Pin zipper strip to cushion bottom, matching clip marks to the corners. Stitch length plus 1½" beyond both corners.

Mark the center of the front short end of each side of the boxing strip; round the front corners slightly. Mark the outer edges of the top/bottom cushion piece even with the crease marking on the pattern. Staystitch ½" from the edge, a distance on either side of the marks equal to the cushion height.

Clip the seam allowances to staystitching every ½". Pin the side boxing strip to the cushion piece, right sides together, aligning the center marks. Check to see that the corresponding points on the top and bottom match up directly across from each other on the boxing strip. Sew a ½" seam, beginning and ending 6" from the back corners. Repeat for opposite side.

Follow steps 6 through 9 on pages 274 to 275. Finish sewing the boxing strip to the cushion bottom on both sides. Turn the cushion cover right side out through the zipper opening.

How to Tailor a Pattern for a Knife-edge Cushion

Follow steps 1 and 2 on page 272, adding the cushion height plus 2" to the seat measurements before cutting the muslin. Remove the muslin.

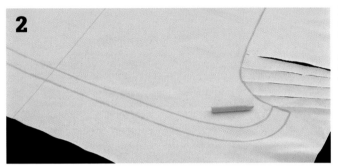

Draw a line along the front of the cushion pattern a distance from the marked line equal to half the finished boxing height. For a T-cushion (shown), extend the line around the front corners to a point even with the line at the back of the T; connect the ends of the lines.

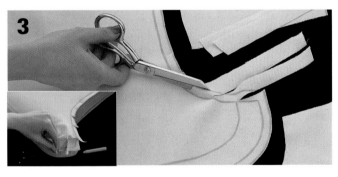

Draw a ½" seam allowance outside the entire pattern and cut out. Fold the pattern in half on the centerline, checking for symmetry. Trim edges as in step 3 on page 272. Lay the pattern over the original cushion, aligning the pattern seam line to the midpoint of the cushion height; pin out corner tucks (inset). Mark tucks; unfold the pattern and transfer marks to the opposite corner.

Knife-edge Cushion Cover Cutting Guide ▸

	Length	Width
Top/Bottom Pieces (2)	See pattern	See pattern
Fabric Strips for Welting	Equal to knife-edge section of cushion	Cording circumference × 2 + 1"
Side Boxing Strips (2)	Side of cushion	Cushion foam + ¼" or width of original strip + 1"
Zipper Tape & Pull	Back of cushion + 8"	
Zipper Closure Strips (2)	Length of zipper tape	Boxing strip width ÷ 2 + ¾"

How to Sew a Knife-edge Cushion Cover

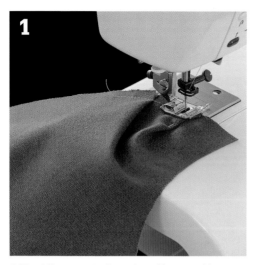

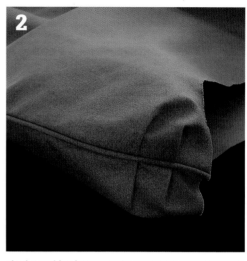

Fold out the corner tucks on the cushion top and bottom; baste. Sew the welting to the desired edges of the cushion top.

Pin the cushion bottom to the cushion top along the welted edge, matching the corner tucks. Stitch the seam, crowding the cording. Complete the cushion cover as for the waterfall cushion on page 276, steps 1 to 4.

How to Prepare & Insert the Cushion

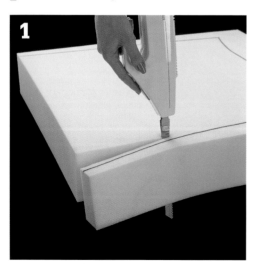

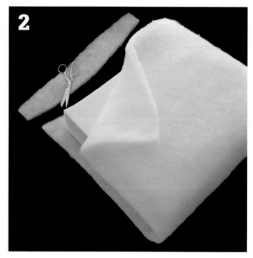

Trace the cutting line of the cushion cover onto the foam and cut using an electric knife. Follow the seam line of the pattern for high-resiliency foam; follow the cutting line for softer foam. Hold the knife blade perpendicular to the foam at all times.

Wrap the polyester batting over the foam from front to back. Trim the sides and back so that the cut edges overlap about 1" at the center.

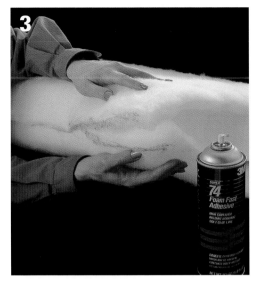

Apply spray foam adhesive to the cut edges of the batting at the back of the cushion; overlap the edges and press firmly to seal, forming a smooth seam. Or whipstitch the edges together using a button needle and heavy thread. Repeat for the sides.

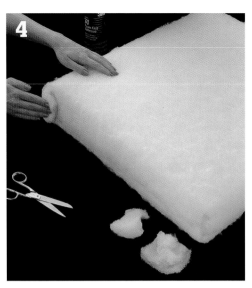

Trim excess batting vertically at the back corners. Fold excess batting over the side seams at the front corners and apply adhesive. Press together firmly to seal or whipstitch in place.

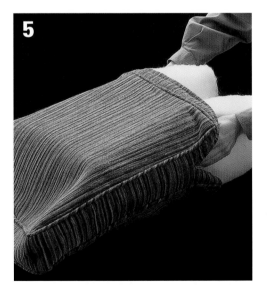

Fold the cushion in half from the front to back. Insert into the cover opening, gradually working the cushion toward the front of the cover. Stretch the cover to fit. Stand the cushion on one side and check to see that the cushion is inserted symmetrically, with equal fullness on both sides.

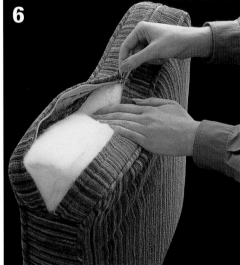

Turn the seam allowances toward the boxing strip all around the cushion. Zip closed, hiding the zipper pull in the pocket.

Button-tufted Cushions

Button-tufted cushions can be custom shaped to fit chairs, benches, or window seats. They have inner cores of batting-wrapped foam and can be anchored to the furniture with fabric ties. Buttons keep the filling from shifting and accent the "stuffed" appearance of the cushion. Since tufted cushion covers are not usually removed, zippers or other closures are not necessary. Tightly woven decorator fabric with a stain-resistant finish, available in endless colors and designs, is a great choice for this project.

Tools & Materials ▸

Fabric	Button and
1" polyurethane foam	carpet thread
Polyester upholstery	Long needle
batting	with large eye
Thread	Felt-tipped pen
Buttons to cover	

Button-tufted cushions can be a cheerful custom addition to chairs in the kitchen and dining room.

How to Sew a Button-tufted Cushion

1

Make a paper pattern of the seat to be covered by the cushion, rounding any sharp corners. Simplify the shape as much as you can. Cut out the pattern and check it for symmetry and fit. Mark the placement of ties.

2

Place the pattern on the right side of the decorator fabric and mark a cutting line 1" from the edge of the pattern. Cut the cushion top out on the marked line, then cut the bottom out, using the top as a pattern. Transfer any marks for ties from the pattern to the wrong side of the cushion front. Use the pattern to cut two pieces of polyester upholstery batting. Trace the pattern on foam using a felt-tipped pen; cut the foam ¼" inside the marked line.

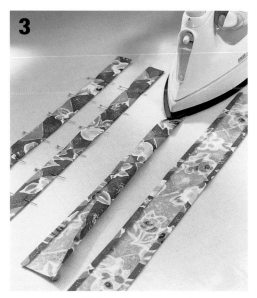

3

Cut two 2½" × 16" fabric strips for each tie, following fabric grainlines. Press under ¼" on the long edges of each strip, then press them in half lengthwise, wrong sides together, aligning the pressed edges. Pin.

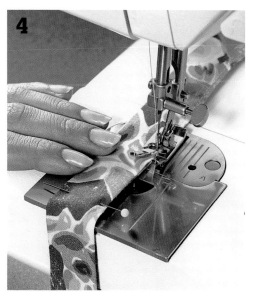

4

Stitch along the open edge of each tie. Leave both ends of the ties open. Tie a single knot at one end of each tie, enclosing the raw edges in the knot.

Velcro Ties ▸

Cut fabric tabs just long enough to go around the chair post plus 1½" for overlap and ½" for seams and twice the finished width plus ½". Cut Velcro tape 1½" long for each tab. Press in ¼" on each edge, then press in half lengthwise and stitch all sides. Attach Velcro to tabs (inset). Press in half horizontally and attach folded end to cushions.

5

Pin the unfinished ends of the ties to the right side of the cushion front at the marked positions. Stitch the ties in place ⅜" from the edge, removing the pins as you come to them.

6

Place the cushion top and bottom right sides together, aligning the outer edges; pin. Leave an opening for inserting the cushion.

(continued)

Place the pieces under the presser foot and stitch ½" from the edge. End the seam at the opposite side of the opening. Clip the seam allowances at any curved areas.

Press the seam flat. Turn back the top seam allowance and press. Press back ½" seam allowance on the cushion cover back in the open area. Reach through the opening to turn the cushion cover right side out.

Press lightly, centering the seam around the outer edge. Make sure ties are sewn securely into the seam at the correct positions.

Place the foam between the layers of upholstery batting. Whipstitch the edges of the batting together, encasing the foam.

11

Fold the cushion in half and insert it into the cushion cover. Unfold the foam, smoothing the fabric over the batting. Slipstitch the opening closed.

12

Mark the button placement on both sides of the cushion. Buttons are usually equally spaced in all directions. Follow the manufacturer's directions for making covered buttons. You will need two buttons for every tuft.

13

Cut two or three 18" strands of button and carpet thread; insert all the strands through the button shank and secure at the middle of the thread with a double knot.

14

Insert the ends of the thread strands through the eye of a long needle. Insert the needle through the cushion to the back side. Remove the strands from the needle and divide them into two groups.

15

Thread a second button onto one group of threads. Tie a single knot, using both thread groups; pull the strands until the buttons are tight against the cushion, creating an indentation. Wrap the thread two to three times around the button shank and tie a double knot. Trim the thread tails. Repeat steps 13 to 15 for each tuft, keeping the indentations equal.

Reupholstering a Drop-in Seat

Reupholstering the seats on dining room or kitchen chairs is a great choice for a first-time upholstery project. The fabric change can give new life to older chairs or can help new chairs better coordinate with the room's décor. Because the seats are easy to remove and reupholster, a set of four chairs can easily be completed in a day.

Drop-in seats usually drop into a recess in the chair seat; some styles rest directly on the surface of the seat and may have welting attached around the lower edge. All styles are held in place by screws attached from the underside of the seat. Regardless of the style, if more than one chair in a set is being reupholstered, always return seats to their original chairs, assuring proper fit and alignment of screw holes.

A set of four chairs like this can easily be reupholstered in a day.

Tools & Materials ▶

Screwdriver
   and tack lifter
   or staple remover
1"-thick foam
Foam adhesive
3 yd. of 27"
   polyester batting
   (for four seats)
Staple gun
   and ⅜" staples
⁵⁄₃₂" welt cording
   (optional)

2 yd. cambric
   (optional)
Upholstery fabric

Cutting Guide ▶

	Length	Width
Upholstery Fabric	Seat + 6"	Seat + 6"
Foam	Seat + 1"	Seat + 1"
Batting	Seat + 4"	Seat + 4"
Cambric	Seat + 2"	Seat + 2"
Welting	Circumference of seat + 3 to 5"	1½"

How to Upholster a Drop-in Seat

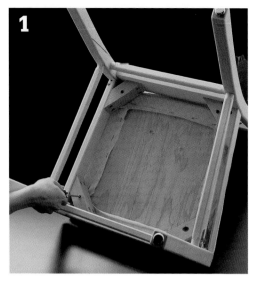

Remove the screws on the underside of the seat; remove the seat. Strip off the existing outer fabric using a staple remover or tack lifter. If the foundation is intact, omit steps 2 and 3.

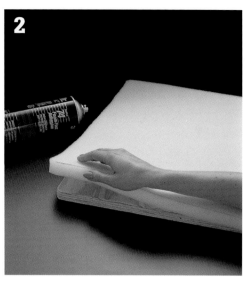

Apply spray adhesive to one side of the foam; affix foam to the top of the seat.

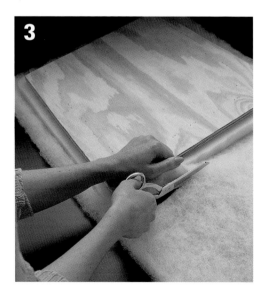

Place upholstery batting on the table; place the seat, foam side down over the batting. Wrap the batting around the top and sides of the seat. Trim excess batting even with the bottom edge of the seat.

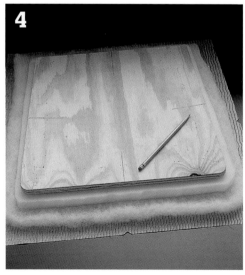

Mark the center of each side on the bottom of the seat. Notch the center of each side of the fabric. Place the fabric on the table wrong side up. Center the seat upside down over the fabric.

(continued)

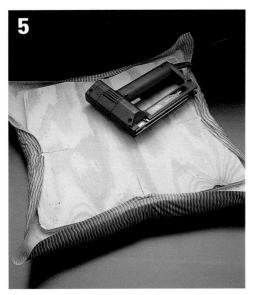

Staple the fabric to the bottom of the seat at the center back, matching the center marks. Stretch the fabric from the back to front; staple at the center front, matching the center marks. Repeat at the center of each side.

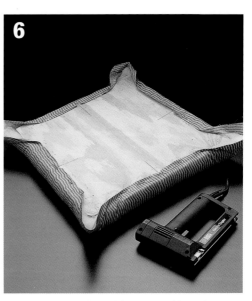

Apply staples to the back of the seat at 1½" intervals, working from the center toward the sides, to within 3" of the corners. Pull the fabric taut toward the front of the seat; staple. Repeat for the sides.

Fold the fabric diagonally at the corner; stretch the fabric taut and staple between the screw hole and the corner. Trim excess fabric diagonally across the corner.

Miter fabric at the corner by folding in each side up to the corner; staple in place. Repeat for the remaining corners. Trim excess fabric, exposing screw holes. If welting is not desired, omit step 9. If cambric is not desired, omit step 10.

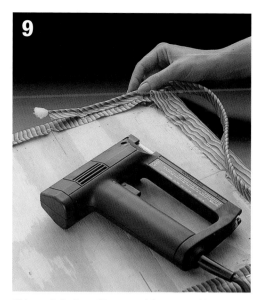

9

Make and staple welting around the seat at ¾" intervals, starting at the back of the seat; align the stitching line of the welting to the edge of the seat.

10

Fold under the raw edges of the cambric; staple to the bottom of the seat at 1" intervals. Puncture cambric at the screw holes in the chair seat. Screw the upholstered seat to the chair.

Reusing Padding Materials ▸

When reupholstering a piece of furniture that was originally padded with natural fiber materials, reuse the materials intact if the foundation is still in very good shape. Most of the time, however, it will be necessary to supplement or replace the padding with cotton or polyester batting.

If you'd like to retain the authenticity of an antique piece, but the padding is in poor shape, reupholster with natural materials. When stripping older furniture, it is common to discover padding materials such as curled hair, moss, tow, and straw. It is possible to reuse these materials, though supplementing them will require a considerable amount of time and expertise. Often, some additional cotton batting is all that you'll need to add to restore the piece to its original shape and firmness.

Inspect the original material and maintain as much of the original material as possible for authenticity, antique resale price, and greater sustainability. Make sure reused materials are dry and free of mold and bugs, though. If the material is suspect, replace it.

Reupholstering a Chair

Reupholstering a chair to better match your room décor can make an old piece functional in a formal room again and can enable you to custom-blend your furniture with your existing style choices. The instructions that follow are a general guide for upholstering a chair, but styles and designs vary greatly from chair to chair. Always refer to the notes, sketches, and photos taken while stripping your chair to help you reassemble it (see page 268).

This particular style of chair, called a Lawson-style chair, is characterized by its boxed arms, boxed and buttoned back, and simple lines. The padding in this chair is fairly minimal, cushioning the corners of the arms and back but allowing the lines to remain fairly sharp. Many of the pieces for this chair are sewn together before they are attached to the frame. Also, the top arms, front arms and front band are cut as one piece and sewn with welted seams to the inside arms, outside arms, and nosing of the chair.

Begin your project by measuring all chair parts and recording their measurements (page 266). Then, determine the cut sizes of all the parts, diagram the fabric layout, and cut out the pieces. Strip the chair as far as necessary. Check the frame for sturdiness and make any necessary repairs (page 270).

Tools & Materials ▸

Upholstery fabric	#18 nylon thread	Foam adhesive	Button twine
Welt cording	Burlap	Staple gun and staples (⅜"	Buttons
Polyester batting	Edge roll	and ½")	Button needle
Webbing and	Deck pad	Lining fabric (such as	Cardboard tack strip
webbing stretcher	Denim	lightweight, inexpensive	Flexible metal tacking strip
Spring twine	High-resiliency foam	upholstery fabric)	Cambric

After

Before

Reupholstering a chair can be a rewarding project, though it is labor and time intensive. Plan carefully and take detailed notes while stripping to ease the re-upholstery process.

Furniture Frame Anatomy ▸

Learning the process of furniture upholstery will be easier if you know the correct names of the frame parts. Familiarize yourself with the basic frame parts shown here. Various chair styles have differently shaped frames, but the basic structure will be consistent from piece to piece.

Frame Parts
(A)   top back rail
(B)   top wing rail
(C)   front wing post
(D)   top arm rail
(E)   front arm post
(F)   arm stretcher rail
(G)   front rail
(H)   corner block
(I)   back rail
(J)   back stretcher rail
(K)   back stretcher post
(L)   side rail
(M)   back leg post

How to Upholster a Chair

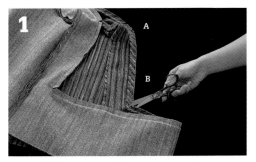

Stitch welting to the front and top edges of the outside arm panel. Stitch boxing to the front and top of the outside arm, aligning the lower edge of the front boxing to the lower edge of the outside arm. Stitch welting to the remaining edge of the boxing and front band. Mark seam allowances of the boxing directly across from the top front corners of the opposite arms (A). Clip the seam allowances at the upper corners of the band (B). Stitch the inside arm to the boxing, aligning the mark to the top front corner of the inside arm. Center nosing on the front band. Stitch nosing to the front band between clips, backstitching at the clips. Stitch the deck to the nosing, matching centers. Mark a placement line for the nosing seam on the spring cover; mark the center. Mark the center of the nosing seam allowance.

Lay the deck piece over the seat. *Note: your piece will look more complete than the pictured piece, with nosing and arm pieces attached.* Fold the nosing back, aligning the seam line to the marked line on the deck, matching the center; pin on each side of the center. Pull the seam allowance taut under the arm; staple to the top of the side rail. Repeat for the opposite side.

(continued)

Use a 6" curved needle and button twine to attach the seam allowance and spring cover, securing both ends. Take 1" running stitches near the seam line; hook springs in the stitches whenever possible.

Pull the deck under the back. Insert extra batting between the deck pad and spring cover to fill in depressions. Pull the deck to the back rail, matching centers. Staple to the top of the rail. Continue stapling the deck to the back rail for several inches on each side of the center.

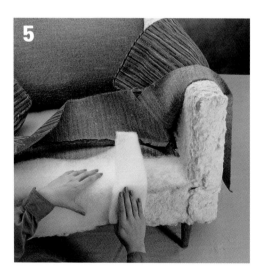

Cut a piece of deck pad ½" narrower than the space between the nosing seam line and the edge roll. Stitch to the spring cover in this position. Cover nosing with one layer of batting. Add a half layer of batting from the nosing seam to the lower edge of the front rail. Replace webbing on the inside arm, if necessary. Cover the inside arms with burlap and attach the burlap to the outside arms, leaving unattached along the lower edge and for a short distance at the lower front and back. Supplement or replace arm padding as necessary.

Turn the arm cover inside out; position the front boxing in place over the arm front. Turn the arm cover right side out; smooth in place over the chair arm, turning the welted seam allowances toward the inside and outside arm panels. Repeat for remaining arm. Then cut a straight Y-cut on the side edge of the nosing, parallel to the front edge, allowing fabric to fit around the front arm post; the front point of the Y-cut is aligned to the nosing seam line.

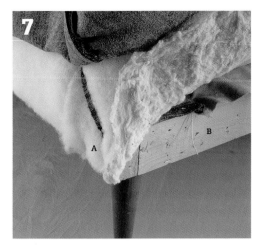

Pull the nosing down to the front and side, straddling the front arm post with the sides of the Y-cut (A and B). Pull taut; staple. Finish stapling the nosing and deck to the top of the side rail. Repeat for the opposite side. Pull the front band taut; staple to the underside of the front rail for several inches at the center. Cut diagonally into the lower front edge of the inside arm, allowing the fabric to fit around the front arm post.

Fold under the cut edge of the inside arm from the corner of the nosing to the point of the cut (A); pull the lower edge of the inside arm under the arm stretcher rail.

Cut a Y-cut in the boxing at the back top of the arm, allowing the fabric to fit around the back post. Cut a second Y-cut on the back edge of the inside arm, allowing the fabric to fit around the back stretcher rail. Fold under the edges of the Y-cut on the boxing. Pull the inside arm through to the back of the chair. Pull taut; staple to the inner side of the back rail.

Pull the lower edge of the inside arm taut to the side rail (A), pulling the welting along the upper arm slightly to the inside (B). Staple the lower edge of the inside arm to the top of the side rail.

Pull the outside arm taut, realigning the welting along the top of the arm. Staple the lower edge to the underside of the side rail up to within several inches of the back corner. Staple the back edge to the outside of the back post, leaving unattached several inches from the top and bottom. Finish stapling the front band to the underside of the front rail.

(continued)

Place the inside back piece over the existing inside back, cutting shallow relief cuts (A) to fit around the arms; pin. Mark a seam line around the outer edge using chalk. Cut out the inside back ½" beyond the marked seam line.

Stitch welting to the outer edge of the inside back, avoiding any welting seams on the top of the back. Stitch the top back boxing to the side back boxing pieces using ½" seams; press open. Pin boxing to the inside back, right sides together, matching boxing seams to the top corners. Stitch.

Supplement or replace back padding as necessary, then place the back cover, inside out, over the padding. Turn the cover right side out, fitting the corners snugly: smooth in place over the chair back, turning the welted seam allowances toward the inside back. Pull taut; secure to the outside of the top back rail at the center.

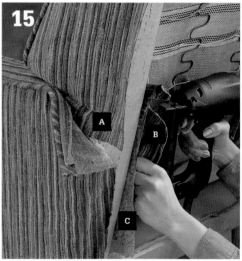

Cut a horizontal Y-cut in the side boxing, allowing the fabric to fit around the top arm rail and arm stretcher rail Pull taut, pulling boxing above the top cut to the outside of the back post (A) and boxing between cuts to the inside of the back post (B); staple over the inside arm fabric (C). Cut the boxing along welting seams at the lower edge of the inside back, allowing the fabric to straddle the back leg post.

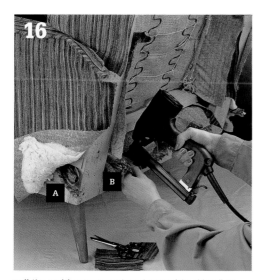

Pull the welting taut; staple to the top of the side rail (A). Pull the remaining lower edge taut; staple to the top of the back rail (B).

Finish pulling and stapling boxing to the back of the back posts and top rail. Pull the top of the outside arm taut over the inside back; staple to the back of the back post. Finish stapling the outside arms under the side rails.

Pin-mark positions of buttons on the inside back. Cut button twine about 25" long for each button. Insert one end of the twine through the button shank; then insert both ends through the eye of the button needle. Insert the needle through the chair back at one pin mark. Pull twine through until the button shank enters the fabric. Separate twines at the back of the chair, straddling a spring, if possible. Tie the twines around a wad of batting, using a slipknot.

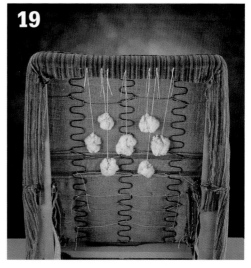

Repeat step 18 for each button. Tighten all knots equally, checking indentations of the buttons on the inside back. Secure knots with overhand knots. Pull twines taut to the top rail and staple securely. Make any final adjustments necessary in tautness of the outer fabric. Trim excess fabric in areas that have not yet been trimmed. Make the cushion (page 272).

(continued)

Attach welting to the outer edges of the back sides and top, beginning and ending at the bottom of the back rail. Encase cording at the ends (inset). Attach lining to the back, trimming even with the cut edge of the welting. Place the outside back fabric over the outside back. Trim to size, allowing a ½" excess along the top, 1" along the sides and 1½" along the bottom.

Flip the fabric up over the back of the chair. Align the cut edge of the fabric to the cut edge of the upper welting, matching centers. Place a cardboard tack strip over the ½" allowance, aligning the outer edge to the welting seam line. Staple across the top.

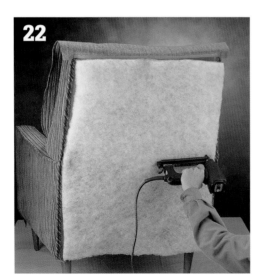

Cut a half layer of batting to fit between the seam lines of the welting at the top and sides and even with the bottom of the back rail. Staple baste at the top and side centers.

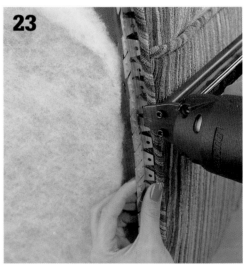

Staple a metal tacking strip to the sides, aligning the outer edge of the tacking strip to the welting seam line. Begin at the upper welting seam line; end at the bottom of the back rail, opening the strip as necessary for ease in stapling. Position the stapler so one leg of the staple goes through each hole in the tacking strip.

Close the tacking strip to about 30°. Wrap batting over the edge of the strip to cushion the sharp edge. Pull down the outside back fabric; staple baste to the bottom of the back rail, matching centers. Trim fabric to ½" along the sides.

Tuck the fabric into the tacking strip opening, using a regulator. Push the tacking strip closed along both sides. Hammer the tacking strip securely using a mallet or tack hammer.

Pull the lower edge taut; staple to the underside of the back rail. Attach the welting to the underside of the rails around the bottom of the chair, joining the ends (inset).

Cut cambric 3" larger than the measurements of the bottom of the chair between the outer edges of the rails. Fold under just shy of the outer edge; staple at the center front, back, and sides. Fold the cambric back at the corner so the fold is even with the inner corner of the leg. Cut diagonally from the corner of the fabric to the fold. Repeat for each corner. Fold under the cut edges so folds are tight against the sides and staple in place. Continue stapling the front, back, and sides.

Upholstered Ottoman

You may never have imagined building your own
furniture—but it's easier than you think! For your first
piece, start with this sturdy tufted ottoman, which will add
comfort and complementary colors to your living space.

Construct a simple frame and upholster with your chosen
fabric. Before you know it, you'll have a handy, attractive
ottoman at a fraction of the cost you would pay in a
store—and it's 100 percent unique, handmade by you.

Tools & Materials ▸

½"-thick plywood
Saber saw
1 × 4 lumber, cut in
  eight 13" lengths
Wood glue
2" coarse-thread
  sheetrock screws

Drill with ⅜" bit
  and 1" spade bit
3" semifirm foam
Electric knife
Approximately
  2½" yd. of
  upholstery fabric

Button needle
3½" yd. polyester batting
Fourteen #22 covered buttons
Nylon button twine
Staple gun and staples
  (⅜" and ½")
Upholstery regulator

1¼ yd. ⁵⁄₃₂"
  welt cording
1½ yd. burlap
2 yd. cardboard
  tack strip
Cambric
Four chair glides

An ottoman is a great addition to large rooms or comfortable living areas in your home.

Fabric Cutting Guide ▸

	Length	Width
Polyester Batting	27"	27"
Ottoman Top Piece	45"	45"
Welting	82"	1½"
Band	17"	82" (piece as necessary)
Cambric	27"	27"

How to Make a Tufted Ottoman

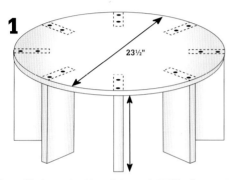 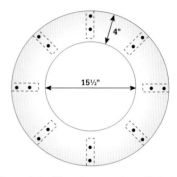

From ½" plywood, cut two circles, each 23½" in diameter. On one piece, draw a circle 4" from the outer edge. Drill a hole large enough to fit the blade of the saber saw inside the inner circle. Use the saber saw to cut out the inner circle to make the ottoman bottom. Draw pencil lines across the second full circle (the top), dividing it into eight equal wedges. Transfer marks to the lower ring.

Apply wood glue to the end of one 1 × 4 support. Center the support over one of the marked lines on the ottoman top, aligning the narrow edge to the outer edge of the circle. Secure the support with two screws inserted through the top of the circle into the support. Repeat for the remaining supports, then turn the top over and attach the bottom ring to the supports in the same way. Make sure the supports are straight and centered on the marked lines.

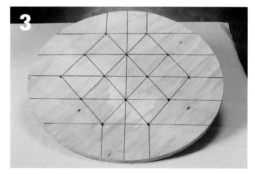

Mark the positions of the tufts on the top of the frame. The example displays a diamond pattern. Drill ⅜" holes at the marked points. Mark a 24" circle on the foam. Using an electric knife with the blade held straight up and down, cut out the circle. Mark out the same button placement pattern on the foam.

(continued)

Using a 1" spade bit and a light touch, slowly drill holes straight down through the foam at the marks. Place the foam over the ottoman frame top, aligning the holes. Center upholstery batting over the foam. On the wrong side, mark a chalk line across the center in both directions.

Place the fabric face up over the batting, aligning the centers and lines. Working on the most central horizontal line of holes, flip back the fabric and cut a small hole in the batting directly over the closest hole to the center. Insert a pin through the fabric and batting at the location of the next hole closest to center to keep the layers from shifting. Turn the fabric back into position. With a finger, push the fabric down through the batting and into the foam hole to the wood. Wiggle a little slack into the fabric, drawing from the outer edge of the fabric while keeping the centerlines aligned.

Thread 24" of nylon button twine through the shank of a button. Thread the ends through a button needle. Push the needle through the fabric and through the hole in the wood. Pull the twines tight so the button rests against the wood.

On the underside of the ottoman top, staple the twines three times as shown.

Cut a hole in the batting over the next hole closest to center. Push the fabric down into the hole as in step 5. Repeat steps 6 and 7. Continue on and complete the buttons in the line of holes closest to center.

Continue to the next row and apply buttons, working from the holes in the center out. Wiggle slack into each hole, drawing fabric from the outside to prevent pulling the fabric too tightly. Apply all buttons in this manner.

Use a regulator to turn all the pleats between buttons in the same direction. The pleats should open out just before they reach the buttons.

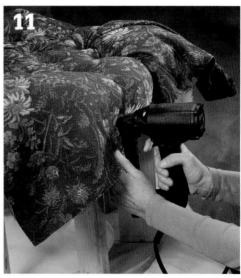

Smooth the fabric over the edge. Beginning at the center front, pull the fabric down in a straight line and staple to the edge of the wood circle. Repeat on the opposite side, then on each side of the horizontal axis. Staple around the ottoman, pulling the pleats straight out to the sides, then easing in other fabric fullness between pleats.

(continued)

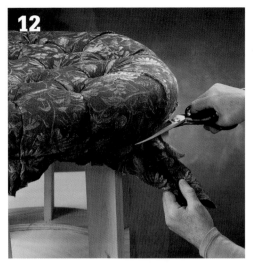

Trim off excess fabric only after you have checked to see that pleat lines are straight and fullness is evenly distributed.

Prepare welting and wrap around the ottoman over the staples. Mark where the ends meet. Sew the welting into a circle. Slide the welting ring back onto the ottoman from the bottom to check the fit and remove. Stitch the welting to the upper edge of the band. Turn the band inside out and with the welting at the bottom pull it over the top of the ottoman until the welting rests just above the top of the wood. Staple in place using ½" staples.

Wrap burlap around the ottoman and staple in place along the edges of the top and bottom circles. Staple the overlapping ends to the edge of a support. Place a cardboard tack strip over the welting seam allowance with the upper edge even with the stitching line. Staple diagonally through the tack strip.

Cut batting 15" × 80" and wrap around the ottoman with 1" extending above the tack strip. Staple the batting along the tack strip and along the lower edge.

Turn the band down and stretch the fabric to the underside of the ottoman. Staple in place using ⅜" staples. Staple at the four center marks first. Then, work out the excess fullness as you finish stapling the rest of the band in place.

Turn under the edge of cambric and staple to the underside of the ottoman. Attach four glides to the underside of the ottoman, evenly spaced and 1" from the edge.

Button Tufting Designs ▸

The pattern shown on page 297 of this project is only one possible layout for the button tufts on a tufted cushion. Four buttons are often laid out in a square, sometimes with a button in the center, in a five-point star, or sometimes the only tuft is one button in the center. Diagram your button layout on graph paper before you mark button placement on the ottoman frame.

Upholstered Headboard

An upholstered headboard can help a bedroom space feel cozy and inviting, and adds color to blank walls. Padded with foam and batting, this headboard also provides comfortable support for reading or watching television. Choose upholstery fabric to blend with the bedroom décor, or to nicely complement your comforter or duvet cover. To avoid having to piece the center padded section on large headboards, choose fabric that can be railroaded.

This project can be custom fitted for any size bed. The headboard attaches to the bed frame, so measure the width of the frame and add 2" to allow room for drilling bolt holes. To determine the height, measure from the bottom of the attachment plate on the frame to the desired height above the mattress. The height of the headboard is completely up to you. Generally, the smaller the bed, the shorter the headboard should be. Lightly outline where you'd like the headboard to rest on the wall before you determine your final measurements.

An upholstered headboard is comfortable to lean against for reading or watching television in bed, and adds warmth and softness to a bedroom.

Tools & Materials ▸

½"-thick plywood	Welt cording
Saw	Polyester batting
Wood glue	Upholstery fabric
1" coarse-thread sheetrock screws	½"-wide cardboard tacking strip
2"-thick firm foam	3" curved needle and #18 nylon thread
Foam glue	
Staple gun and staples (⅜" and ½")	Bolts and nuts

Fabric Cutting Guide ▸

	Length	Width
Central Headboard Foam (cut to fit curve of headboard frame top)	Headboard frame − length of headboard bottom cover − 2"	Headboard frame − 6"
Central Headboard Piece (cut to fit curve of headboard frame top)	Central headboard foam + 3 to 4"	Central headboard foam + 3 to 4"
Welting	Outer edge of headboard − 2 × the length of headboard bottom cover + 6 to 8"	1½"
Border Strip (piece as necessary)	1½ × welting	6½"
Headboard Bottom Cover	Bed frame + box spring + mattress + 1"	Headboard frame + 6 to 8"
Headboard Back (cut to fit curve of headboard frame top)	Headboard frame + 1"	Headboard frame + 1"

How to Make an Upholstered Headboard

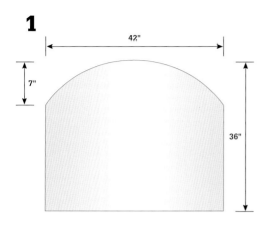

1

42"

7"

36"

Cut a rectangle of ½" plywood in the desired width and height. Mark a point 7" down from the top corner on each side and draw a gentle curve from these points across the top of the board. Check for symmetry and then saw on the marked line. Cut another rectangle of plywood 8" by the headboard width. Shape the upper edge to match the headboard curve. Cut 3" support strips of plywood for the bottom, sides, and center.

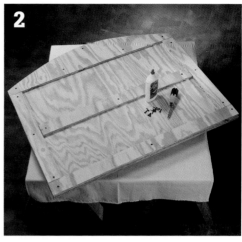

2

Glue, then screw the support pieces to the back of the headboard. Take care not to insert screws where you will need to drill bolt holes to attach the headboard to the bed frame. Measure the height of the bed frame, box spring, and mattress. Mark a line across the front of the headboard at this distance from the bottom. Draw a line 3" from the edge along the sides and top, beginning at the first marked line. This marks the width of the gathered border.

3

Cut a piece of foam to fit the center section of the upper headboard, glue it in place, and lay a half layer of batting over the foam. Staple it in place. Cut fabric several inches larger than the foam. Mark the center of each side. Mark the center of each side of the padded section of the headboard.

4

Pull the fabric evenly and staple it to the frame, starting in the centers and working out toward the corners. Trim off the excess fabric. Measure the outer edge of the headboard, beginning and ending at the bottom of the padded section. Prepare welting slightly longer than this measurement and cut border strip according to cutting directions. Stitch the welting to one edge of the border strip.

(continued)

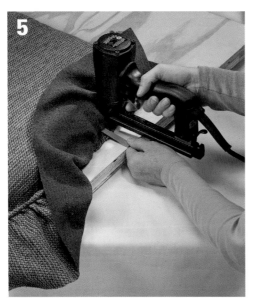

Using ⅜" staples, staple the border strip to the headboard around the padded section with the welting seam 3" from the edge. Use a 3" strip of cardboard tack strip as a gauge.

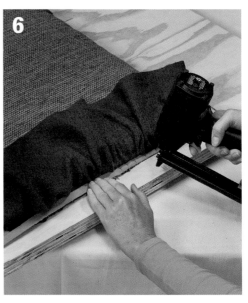

Place the cardboard tack strip over the welting seam allowance with the upper edge even with the stitching line. Staple diagonally through the tack strip using ½" staples.

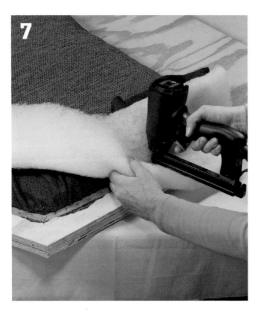

Center 8" strips of batting long enough to cover the border on the tack strip and staple in place.

Wrap the border strip to the back of the headboard and staple it in place using ⅜" staples. Don't pull the fabric too tightly. It should look full and padded. Staple frequently, distributing the fullness evenly.

9

Mark the centers of the sides of the bottom headboard cover. Place the fabric face-down over the padded section. Staple in place along the bottom of the padded section. Place a cardboard tack strip over the edge, with the upper edge aligned with the line drawn in step 2. Staple through the tack strip.

10

Turn down the fabric, wrap it to the back of the headboard and staple in place using ⅜" staples. This area is unpadded to allow it to fit closely to the frame, box spring, and mattress. Place the headboard back piece wrong side up over the lower edge and staple in place through the tack strip. Turn under the sides even with the sides of the headboard.

11

Attaching the Headboard ▸

Hold the headboard to the head of the bed, aligning the lower edge to the lower edge of the attachment plates on the frame. Mark the placement of holes for bolts. Punch holes in the fabric before drilling to prevent catching and tearing the fabric. Secure the headboard to the frame with bolts and nuts.

Turn the fabric up, turn under the edges and pin in place. Blindstitch the outside of the headboard using a 3" curved needle and #18 nylon thread.

Reversible Seat Covers

Making your own seat covers is a quick way to dress up your kitchen or dining room chairs. Plus, these covers are made with two coordinating decorator fabrics so they can quickly be flipped over for an instant décor change. Darts sewn at the front corners shape the covers to fit the chair seats smoothly. The back corners are held in place with a button tab that wraps around the back of the chair leg.

These covers are suitable for armless chairs with straight sides and fronts that are open between the back posts. Make the pattern before you buy fabric so you'll know how much fabric you'll need. If you're making covers for two or more chairs, be sure to center the printed motif on each seat cover. Sometimes it helps to bring the pattern with you to the store to make sure you buy enough fabric to do this.

Tools & Materials ▸

Two coordinating decorator fabrics

Four buttons for each cover, ⅞ to 1" in diameter

½ yd. grosgrain ribbon ⅞" wide, in a color to match the fabrics

Muslin

Reversible seat covers are a quick way to transform the look of your chairs and are as quick and easy to change as your placemats.

Tip ▸

Choose reversible dining chair seat cushions. In this way, it's possible to enjoy two distinct looks—one for the dining room and one for the living room, or one for summer and one for winter—without requiring storage for the extra set of cushions.

How to Sew a Reversible Seat Cover

Measure the chair seat side to side and front to back. Add 10" in each direction. Cut muslin to this size to make a pattern. Press the muslin pattern in half in both directions. Unfold. Center the pattern on the chair seat, allowing it to fall down over the front and sides. At the back, turn the pattern up along the posts. If necessary, tape the pattern in place.

Mark a dot at one front corner. Pinch the fabric together from the dot down, bringing the front to meet the side. Pin out excess fabric, inserting the pins parallel to the chair leg, forming a dart. Mark lines on both sides of the dart from the dot down to the bottom. Repeat on the other front corner.

Mark dots at the back of the seat, at the inside front corners of the back posts. (If your posts are round, mark each dot at a point in line with the front and side of the post.) Trace the outline of the chair seat on the pattern.

Remove the pattern from the chair; remove the pins. Draw lines 4½" outside the traced seat lines. At the back corners, draw lines from the dots to the outer lines, forming squares. (These will be the stitching lines.) Mark pivot points (shown in blue) on the stitching lines ½" from the outer edge. Draw cutting lines (shown in red) ½" outside the stitching lines at the legs and the front darts. Fold the pattern in half to make sure it is symmetrical, and make any necessary corrections. Cut out the pattern on the outer lines.

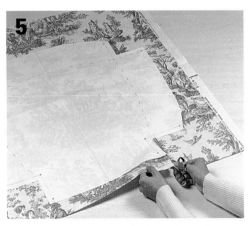

Place the pattern on the top fabric, aligning the front-to-back crease with the lengthwise grain and the side-to-side crease with the crosswise grain. Position the pattern so that the intersection of the creases is at the exact center of the design motif, if you're using a large print. Cut out the seat cover top. Transfer the pivot points and dart dots to the wrong side of the fabric. Cut out the remaining seat cover tops using the first piece as a guide.

(continued)

6

Place each top piece on the bottom fabric, right sides together. Pin near the outer edges. Cut out bottom pieces; remove the pins.

7

Fold the dart on one front corner, right sides together, aligning the raw edges; pin. Stitch the dart. Repeat for the remaining front corners on the top and bottom pieces.

8

Press the seam allowances of the darts open.

9

Place the top and bottom seat covers right sides together, aligning the raw edges; pin. Align the seams of the front darts. Stitch the layers together ½" from the edge all around, pivoting at the corners. Leave a 6" opening along one straight edge for turning.

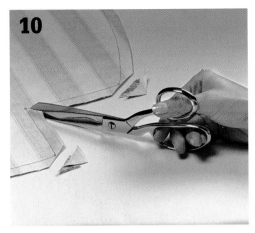

Trim the seam allowances diagonally at the outer corners. Clip to, but not through, the stitches at the inner corners.

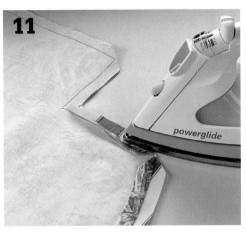

Turn back the top seam allowances and press, applying light pressure. In the area of the opening, turn back and press the seam allowances ½" where they meet. Turn the cover right side out through the opening. Gently push the pivot points out to form perfect corners (use a pointed object, like a crochet needle, to help if necessary). Push the seam out so that it is centered all around the outer edge; press. Align the folded edges of the opening and pin them closed.

Edgestitch around the seat cover, stitching the opening closed; pivot at the corners.

Mark placement lines for the four buttonholes parallel to and 1" above the lower side and back edges. Mark lines that equal the diameter plus the thickness of the buttons, with one end 1" from the vertical edges. Attach a buttonhole presser foot or buttonhole attachment. Stitch the buttonholes over the marked lines. Cut the buttonholes open, using a buttonhole cutter or small, sharp scissors.

Place the cover on the chair seat. At the back of one chair leg, measure the distance between buttonholes. Cut ribbon 4" longer than this measurement. Turn under 1" twice on each end of the ribbon; press. Stitch across the inner folds, forming double-fold hems. Stitch a button to the center of each hem. Repeat for the other leg. Button the chair seat cover in place.

Ottoman Slipcover

Rectangular ottomans with attached cushions are often used with upholstered chairs and sofas. Their styling is so simple that they easily blend with various furniture styles, and their shape fits perfectly into a fitted slipcover.

This slipcover features a tailored skirt with inverted box pleats at the corners and is suitable for an ottoman that has short legs or bun feet (with or without a skirt). A hidden lip of fabric that extends from the boxing strip under the skirt helps you pull the cover firmly in place and secure it to the existing upholstery. Twill-tape ties sewn to this lip are tied around the legs to keep the slipcover from sliding up. The skirt is lined for body and to avoid a noticeable hem around the bottom.

Making a slipcover for an ottoman is a quicker project than reupholstery—with equally classy, polished results.

Tools & Materials ▸

Decorator fabric
Lining
Welt cording

Fabric Cutting Guide ▸

	Length	Width
Top	Ottoman top + 1"	Ottoman top + 1"
Boxing Strip (2)	½" Circumference + 1"	Width of existing strip + 2"
Skirt Pieces (4)	Lower seam of boxing strip to the floor	Side of ottoman top + 16"
Lining Pieces (4)	Skirt piece - 2"	Skirt Piece width
Welting	Circumference of ottoman × 2 + 8 to 10"	1½"
Twill-Tape Ties (8)	18"	

How to Sew a Slipcover

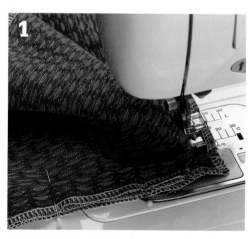

Make the welting and stitch to the outer edge of the slipcover top, then sew the boxing strip pieces together in ½" seams. Finish the lower edges with zigzag stitches or serging. Pin the boxing strip to the slipcover top, matching the print on one side, if necessary. Clip into the boxing strip seam allowance at the corners to allow the fabric to spread. Stitch the boxing strip to the top.

2

Mark a chalk line 1" from the lower edge of the boxing strip. Stitch the welting to the boxing strip, aligning the raw edges of the welting to the line. Mark the lower edge of the boxing strip at the corners, even with the pivot points of the stitching on the top edge. Then sew the skirt pieces together in a big circle using ½" seam allowances. Repeat for the lining pieces. Press seam allowances open.

3

Pin the lower edges of the skirt and lining right side together, matching seams. Stitch ½" from the edges. Press the seam allowances toward the lining.

4

Fold the lining and skirt, wrong sides together, aligning the upper edges. Press. Baste the upper edges together.

5

At each seam at the upper edge of the skirt, place one pin 1" to the left of the seam, one pin 7" to the right of the seam, and one pin 15" to the right of the seam. Fold each pleat, bringing the outer pin marks to the center pin mark; pin them in place. The seams will be hidden in the folds of the pleats. Check the skirt for fit and adjust the pleats if necessary. Baste across the top of each pleat. Pin the upper edge of the skirt over the welting at the lower edge of the boxing strip, right sides together, aligning the raw edges and matching the marks on the boxing strip to the centers of the pleats. Stitch. Stitch the ties to the extension of the boxing strip, 2" from each corner.

6

Place the slipcover on the ottoman, pulling on the boxing strip extension to position it snugly in place. Tie the ties behind the ottoman legs. If the ties are impractical for your ottoman, secure with screw pins through the boxing strip extension into the upholstered sides of the ottoman.

Chair Slipcover

A custom-fit slipcover is made to fit your chair to a T, and covers as beautifully and drapes as nicely as a complete reupholstery—without the mess of stripping. Slipcovers can be made from a single fabric or several coordinating fabrics. For added detail, add contrasting welting in the seams. Choose between a fully gathered or box-pleated skirt to best complement the rest of your furniture.

Chairs with a concave back design may be difficult to slipcover and the cover may not fit well. For best results, a concave back should be wrapped or covered in a thick upholstery batting before you pin-fit your pattern. To help the slipcover stay in place, this technique adds a fabric strip pinned to the existing upholstery, hidden under the skirt, which keeps the cover from pulling out of place. Also, polyurethane foam pieces can be tucked along the sides of the deck to provide a tight fit. These same instructions can be used for sofas or loveseats as well.

Tools & Materials ▸

Muslin	Tacks or heavy-
Decorator fabric	duty stapler
Welt cording	and staples
Upholstery batting	Zippers
Polyurethane foam,	(one for chairs,
cut in 2" strips	two for sofas
T-pins	and love seats)

Making Patterns for Fitted Slipcovers

The easiest way to make a slipcover pattern is by pin-fitting muslin on the chair you plan to cover. Before you start, look carefully at the chair and note the placement of all of the seams. Usually the seams in the slipcover will be in these same locations, but you may be able to add or eliminate some details if it will not affect the fit of the cover. For example, cover a waterfall cushion with a box cushion cover with welting (page 272). Or a chair with a pleated front arm can be slipcovered with a separate flat front arm piece (page 322).

Make your slipcover with a fully gathered skirt (upper) or box pleats (lower).

Pin-fitted Slipcover Pattern Cutting Guide* ▸

Cut pieces from muslin, then mark the center line on each piece, following the lengthwise grain.

	Length	Width
Outside Back	Outside back length + 3 to 4"	Outside back width + 3 to 4"
Inside Back	Inside back length + 10" (allows for 6" at the lower edge to tuck into the deck and hold in place)	Inside back width + 15"
Outside Arm (2)	Outside arm length + 3"	Outside arm width + 3"
Inside Arm (2)	Deck to upper edge of outside arm + 9"	Inside back to front + 9"
Arm Front (2) optional	Arm front length + 2 to 3"	Arm front length + 2 to 3"
Deck	Front of chair to skirt seam + 9"	Width at deck front + 15"
Skirt	Length of skirt + 1"	Circumference + pleats

*Measure existing pieces between seam lines.

How to Pin-fit the Pattern

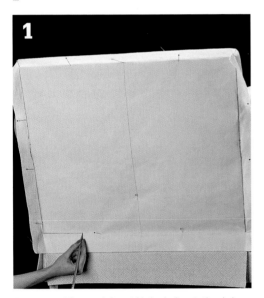

Remove cushions and pin outside back piece to the chair, smoothing fabric. Mark seam lines.

Pin the outside back and inside back together along the top of the piece, matching center lines. Fold out excess fabric on the inside back piece at the upper corner, forming a dart. Pin muslin snugly, but do not pull tight.

Tip ▸

Zipper length should be 1 to 2" shorter than the length of the vertical seam at the side of the outside back. Additional zippers will be needed for cushions.

(continued)

Trim excess fabric on sides of the inside back to 2"; clip along the arms as necessary for a smooth curve. Push about ½" of fabric into crevices on sides and lower edge of the inside back, and mark seam lines by pushing a pencil into the crevices.

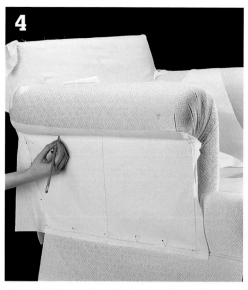

Pin an outside arm piece in place with the grain line perpendicular to the floor and the lower edge extending ½" beyond the seam line at the upper edge of the skirt. Smooth fabric upward; pin. Pin the outside arm to the outside back. Mark the seam lines.

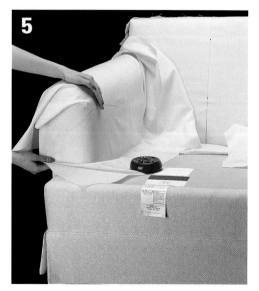

Pin an inside arm piece in place, with 7" extending at inside back and grain line straight across the arm, smoothing fabric up and around the arm.

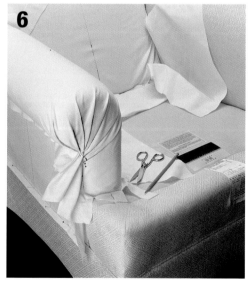

Pin the inside arm to the outside arm at front; clip and trim fabric at the front lower edge as necessary for a smooth fit. Pleat out fabric for the rolled arm to duplicate pleats in the existing fabric. Mark radiating fold lines of pleats.

7

Mark tucks on the inside arm at the back of the chair to fold out excess fabric; clip the inside arm as necessary for a smooth fit.

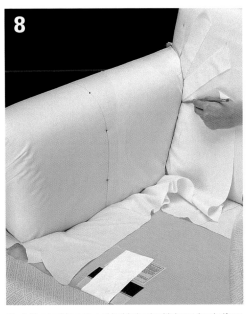

8

Mark the inside arm and inside back with large dots halfway up the arm. Push about ½" of fabric on the inside arm into crevices at the deck and back.

Variation: Pin-fitting an Arm with a Front Section ▸

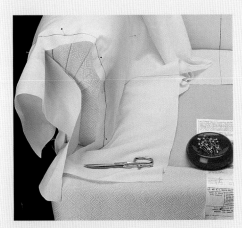

After the inside arm piece has been placed (see step 5), mark seam line at front edge of the arm and trim away excess fabric not needed for seam allowances.

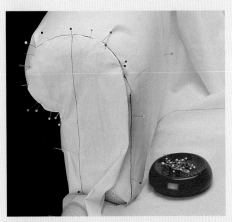

Pin the front arm piece in place. Fold out excess fabric on the inside arm as necessary to fit the front arm piece, making two pleats. Mark the seam line for the curve of the arm, following existing seam line on the chair. Complete the arm pattern as in steps 7 through 9.

(continued)

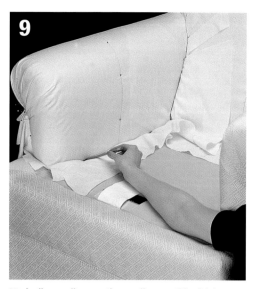

Mark all seam lines on the muslin, smoothing fabric as you go.

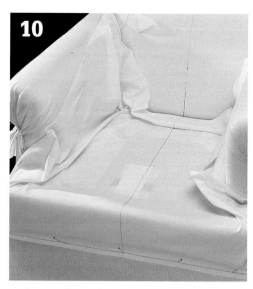

Mark a seam line on the front edge of the deck piece on the straight grain, ½" from the raw edge. Pin the marked line to the welting of the skirt seam, with the center line centered on the skirt. Smooth muslin over the front edge and deck and match center lines of deck and inside back.

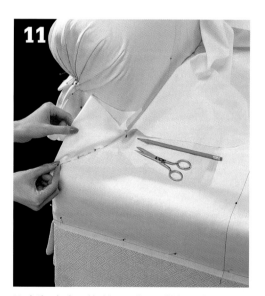

Mark the deck and inside arm pieces with large dots at the point where the deck meets the front of the inside arm. For furniture with a T-cushion, clip excess fabric to the dots. Fold out excess fabric on the deck at the front corner, forming a dart; pin and mark.

Pin the deck to the outside arm piece at the side of the chair; mark the seam line. Do not fit the deck snug. Push about ½" of fabric into the crevices at the sides and back of the deck; mark seam lines by pushing a pencil into the crevices.

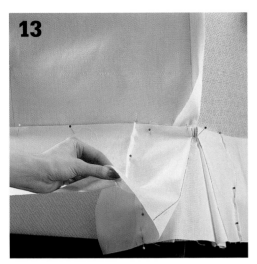

13

Place raw edge of the first skirt piece just below the lower edge of the skirt; pin at the upper edge of the skirt, keeping the muslin straight and even. Pin seams as you come to them; pin out fullness for pleats or gathers. Pin vertical tucks in the skirt, pinning ⅛" tuck near back corner on each side of the chair and ¼" tuck near each corner on back of the chair; tucks will be released in step 16, adding ease to the skirt. Mark seams and placement of pleats or gathers.

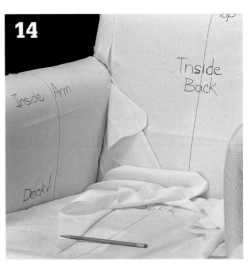

14

Mark the direction of the upper edge on all muslin pieces; label pieces. Check that all seam lines, darts, gathers, and pleats are marked. Mark dots at intersecting seams; label.

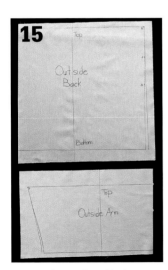

15

Remove the muslin. Add ¼" ease to back edge of the outside arm at lower corner. Add ½" ease to sides of the outside back at lower corners. Taper to the marked seam lines at upper corners.

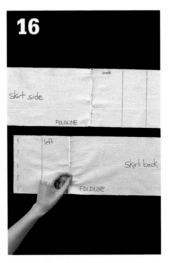

16

Remove the pinned tucks near the back corners of the skirt pieces. Mark "fold line" at lower edge of the muslin for a self-lined skirt.

17

True straight seam lines using a straightedge; true curved seam lines, drawing smooth curves. Do not mark seam lines in pleated areas.

(continued)

18

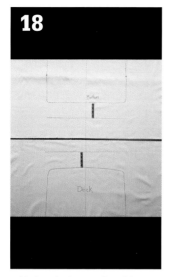

Add 4" to the lower edge of the inside back and back edge of deck.

19

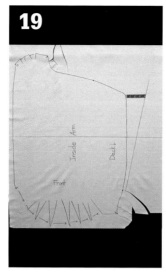

Mark the lower edge of the inside arm from a point 4" away from seam line at the back edge to ½" from large dot at front edge; repeat for the sides of the deck.

20

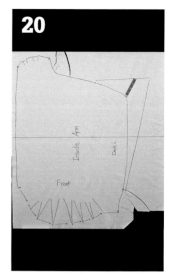

Mark the back edge of the inside arm from a point 4" away from the seam line at the lower edge to ½" from the large dot; repeat for the sides of the inside back.

21

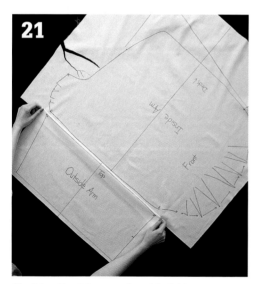

Check lengths of the seam lines for adjoining seams; adjust as necessary to ensure that seam lines match.

22

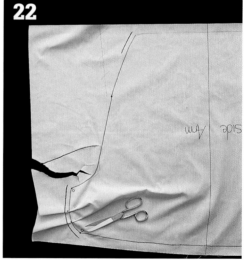

Fold pleats on marked lines. Mark seam lines in pleated area; add ½" seam allowances. Trim on the cutting line through all layers of the pleats. Add ½" seam allowances to any remaining seams and cut pieces out on the marked cutting lines. Before cutting, double-check that you cut on the cutting line, not on the seam line.

Making a Quality Slipcover

- When laying out the pattern for cutting, center large motifs in your fabric on the back, sides, cushions, and on the top of the arms. On a striped fabric, center the prominent stripe on the center placement line on the back and cushion pieces. Position arm pieces on striped fabric so the stripes will run in the same direction as the skirt.
- Cut the skirt pieces to make a self-lined skirt, placing the fold line at the lower edge of the pattern on a crosswise fold. Self-lined skirts generally hang better than single-layer skirts with a hem.
- Mark names of pieces on wrong side of fabric and transfer all markings, including notches and dots.

- Although your slipcover may be slightly different from the project shown, familiarize yourself with the basic construction steps, as the general order of assembly will be the same.
- Stitch small details, such as darts, before assembling pieces.
- Use strong thread, such as long-staple polyester, a medium stitch length, and a size 90/14 or 100/16 sewing machine needle.
- Add welting to any seams that will be subjected to stress and wear. Welting can also be added for decorative detail to seams such as around the outside back and the upper edge of the skirt.

Fitted Slipcover Cutting Guide ▸

	Length	Width
All Slipcover Pieces	See pattern	See pattern.
Tacking strip (cut on straight grain)	Circumference of chair at upper edge of skirt	3"

How to Sew a Fitted Slipcover

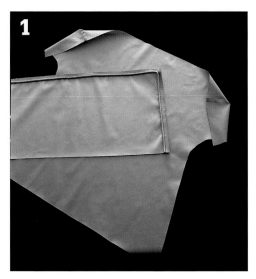

Stitch darts at the upper corners of the inside back. If welting is desired, apply it to the upper front edges of the outside arm, pivoting at the corner.

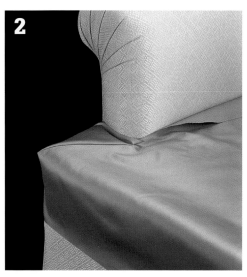

Stitch darts at the outer front corners of the deck; stop stitching ½" from the raw edges at the inner corner.

(continued)

Stitch the deck to the front of the arm and the inside arm; this can be stitched as two separate seams.

Pin pleats in place at the front and back of the arm. Check the fit over the arm of the chair. Baste in place on seam line.

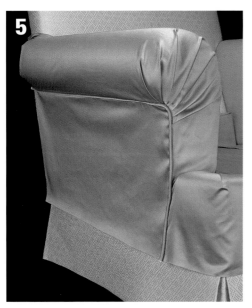

Stitch the horizontal and vertical seams, joining the outside arm to the inside arm; pivot at corner.

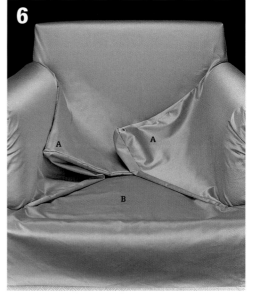

Pin the inside arms to inside back on both sides (A). Pin lower edge of the inside back to back edge of the deck (B). Make tucks in seams at the corners, if necessary, so pieces fit together. Stitch seams.

7

Apply welting around the sides and upper edge of the slipcover unit; curve ends of the welting into seam allowance ½" from the lower edges (arrow). Join slipcover unit to outside back, leaving the seam open for zipper application. Apply welting to the lower edge. Stitch skirt pieces together, leaving the seam at the back corner unstitched for the zipper; press seams open. Fold the skirt in half lengthwise, wrong sides together and press.

8

Press pleats for the pleated skirt. For a gathered skirt, stitch gathering stitches by zigzagging over a cord; for a skirt with bunched gathers, stitch gathering stitches between the markings.

9

Pin the tacking strip to the upper edge of the skirt on the wrong side. Join the skirt to adjoining pieces; for a gathered skirt, pull the gathering threads together to fit. Insert the zipper (page 322) and sew cushion covers (page 272).

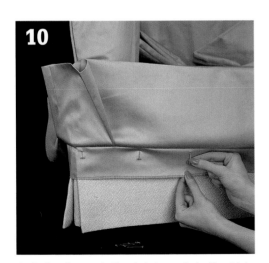

10

Apply the slipcover to the chair. Secure the tacking strip to the chair by pinning into upholstery with T-pins.

11

Push extra fabric allowance into crevices around the deck and inside back. Stuff 2" strips of polyurethane foam into crevices around the deck to keep fabric from pulling out. Insert the cushions.

Sewing a Fitted Slipcover with a Front Arm Piece ▶

  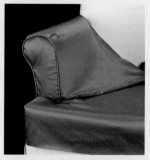

Stitch darts at the upper corners of the inside back. Apply welting to the upper edge of the inside arm, if desired. Stitch the horizontal seam, joining the outside arm to the inside arm. Pin and baste tucks at the front edge of the inside/outside arm.

Stitch the front arm piece to the front edge of the inside/outside arm; stop stitching 2" from the outer end of the front arm piece.

Follow steps 2 and 3 on page 319 to 320. Pin the pleats in place at the back of the arm; baste in place on the seam line. Complete the vertical seam at the front edge of the outside arm. Finish the slipcover as in steps 6 to 11 on page 320 to 321.

How to Add a Zipper to a Slipcover

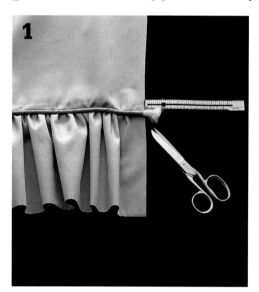 

Pull the cording out slightly from the ends of the skirt opening; trim off the ends 1". Pull the seam to return the cording to its original position.

Press under the seam allowances on the zipper opening. Place the open zipper on the welted side of the seam, so the welting just covers the zipper teeth and with the zipper tab at the lower edge. Pin in place; fold in the seam allowance at the lower edge of the skirt to miter. Fold up the end of the zipper tape.

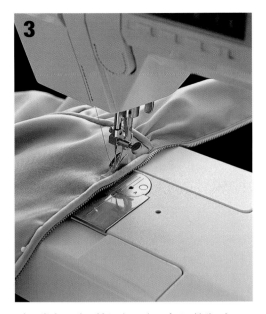

Edgestitch on the skirt using a zipper foot, with the zipper teeth positioned close to the folded edge. Stitch in the ditch of the welted seam.

Close the zipper. Place the remaining side of the zipper under the seam allowance, with the folded edge at the welted seam line. Pin in place; fold in the seam allowance at the lower edge of the skirt to miter. Fold up the end of the zipper tape.

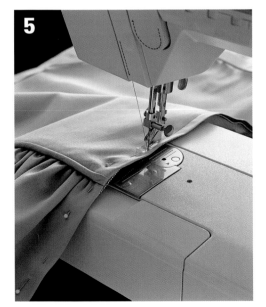

Open the zipper. Stitch ⅜" from the folded edge, pivoting at the top of the zipper.

Pleated Skirt ▸

Break the stitching at the upper edge of the skirt. On the skirt, stitch through the lower layer of the box pleat; stitch as close as possible to the seam at the upper edge of the skirt.

Futon Slipcover

Futons are wonderfully practical, especially for small spaces. With the addition of this simple slipcover, your futon can complement your décor as well. Use flat cotton sheets or decorator fabric to stitch together this practical fitted cover.

Futons are a comfortable addition to guest rooms, vacation homes, basements, and small spaces. Dress them up with a slipcover to match your room's décor.

Tools & Materials ▸

Two cotton sheets the same size as the mattress, or decorator fabric

Zipper tape
Zipper pull
¾"-wide transparent tape

Futon Slipcover Cutting Guide ▸

	Length	Width
Front/Back Piece (2)	Length of futon mattress + 1"	Width of futon mattress + 1"
Boxing Strip	Length of futon mattress + 1"	Width of futon mattress + 1"
Zipper Tab	4"	Width of boxing strip
Long Zipper Strip (2)	Length of futon mattress + 1"	Width of boxing strip ÷ 2 + 1½"
Short Zipper Strip (4)	Length of mattress end + 1"	Width of boxing strip ÷ 2 + 1¼"
Zipper Tape	Length of mattress end × 2 + length of mattress side + 1"	

How to Sew a Futon Cover

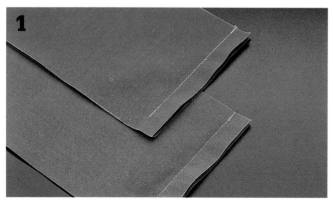

1

Stitch one short zipper strip to each end of one long zipper strip, right sides together, with ½" seams. Stitch from raw edge to ½" from the opposite edge. Finish seams, using a zigzag stitch or serging; press open. Repeat, using the remaining short and long zipper strips.

Place the zipper strips right sides together, matching the raw edges and seams. Machine-baste ¾" from the long edge, where stitching of the end seams extends to the raw edge. Finish seams; press open.

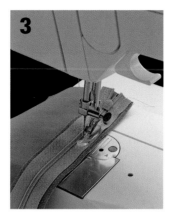

Fold the strip in half, right sides together, with one seam allowance extending. Place the closed zipper facedown over seam allowances, with the teeth centered on the seamline and the ends of the zipper tape even with the ends of the strip. Machine-baste the zipper tape to the extended seam allowance. Unfold. Center a strip of transparent tape over the seam line. Stitch on both sides of the tape, securing the zipper. Remove the tape and basting stitches.

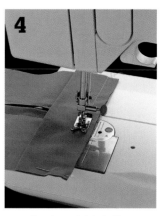

Press the zipper tab in half, wrong sides together. Open the zipper about 2". At the top end of the zipper, place the tap over the zipper strip, right sides up; stitch across the end ½" from the raw edges, stitching carefully over the zipper teeth.

Stitch the ends of the boxing strip to the ends of the zipper strip, right sides together with ½" seams. Start and stop ½" from the raw edges. Finish the seams and press open.

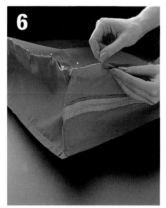

Pin the boxing strip to the futon cover front, right sides together, matching seams to corners. With the boxing strip face-up, stitch a ½" seam, pivoting at the corners. Pin the opposite side of the boxing strip to the futon cover back, right sides together, matching seams to corners; stitch. Finish remaining seams.

Open the zipper; turn the futon cover right side out. Insert the futon mattress; close the zipper, hiding the zipper pull under the tab.

Furniture Refinishing

Refinishing furniture pieces not only improves the appearance and value of rare, well-loved, or rescued furniture, but it can also be a fun hobby. The techniques described in this chapter are easy to master, but will require time, patience, and diligent attention to detail for a truly excellent end result. Always spend time stripping, sanding, and preparing the surface, as well as making any minor repairs, before you apply the final stain or paint color. If you spend time preparing your piece, you will not be disappointed with the final result. A unique furniture piece with a professional, high-quality surface has lasting appeal and can add immense character, spark, and sophistication to your living spaces.

In this chapter:

- Heat Stripping
- Chemical Stripping
- Surface Prep
- Stain & Top Coat
- Painting Furniture
- Faux Leather Finish
- Photo Montage Table
- Spray-painting Metal Furniture
- Painting Radiators

Heat Stripping

Before painting or refinishing, wood should be cleaned, repaired, and sanded. If the old paint is heavily layered or badly chipped, it should also be stripped before the wood is repainted. Using heat to strip an old finish is safe and effective; heat encourages paint to blister and pull away from the wood so it can easily be scraped away with a putty knife. You just need to use the proper techniques and safety measures.

An electric heat gun looks much like a hand-held hair dryer and forces a stream of hot air against the piece. This stripping technique works best when stripping multiple layers of paint but can also be used on thick layers of varnish, lacquer, and other top coats. If you plan to use a chemical stripper, you may want to heat strip the wood first—you'll use less of the chemical stripper if you do. Never use a heat gun after using chemical strippers, however. The chemical residue could become vaporized or ignited by the heat.

Heat-Stripping Tip ▸

A heat shield keeps the heat gun from damaging or blistering the finish on surrounding areas. For a shield, use a piece of sheet metal or cover cardboard with heavy-duty aluminum foil.

Tools & Materials ▸

Heat gun	Heavy-gauge extension cord	Goggles	Aluminum foil
Putty knife	Fire extinguisher	Work gloves	Cardboard
Assorted scrapers	Coffee can		

Heat stripping can scorch the wood if applied unevenly—watch the painted surface carefully. If the paint looks gummy, it may be becoming overheated.

How to Heat-strip Paint

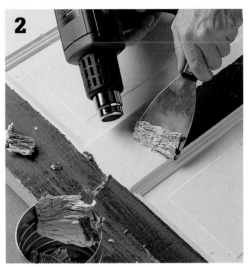

Scrape off all loose paint flakes using a paint scraper. Hold the heat gun about 2" above the surface, and then turn it on, starting at the lowest setting. Move the gun in a circular motion until the paint begins to blister. If the paint doesn't blister, try the next higher heat setting.

Follow the heat gun with a metal scraper. Hold the scraper at about a 30° angle, and move both the scraper and the heat gun at the same speed. (Always move the heat gun in a circular motion.) Strip all the large, flat surfaces. Deposit the ribbons of paint in a coffee can or other heat-proof container.

Heat strip the contoured and uneven areas using specialty scrapers, where needed, to remove the loosened paint. Do not overheat or use too much pressure around detailed areas—they are more vulnerable to scorching and gouging than flat areas.

Dry scrape all wood surfaces to remove any remaining loosened paint flecks after you are done heat stripping. In most cases, you will need to use chemical solvents or strippers to remove the rest of the finish.

Chemical Stripping

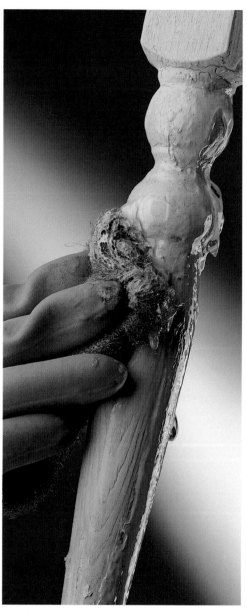

Chemical solvents are fast and thorough. They can remove just about any finish material, from varnish to polyurethane or paint. Before choosing a solvent or stripper, identify the old finish type. Remember that most finishes are composed of several layers; try to select a chemical that is effective on the materials in all of the layers.

The primary solvents used for stripping are mineral spirits, denatured alcohol, and lacquer thinner. These chemicals are inexpensive and relatively safe, so use them instead of commercial strippers whenever possible. Many commercial strippers and older strippers contain hazardous chemicals, and will require you to wear a respirator and other protective equipment when in use. These strippers are very effective but always follow the recommended precautions and try to use a less abrasive product if you can. Newer products without hazardous chemicals dissolve most finishes with far less risk, although they work somewhat slower than their more hazardous counterparts.

Tools & Materials ▸

Paintbrushes
Putty knife
Assorted scrapers
Safety equipment
Stripper or solvent
Medium abrasive pads
Newspapers and rags
Sawdust
Rinsing agent

Refinishing Safety Tip ▸

Protect yourself and your home, and help ensure good finishing results by using sensible safety, cleanup, and disposal methods. Contact your local city office or the Environmental Protection Agency (page 444) for disposal regulations. Also see "Safety Equipment" on page 346.

Chemical stripper dissolves thick finishes so they can be wiped or scraped off easily. Coarse abrasive pads are effective removal tools for contours.

How to Chemically Strip a Finish

Pour some stripper into a small, easy-to-use container (no more than you can use in 15 minutes). Read the label and select a brush for applying the stripper—most brands can be applied with inexpensive polyester-bristle brushes.

Wearing rubbers gloves (and a respirator if the label advises you to use one), apply a thick coat of stripper to the workpiece, beginning at the top of the project and working down from there. Do not overbrush the stripper.

Let the stripper work for the length of time suggested by the manufacturer. Remove the sludge with a putty knife or stripping knife, and deposit it on old newspapers. *Tip: Just before you start to scrape away the sludge, sprinkle sawdust on the stripper to make it easier to remove.*

Strip the detailed and contoured areas, using specialty scrapers and abrasive pads to remove the sludge. Use light pressure on the scrapers so you do not gouge the wood.

Apply a thin coat of stripper to the wood, and then scrub off any remaining finish, using a synthetic-bristle stripping brush or medium abrasive pads.

Clean the wood with a medium abrasive pad dipped in the rinsing agent recommended by the stripper manufacturer (often denatured alcohol). This removes most traces of the finish and the stripper.

Surface Prep

Surface preparation ensures an even, high-quality finish. Finish sand with progressively finer grits of sandpaper, starting with 150-grit. Generally, hardwood requires finer-grit sandpaper than soft wood. To speed up the process, use a power sander for the first stages of the sanding, then switch to hand sanding to complete the process.

Finish sanding alone creates a smooth surface, but because wood absorbs stain at different rates, the color can be blotchy and dark. Sealing wood with sanding sealer evens out the stain-absorption rates and yields a lighter, more even finish. Filling the grain creates a finish that feels as smooth as it looks.

Tools & Materials ▸

Fine-grit sandpaper
Power sander
Sanding blocks
Rags
Abrasive pad

Putty knife
Grain filler
Plastic scraper
Mineral spirits

Use sanding sealer or grain filler for a fine finish. Finish sanding alone (left) can leave a blotchy surface, but sanding sealer (center) plus grain filler (right) give progressively finer finishes.

Using Sanding Sealer ▸

Make your own sanding sealer by blending one part clear top coat material (not water based) with one part top coat solvent. Use the same top coat material you plan to apply to the project. Wipe on a heavy coat of the sealer, then wipe off the excess after a few minutes. When dry, sand lightly with 200-grit sandpaper.

How to Finish Sand

Finish sand all surfaces with 150-grit sandpaper, following the direction of the grain. Use a finishing sander on flat surfaces and specialty sanding blocks on contours. When sanding hardwood, switch to 180-grit paper and sand again.

Raise the wood grain by dampening the surface with a wet rag. Let the wood dry, then skim the surface with a fine abrasive pad, following the grain.

Use sanding blocks to hand sand the entire workpiece with the finest-grit paper in the sanding sequence. Sand until all sanding marks are gone and the surface is smooth. (Use bright sidelighting to check your progress.) If using sanding sealer, do that now.

How to Apply Grain Filler

After finish sanding, use a rag or putty knife to spread a coat of grain filler onto the wood surface. With a polishing motion, work the filler into the grain. Let the filler dry until it becomes cloudy (usually about 5 minutes).

Remove excess filler by drawing a plastic scraper across the grain of the wood at a 45° angle. Let the grain filler dry overnight.

Lightly hand sand the surface, following the direction of the grain, with 320-grit sandpaper. Finally, dampen a clean cloth with mineral spirits and use it to thoroughly clean the surface.

Stain & Top Coat

Applying stain shows off a fine or distinctive grain pattern and creates a beautiful wood tone. Stain and penetrating oil, the two most basic coloring agents, also help conceal uneven coloration and can blend different wood types on the same piece. When selecting a coloring agent, consider oil-based stains, water-based stains, wipe-on gel stains, penetrating oils, and one-step stain-and-sealant products. To sort through the options, start by finding a color you like, and then read the label to determine if it's the best product for your project and that it is compatible with the top coat you'd like to use.

Top coats seal the wood and protect the finish from scratches and other wear as they highlight the coloring of the wood. For most projects, a top coat of tung oil, polyurethane, or paste wax will protect the wood and give it the appearance you want. When choosing the best top coat for you, consider durability, sheen, and compatibility with the stain color you've selected.

For both the stain and top coat you choose, pay careful attention to drying times, safety advisories, application techniques and cleanup methods on the product label, as these aspects vary greatly from product to product.

Tools & Materials ▶

Protective gloves
Penetrating oil
Staining cloths
Soft buffing cloth
Fine abrasive pad
Liquid stain
Paintbrush

Stiff-bristled brush
Mineral spirits
Polyurethane
600-grit wet/dry
　sandpaper
Paste wax

A well-chosen, properly applied color layer and protective top coat will highlight the natural beauty and prolong the life of your furniture. Regularly dust and maintain the furniture and it will serve you for life.

Masking Discoloration ▶

Evening out the color with dark stain is easier than trying to sand out discolorations. Because stain forms a more opaque color layer than penetrating oil, it's generally a better product for covering wood problems.

How to Use Penetrating Oil

Apply a heavy coat of penetrating oil to all prepared surfaces using a staining cloth. Wait 15 to 30 minutes, recoating any areas that begin to dry out. Apply oil to all surfaces, and let it soak into the wood for 30 to 60 minutes.

Wipe the surface dry with a clean cloth, rubbing with the wood grain. Apply another coat of oil with a clean cloth, then let the oil dry overnight. *Note: Two coats are sufficient in most cases, since further coats will not darken the finish color.*

Dab a few drops of penetrating oil onto a fine abrasive pad, then rub the surfaces until smooth. Let the oil dry for at least 72 hours before applying a top coat. If you do not plan to top coat the finish, buff with a soft cloth to harden the oil finish.

How to Apply Liquid Stain

Stir the stain thoroughly and apply a heavy coat with a brush or cloth. Stir the stain often as you work. Let the stain soak in according to manufacturer's instructions.

Remove the excess stain with a clean, lint-free cloth. Wipe against the grain first, then with the grain. If the color is too dark, try scrubbing the surface with water or mineral spirits. Let the stain dry, then buff with a fine abrasive pad. Repeat with light coats of stain until the desired color is achieved. Buff between coats and after the final coat.

How to Apply Gel Stain

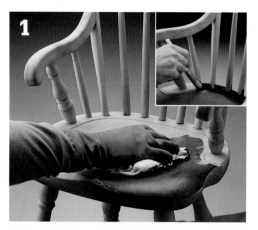

Stir the stain, then work it into the surfaces of the workpiece with a staining cloth, rubbing in a circular motion. Recoat any areas that dry out as you work and cover as much of the piece as possible. Use a stiff-bristled brush, such as a stencil brush, to apply the gel in hard-to-reach areas (inset).

Let the stain soak in according to manufacturer's directions, then wipe off excess with a clean rag using a polishing motion. Buff the stained surface with the wood grain using a soft, clean cloth. Apply additional coats until the desired color has been achieved; three coats are typically recommended. Let the stain dry, then buff the piece with a fine abrasive pad.

How to Apply Polyurethane Top Coat

Seal unstained wood with a 1:1 mixture of polyurethane and water or mineral spirits (check the product label for its recommendation). Apply the sealer with a clean cloth or brush and let it dry. Wipe off excess sealer using a clean cloth. *Note: If you used stain or penetrating oil to color your piece, skip this step.*

Apply a coat of polyurethane, starting at the top of the project and working your way down. When the surface is covered, smooth out the finish by lightly brushing in one direction only, parallel to the grain. Let dry, then sand the surface with 600-grit wet/dry sandpaper.

Apply the second coat. To keep the finish from running, always try to position the workpiece so the surface being top coated is horizontal.

How to Apply Paste Wax

Apply a moderate layer of paste wax to the wood using a fine abrasive pad or a cloth. Rub the wax into the wood with a polishing motion.

Allow the wax to dry until it becomes filmy in spots. Gently wipe off any excess, undried wax, and then allow the remaining wax to dry until filmy (usually within 10 to 20 minutes). *Note: Do not let the wax dry too long or it will harden and become very difficult to buff.*

Begin buffing the wax with a soft cloth using a light, circular motion. Buff the entire surface until the filminess disappears and the wax is clear. Continue buffing the wax until the surface is hard and shiny. Apply and buff another coat, then let the wax dry for at least 24 hours before applying additional coats. Three coats are recommended for a fine finish.

How to Apply Tung Oil

Apply a thick coat of tung oil with a cloth or brush. Let the tung oil penetrate for 5 to 10 minutes, then rub off the excess with a cloth using a polishing motion.

After 24 hours, buff the tung oil with a clean cloth, and then reapply additional coats as necessary to build the finish. (Three coats are generally considered the minimum for a good finish.) Use a clean cloth to apply each coat.

Painting Furniture

The key to a beautiful painted finish is detailed surface preparation, so spend time sanding your piece to a fine finish, making any small repairs, and filling any nicks or dents with wood putty before you begin. For a truly professional finish, sand after priming and between coats as well. Use a power sander for large surfaces and plan to hand sand detailed areas.

After initial sanding, apply a high-quality primer as your first coat. If you will be painting your piece a bold color, ask your retailer about tinting the primer—this may result in fewer coats of your final paint color later on. Finally, apply several coats of high-quality paint for a shined-up, refreshed, good-as-new piece.

Tools & Materials ▸

Extra fine-grit
    and fine-grit sandpaper
Extra fine sanding sponge
2" paintbrush
Tack cloth
Latex primer
Semigloss latex paint
Polyurethane spray

Sanding Tip ▸

To check a sanded surface for flaws, shine a bright light sideways over the piece and run your hands over the surface, feeling for flaws that can't be seen.

A coat of paint can unlock the potential of an old or neglected table or chair, transforming it in a matter of hours.

How to Paint a Furniture Piece

Sand the piece thoroughly using fine-grit sandpaper. Switch to the extra fine-grit paper and sand again. Wipe away the sanding dust with a tack cloth.

Apply the first coat of primer and let it dry overnight.

Lightly sand the surface using an extra fine-grit sanding sponge. Wipe the piece down with a tack cloth and apply a second coat of primer. Let the second coat of primer dry overnight.

Brush the first coat of paint onto the piece and let it dry. Sand the piece using the extra fine sandpaper. Wipe away the sanding residue with a tack cloth. Apply a second coat of paint and let it dry.

Spray a light coat of polyurethane onto the entire piece and let it dry thoroughly. Add a second coat and let it dry.

Faux Leather Finish

legant and easy, this finish works well as an inlay on large tables or desktops and complements both painted and stained surfaces. Leather hides tend to be smaller than 19 × 30", so inlays with dimensions smaller than that most successfully mimic real leather. Color variations in tanned leather range from reddish Cordova to a deep brown/black. Experiment with different latex paints and mediums to create this finish, but the oil glaze is an essential component and gives the finish a richness that the latex just cannot quite achieve.

Apply the faux leather finish to the entire project piece, allowing the tape lines to form panels, or use 3" painter's paper to protect the outer surface to create an inlaid look. Use a clear ruler and T-square to keep your tape lines straight when planning out your panels.

To begin, basecoat the project or inlay surface with a paint color that is about 50 percent lighter than your glaze color. Allow it to dry, then apply tape lines where they'd best help to frame your panels.

Tools & Materials ▸

½"-wide painter's tape
3" painter's paper
Flat oil-based paint, brown
Flat oil-based paint, golden brown
   (for base coat)
Alkyd glazing liquid
Paint thinner
3"-wide flat oil paintbrush
Newspaper
90-weight, 24" cheesecloth

Leather colors range from reds to warm black; although the table shown here was painted in brown tones, your choice of colors for this finish is quite broad.

How to Apply a Faux Leather Finish

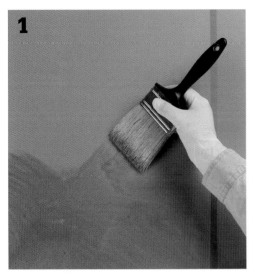

Mix a glaze using one part brown paint, one part glazing liquid, and one part paint thinner. After the basecoat has dried, use a paintbrush to apply glaze to the entire project surface.

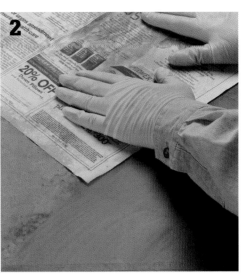

While the glaze is still wet, smoothly lay the sheet of newspaper onto the glazed surface. Keep the newspaper flat. Lift the paper, then replace it on the project surface overlapping the first area slightly and avoiding right angles. Repeat this process over the entire surface.

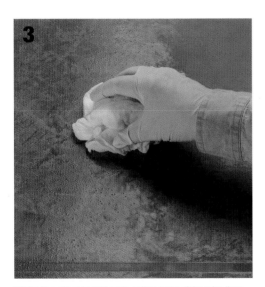

While the glaze is still wet, soften some of the edge lines by patting with the smooth side of a cheesecloth wad. Soften the lines and fold the texture into the finish. Allow the paint to dry, then remove the tape.

Top coat the surface with one or two coats of wax. For greater protection, apply a satin oil-based varnish before waxing.

Photo Montage Table

Display your photos proudly as a creative, professional-grade finish on a desk or tabletop! This technique is not decoupage but a modern application of paper to a piece of furniture. Whether following a theme or choosing random much-loved photos, your work is sure to be a conversation piece. A computer, a basic photo-editing program, and a printer will enable you to manipulate the size and color of the images, but photocopies can be used as long as they are produced on matte-finsh photo-grade paper.

When working with photographic images, never use your originals. Store them in a safe place and use reproductions for this project. For best results, print your images on matte-finish photo-grade computer printing paper, or send them to a professional photo printer.

Tools & Materials ▸

Flat latex paint, black
Matte finish photo-grade
    computer printing paper
Wallpaper cutting blade
Metal straightedge or ruler
White chalk
Painter's masking tape
18 × 24" acid-free artist sketchbook pad
Spray adhesive
Wax paper
Rubber roller
Satin oil-based varnish

A photo montage table or chair can be the perfect accent to add spice and artistic interest to any space in your home.

Composition Tip ▸

To help you arrange a pleasing composition on your piece, draw two diagonal lines with chalk to find the center intersection of the surface. Work off the center for a balanced composition. Also, determine which photos will be placed portrait or landscape, then size and crop photos appropriately before printing.

How to Make a Photo Montage Table

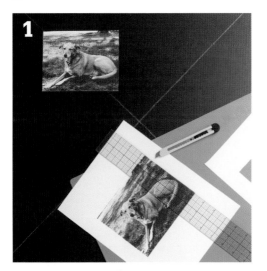

Basecoat the project surface with the black paint. Trim the white borders from all images using the cutting blade and a straightedge.

Place a number of images on the surface and move them around until you find a pleasing composition, holding images in place temporarily with a small loop of painter's tape. When your composition is complete, lift one image and lay it back side up on a clean sketchbook page. Lightly apply an even coat of spray adhesive across the entire back. Place the image in its final position carefully, for you will not be able to reposition it.

Place a sheet of wax paper over the image. Roll it smooth using the rubber roller and flatten any bubbles or air pockets. Smooth with clean fingers, if necessary. Repeat adhering and rolling procedure for all images. Allow the surface to dry for 24 hours.

Top coat with one or two coats of satin oil-based varnish. When applying varnish, the photo paper may bubble. Not to worry—just press the image flat with a fingertip once the varnish is dry.

Spray-painting Metal Furniture

Spray-painting metal furniture can help unmatched pieces coordinate and bring new life to old pieces. Spray paint is available in a wide variety of colors, styles, and finishes, and there's certainly a color or finish perfect for your furniture. As with every other painting project, preparation is the most important aspect of spray-painting. Spray paint adheres best to clean, rough surfaces, so cleaning is the first and most important step in this project. For best results, shake the can and clean the nozzle often and maintain a distance of about 12" to ensure a smooth, even spray.

Also, it's important to spray-paint in a well-ventilated space. When concentrated, paint fumes are both dangerous to breathe and flammable.

There are many spray paint options for metal furniture—consider brush-on, crackle, stone, hammered metal, and suede effects in several shades.

Tools & Materials ▸

Drop cloths	Mineral spirits
Spray primer	Wire brush
Spray paint	Newspaper

HVLP (High Volume Low Pressure) Sprayers ▸

Turbine-driven HVLP sprayers have a self-contained turbine blower that supplies a large volume of uncompressed air through the sprayer nozzle, atomizing the finish material and dispensing it in a soft, manageable mist.

Compressor-driven HVLP sprayers are supplied by an air compressor, usually at least 3 hp and 20 gal. in size. They function similarly to turbine-style models, except the product is not warmed up (which can cause the finish to dry too quickly).

Gravity feed HVLP spray guns have a small finish cup that's mounted at the top of the gun so it flows down into the nozzle unassisted. Guns with bottom-mounted cups rely on suction created by the sprayer turbine or comrpessor to siphon the material up and into the nozzle.

How to Spray-Paint Metal Furniture

Remove any hardware and dismantle furniture, then wash thoroughly with a scrub brush and mild detergent. Rinse and allow to dry completely.

Scrape away rust and loose paint with a wire brush. Wipe down all pieces with mineral spirits and inspect for any surface bubbles. Use a putty knife to scrape bubbles away, then brush the surface for a second time and continue to wipe with mineral spirits until your rag stops picking up grime.

Spray a very light coat of primer using a wide-spray nozzle attachment to the can. Bear in mind that the primer is meant to create a rough surface that will be easy for the final coat to adhere to. Shake the can and hold about 12" away while you spray. Clean the nozzle every few minutes according to the manufacturer's directions. Let the primer dry, then apply a second coat.

After the primer has cured, apply the first coat of paint. Shake the can well before you start and hold it about 12" away while you spray, cleaning the nozzle periodically. Allow the first coat to dry, then reapply additional coats as necessary. After your final coat has dried, reassemble your piece.

Painting Radiators

Painting radiators can help these ornate, functional pieces add decorative flair, as well as warmth, to your décor. Before you prepare the surface, remember that many radiators are old enough that they could be coated with lead paint, so always test for lead before beginning this project. If tests indicate the presence of lead, consult a lead-abatement expert, and do not attempt to paint the radiator yourself.

Top-of-the-line interior eggshell, satin finish latex paint, or high heat-resistant paint can all be used for this project. Before you begin, make sure your radiator is clean and grease free and has a slightly rough surface. Also, radiators should be warm, rather than hot or cold, while being painted, and should be allowed to remain cool for 2 to 3 hours after painting. Take on this project in late spring or early fall, when the heating system in your home won't be necessary.

A new coat of paint can help coordinate a radiator with the rest of the room, rescue it from shabbiness, or turn it into a showpiece.

Tools & Materials ▸

Drop cloths
Latex paint
Plastic sheeting

Tack cloth
Lead-testing kit

Scrub brush
Painter's tape

Bendable paint pad
1½" tapered paintbrush

Safety Equipment ▸

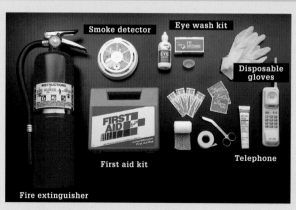

Smoke detector
Eye wash kit
Disposable gloves
First aid kit
Telephone
Fire extinguisher

Basic safety equipment for the work area includes a fully charged fire extinguisher rated for type A and B fires, a smoke detector, a first aid kit, an eye wash kit, disposable latex gloves, and a telephone for emergency use.

How to Paint a Radiator

Use a lead-testing kit, following the manufacturer's instructions, to test the paint on the radiator. If test indicates the presence of lead, stop and consult a lead-abatement specialist. If lead is not detected, prepare your work area with drop cloths and plastic sheeting.

Wash the radiator using a scrub brush and mild detergent. Rinse the radiator with clear water and allow it to dry completely.

Scrape away loose paint using a wire brush. Sand the surface of the radiator, paying special attention to areas where the old paint is cracking or peeling. Wipe the surface with a tack cloth to remove sanding dust and debris.

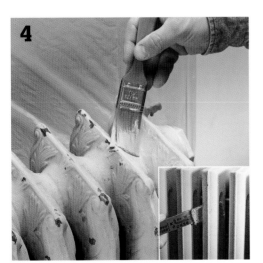

Turn on the radiator until the surface is slightly warm. Apply paint using long, smooth strokes. Use a bendable painting pad to reach the back of the radiator fins (inset). Do not run the furnace for 2 to 3 hours after the paint is dry.

Variation: Heat resistant paint is designed to resist heat as high as 2,000°. This type of paint comes in spray cans, which makes it easy to apply. Always apply two coats of sprayed paint for best adherence, cleaning the nozzle regularly and holding the can about 12" away from surface.

Window Treatments

Window treatments can transform a room from an architecturally stunning, well-decorated space to a complete, inviting corner of your home by softly framing windows, accenting decorating colors, and reflecting your personality. Hundreds of window treatment styles are available, and each can be customized to fit your style. Select coordinating decorator fabric, add trim and hardware, and mix and match over- and under-treatments for the best marriage of form and function in each room.

Protect your privacy, control light, and insulate rooms from heat and cold while you add a splash of color, a sweep of elegance, or draped sophistication to your windows with any of the following projects.

In this chapter:

Window Treatment Basics

Before you design new window treatments, always take accurate measurements of the window to determine the amount of fabric you'll need to purchase. First, choose the style of your treatment, the installation type, and determine the type of hardware you'll need. Then, take careful measurements of your window, including space for mounting hardware, to estimate the yardage of fabric you'll need. Once you have this basic information gathered, you'll be well prepared to make custom window treatments in any style.

Measuring Windows

Measure the window to determine the finished length and width of the treatment. These measurements will help you determine the cut length and width, which is the finished measurement plus the amount of fabric needed for hems, rod pockets, seams, matching repeats, and fullness.

Finished Length: Top of the heading or rod pocket to bottom of the hem.

Finished Width: Width of the rod plus returns and overlap for draperies.

Curtains and draperies can be sill length, apron length, or floor length. For good proportion, valances and swags are often one-fifth the length of the window or the completed window treatment. Swags are usually one- or two-thirds the length of the window. Whatever your desired measurement, avoid dividing any window directly in half with a window treatment.

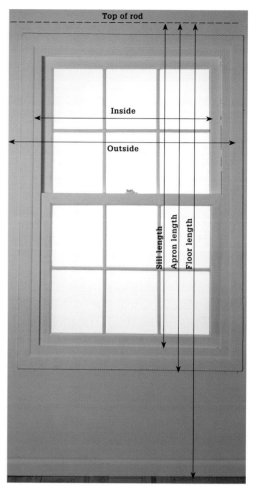

Always measure and record the measurements for each window you plan to dress, even if windows appear to be the same size. Use a folding ruler or metal tape for measuring; cloth tapes may stretch or sag.

Measuring Tips ▶

- **For floor-length draperies,** allow ½" clearance between the bottom of the drapery and the floor.
- **For loosely woven fabrics,** allow 1" clearance to allow extra room for stretching.
- **If you have baseboard heaters,** allow 4 to 6" drapery clearance above heaters for safety.
- **If carpeting has not yet been installed,** allow 2½" clearance.
- **If windows are varying heights in one room,** use the highest window as the standard for measuring others. Place all draperies in the room at the same height from the floor, if possible.

Estimating Yardage

Fabric widths vary, so wait to calculate yardage until you have selected your fabric. After you take the necessary measurements and determine the finished size of the treatment, calculate the cut length and width of the project.

To determine the cut length, add the amount of fabric needed for lower hems, rod pockets, headings, and pattern repeat to the finished length:

Lower hems: Because many lower hems are doubled, add double the desired finished hem length. For medium-weight fabrics, add 8" to make a 4" hem. For sheer or lightweight fabrics, add 11 to 12" for a 5 to 6" hem. For short curtains or valances, add 2 to 6" for a 1 to 3" hem.

Rod pockets and headings: For rod pockets with no headings, add an amount equal to the diameter of the rod plus ½" to turn under and ¼ to 1" ease, depending upon the thickness of the fabric and the size of the rod. Lightweight fabrics require less ease; rod pockets for large rods require more. For rod pockets with headings, add twice the depth of the heading to the rod pocket measurement.

Pattern repeat: Prints must match across the width of the panels. Measure the distance between motifs and add that amount to the cut length of each panel.

To determine the cut width, add the amount needed for seams, side hems, and fullness to the finished width:

Seams: For multiwidth panels, add 1" for each seam. If your panel is not wider than the fabric, you will not require extra fabric for seams.

Side hems: Add 6" per panel for a 1½" double-fold hem on each side of the panel.

Fullness: Fabric weight determines fullness. For lace and medium-weight to heavyweight fabrics, use 2 to 2½ times the finished width of the curtain. For sheer and lightweight fabrics, use 2½ to 3 times the finished width.

Make a copy of the chart at right and fill it in to help determine the yardage needed for your window treatment project. If you are working on draperies (with lining), see pages 402 to 403.

Estimating Yardage ▶

Cut Length	in.
For fabrics not requiring pattern match	
1) Finished length	
2) Double-fold bottom hem	+
3) Rod pocket/heading	+
4) Cut length for each width or part width	=
For fabrics requiring pattern match	
1) Cut length (see above)	
2) Size of pattern repeat (distance between motifs)	÷
3) Number of repeats needed*	=
4) Cut length for each width or part width: multiply size of repeat by number of repeats needed	

Cut Width	
1) Finished width	
2) Fullness (how many times the finished width)	×
3) Width times fullness	=
4) Double-fold side hems	+
5) Total width needed	=
6) Width of fabric	
7) Number of fabric widths: total width needed divided by width of fabric*	

Total Fabric Needed	
1) Cut length (see above)	
2) Number of fabric widths (see above)	×
3) Total fabric length	=
4) Number of yd. needed: total fabric length divided by 36"	yd.

For wide sheers, which can be railroaded	
1) Finished width times 3 (fullness)	×
2) Number of yd. needed: Total width needed divided by 36"	yd.

* For fabrics requiring pattern match, see page 28.

Window Treatment Styles

Window treatments infuse a room with color, pattern, and personality. They also provide privacy, control light, conserve heat, minimize noise, and obscure or draw attention to a view.

There are hundreds of variations on each window treatment style, depending on the fabric and combination you choose to best suit your home and personal style. Also see pages 361, 379, 401, 411, 425.

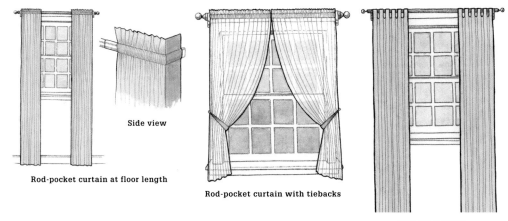

Side view

Rod-pocket curtain at floor length

Rod-pocket curtain with tiebacks

Tab-top curtains

Curtains are straight fabric panels, usually unlined, that hang on the sides of the window. Change up your curtains by choosing a creative heading or layering them over window shades or under a top treatment. Lightweight cottons, cotton/polyester blends, and some fashion fabrics are a good choice for curtains.

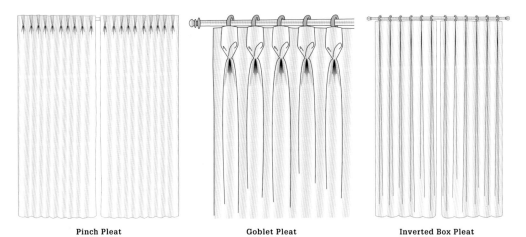

Pinch Pleat

Goblet Pleat

Inverted Box Pleat

Draperies are long, straight fabric panels with pleated headings that are almost always lined. Draperies are hung from drapery hooks, usually on traversing rods, which makes them easy to open and close. Medium-weight to heavyweight cottons and formal fabrics, such as damask, toile, antique satin, and brocade work well for draperies.

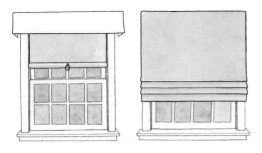

Roller shade   Roman shade

Balloon shade   Padded cornice

Fabric shades are mounted inside or outside the window frame and are used to block or filter light. They can be flat, gathered, or pleated, and they are generally raised from the bottom by pulling a cord. Use firmly woven cloth for flat shades and soft, drapable fabric for gathered shades.

Valances are window toppers that hang alone or over curtains, draperies, or shades, cleverly camouflaging mounting hardware. Valances can be made in a variety of styles to best match your décor; choose fabric that will work best for the valance style and formality of the room.

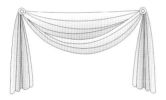

Freeform Scarf Swag

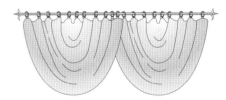

Bias Swag

Swags are pleated or draped to hang across the top of a window, and they are usually lined because both sides are part of the design. Soft, drapable fabrics, such as lace, silk, or linen drape beautifully as swags.

Window Treatment Hardware ▸

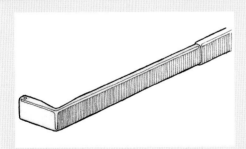

Curtain rods work well for rod-pocket window treatments or for any treatment that will cover most of the rod. These rods are functional, not decorative and don't allow you to easily open and close curtains.

Decorative rods are made of a variety of materials and are often sold in kits that include brackets, finials, and rings. These rods are meant to be seen—pair them with treatments that will showcase their material and styling. Hang window treatments from decorative rods with pleat hooks, fabric tabs, ribbons, grommets, rings, or clips—depending on the best look for your room.

Blinds & Shades

Horizontal blinds and shades can be opened or closed with the push of a button or a tug of a cord. They also help control the amount of light that is filtered into a room, and they can help insulate a room against heat or cold. The key to easy blind or shade installation is careful measurement and good preparation.

Blinds or shades can be mounted inside or outside of the window frame on the hardware provided with the item. Custom shades or blinds are often installed on mounting boards, which are covered and custom-cut to fit your project.

Tools & Materials ▸

Shade or blind	Wall anchors
Tape measure	Hanger brackets
Drill	Screws
Stud finder	

Mounting Styles ▸

First, decide if the new shade or blind will be placed inside or outside of the window frame. For an inside mount (shown), install the hardware inside the top of the window frame so the molding is exposed; this is a good choice when you've installed decorative molding, or if your window treatment fits nicely inside the window frame. An outside mount is installed at the top of the window frame or on the wall above the window; treatments installed on an outside mount add height to the window and can let more light into the room. Inside or outside mounts can be used for either blinds or shades.

Inside mount

Horizontal blinds and shades improve energy efficiency and provide privacy and light control. Many retailers will cut them to fit while you wait, so always bring your measurements to the store with you.

Blind and Shade Installations to Consider

Stationary blinds (shutters, here) are installed like other inside-mount blinds only they do not require space above for hardware—they are typically flush with the top window frame, as shown here.

Inside-mount blinds allow window trim to complement the décor. Here, a simple matching wood valance was provided with the blinds to conceal the hardware along the top edge.

Outside-mount shades are often used for window top-to-floor coverage. Covering the window trim on both sides and the bottom maintains a balanced look.

Center inside-mount shades are often used if windows on an upper-level floor require privacy only on the lower half of the window. Outside-mount curtains complement this scenario well for those times when full light filtration is desired.

How to Install Shades (Inside Mount)

Measure the opening between the side jambs at the top, bottom, and middle of the window frame. Make a quick diagram of the window and note the smallest of the three measurements.

Measure the height of the window frame (between the top and bottom) at each side and in the middle. Add the largest of these measurements to your diagram. With your diagram in hand, purchase blinds or shades to fit the window. If possible, have the retailer cut the blinds or shades to your specifications. If that's not possible, buy the closest size (a bit smaller) to the window opening.

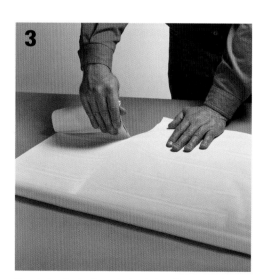

To cut standard roll-up shades to length, remove the slat from the bottom edge and cut through the hem with scissors. Carefully tear the material until you reach the roller tube. Follow the manufacturer's specific instructions.

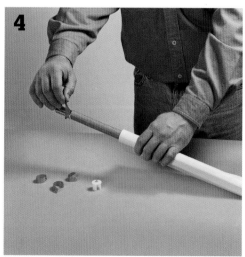

Remove the excess cardboard, and then remove the roller end from the tube. Cut the tube to length with a hacksaw (for metal tubes) or finetooth wood saw (for cardboard tubes).

5

Roll the shade material back up, and then push the roller end inward and replace the end cap.

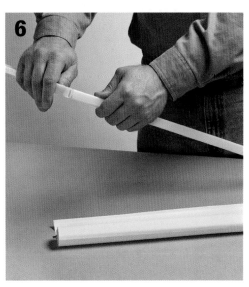

6

Cut the slat (that fits into hems) to length, according to manufacturer's instructions. For basic roller shades, you simply snap the slat apart at the desired location.

7

Position the first bracket flush with the upper front corner of the window frame, and mark its screw holes. Drill a pilot hole at each mark, hold the bracket in place, and then drive in the screws to secure it. Repeat for the other bracket, making sure the two brackets are level. Inset: slide the pin end of the head rail into the bracket on one end, and then slide the slatted end into the other bracket.

Dress Up Plain Roller Shades ▸

It's easy to dress up inexpensive roller shades. Simply add grommets to the lower edge for a designer detail. Follow the same basic instructions for installing curtain grommets on page 391.

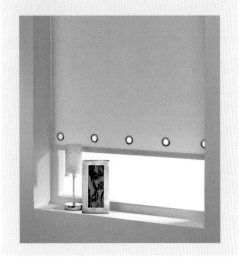

How to Install Blinds (Outside Mount)

To mount blinds outside the window frame, measure the width from the outside edges of the window frame and the height from 2 to 3" above to 2 to 3" below the frame. If the window doesn't have a frame, measure the opening and add a few inches on each side. Make a diagram of the measurements and refer to it when purchasing blinds to fit.

Position the first bracket as indicated by the diagram you made in step 1, and mark its screw holes. Use a stud finder to locate nearby studs. If a stud is in the bracket area, drill pilot holes at the marks and attach the bracket to the wall. If no stud is available, use an awl to make a small hole at each mark, and then drive a self-tapping hollow wall anchor into each. Finally, drive a screw into each anchor.

Shoot a line with a laser level or use a standard level to draw a level line across the wall from the top edge of the bracket to the planned position for the second bracket. Position the second bracket and fasten it to the wall as described in step 2.

Lift the blinds into place and install them in the brackets on the wall. Follow the manufacturer's instructions to ensure a secure fit.

How to Install a Mounting Board (Outside Mount)

Many valances and simple stationary shades are mounted on boards instead of window hardware. The mounting board is covered with fabric; then the valance is styled to the board. The board size depends on the strength required (based on fabric weight × span)

Cut window treatment fabric to fit around a 1 × 2 board, adding 3" to the length and 1" to the width. Center the board on the wrong side of the fabric and staple it to the long edge, spacing staples about 8" apart. Wrap fabric under the board, and then fold under ⅜" on the long edge and staple.

Miter fabric at the board end corners. Finger press and staple miters in place. Fold under excess fabric at ends and staple near the fold.

Mark screw holes for the angle irons on the bottom of the board, positioning them within 1" of each end and at 45" intervals or less. Snip a hole in the fabric at screw positions using scissors, then predrill screw holes into the board at marked locations.

Hold the board level at the desired placement and mark the screw holes on the wall. Predrill holes into the wall studs, and then fasten brackets to the wall with 1½" flathead screws using a handheld screwdriver or drill.

Align the board onto brackets, and then secure board with ¾" screws using a handheld screwdriver or drill.

Option: Mounting boards can also be installed flat against the wall for Roman shades, or secured to the top of the window frame (inset), if an inside mount is preferable.

Window Shade Styles

Window shades control light, provide privacy, can be used alone or with curtains, and are one of the most affordable window treatments to make—fabric cost is minimal and hardware is inexpensive. Window shades also fit close to the window and help keep your house cool in the summer and warm in the winter, improving your home's energy efficiency.

Dress up traditional shades with gathers, tabs, sophisticated tucks, complex layers, and bold color and pattern choices.

Tools & Materials ▸

Drapery pull (optional)
Decorator fabric(s)
Angle irons with screws
    or nuts and bolts
Drapery lining (optional)
⅜ or ½" plastic rings
Staple gun and staples
Mounting board
Screw eyes
Shade cord
White glue
Awning cleat

Depending on the project you choose, you may also need:
Roller kit (includes
    roller, mounting
    brackets, fusible
    backing, and
    hem stick)
Paper-backed
    fusible adhesive
Carpenter's square
Awl

Iron and large
    pressing surface
Liquid fray preventer
    and small paintbrush
Decorative trim
Fabric glue
⅜ to ⅞" wooden dowel
½"- or ⅜"-wide flat
    metal weight bar,
    cut ½" shorter than
    the finished width
    of the shade

Graph paper
Round ball finials
    or drawer pulls
Paint and paintbrush
Masking tape
    or vinyl tape
Adding machine paper
Self-styling tape
Adhesive-backed hook
    and loop tape

Window shades are a beautiful, formal alternative to blinds. They can be customized with decorator fabric to complement your décor and draw attention to your windows.

Shade Styles to Consider

Roller shade: This traditional style can be customized with dynamic decorator fabric, tabs and decorative hardware, painted designs, tassels and pulls—the options are limitless!

Roman shade: These shades are raised and lowered by a system of cords and rings, which also cause them to pleat into soft folds when raised. Shown here are tucked (or "flat") roman shades.

Hobbled shade: Twice the length of a roman shade, excess fabric is taken up in permanent soft folds between each row of rings, giving the shade a bubbled look when lowered.

Butterfly shade: When drawn up, folds stack in the center and flare at the sides in this classic version of the Roman shade.

Cloud shade: Cut two to three times the width of the window, then shirred across the upper edge to create a soft heading, the lower edge of cloud shades fall into gentle poufs.

Balloon shade: Cut two to two and a half times the width of the window, fullness is folded into oversized inverted pleats at the heading and lower edge. This shade has permanent poufs at the bottom.

Coach shade: Two fabrics fused together roll up around a wooden pole at the bottom and flip over the mounting board to form a valance.

Roller Shades

Roller shades are the most common of all shade styles—but that's because they work! Roller shades provide total privacy, they're affordable, and they're easy to install and operate. This style can be beautifully decorative as well, especially when made with the fabric of your choice and designer details, such as a sculpted bottom edge, decorative trim, or painted motifs.

Roller kits, which are sold in fabric and craft stores, include the roller, mounting hardware, hem stick, fusible adhesive strips, and fusible backing. Some shades have a pulley system with a cord for raising and lowering the shade; others operate by means of a spring inside the roller. Use firmly woven, lightweight to medium-weight fabric; avoid glazed, stain-resistant, or water-repellant fabrics, because these finishes will prevent the fabric from bonding well to the fusible backing. Before you make your shade, test a scrap of the fabric with the fusible backing to ensure a good bond.

Add customized details and bold drapery fabric to best complement decorative (and functional!) window shades.

Cutting Guide ▸

	Length	Width
Decorator Fabric	Finished length + 14"	Finished width + 2"
Fusible Backing	Finished length + 12"	Finished width + 1"

How to Make a Roller Shade

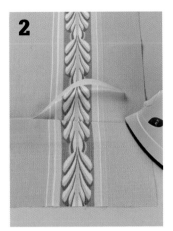

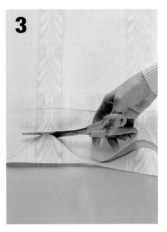

Install the mounting brackets and roller inside or outside the window frame (see page 359), and measure the roller to determine the finished width of the shade. Steam-press the fabric thoroughly to prevent shrinkage during fusing. Cut the fabric and use a carpenter's square to ensure square corners.

Turn up the lower edge of the fabric 6" from the bottom, wrong sides together, and press a crease. Turn the lower edge back down, right sides together 1½" from the first crease, forming a pocket. Using a ⅜"-wide strip of fusible adhesive, fuse the upper edge of the pocket closed. Fuse the backing to the wrong side of the fabric, following the manufacturer's instructions. Center on the width of the fabric.

Mark the finished width on the shade backing. Square off the upper and lower edges using a carpenter's square. Draw a symmetrically shaped, decorative hem. Cut along the marked lines.

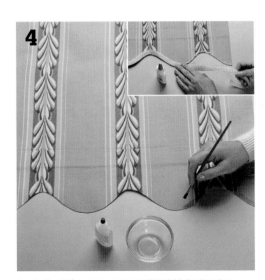

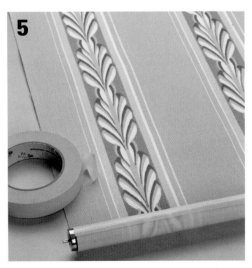

Apply liquid fray preventer or diluted fabric glue along the cut edges using a small paintbrush. Apply decorative trim along the cut edge of the shaped hem using fabric glue, if desired (inset).

Mark a straight line down the center of the roller and attach the shade to the roller by taping the upper edge in place along the marked line. Trim the hem stick to fit the pocket and slide in. Mount the roller on the brackets.

Roller Shade with Tabbed Hems

Adding a tabbed hem and decorative dowel to the bottom of a roller shade increases the stability and detail of the standard roller shade shape. Select a dowel with decorative finials that are larger than the tab openings to hold the shade bottom securely in place. Paint or stain the dowel in a color that complements your fabric before insertion.

A tabbed hem and decorative rod at the bottom of a window shade is one creative way to dress up this standard window treatment.

Cutting Guide ▸

	Length	Width
Decorator Fabric	Finished length + 14"	Finished width + 2"
Fusible Backing	Finished length + 12"	Finished width + 1"
Tabs (desired number)	4½"	3"
Facing Strip Note: cut from decorator fabric after it has been fused to backing	2"	Finished Width

How to Make a Roller Shade with a Tabbed Hem

Cut tabs. Follow steps 1 to 3 on page 363, then cut the 2" facing strip from the lower edge of the fused shade.

Fold the long edges of the tab to the center, wrong sides together; press. Fuse in place using a ⅜" strip of fusible web. Repeat for all tabs.

Fold the tabs in half; pin to the lower edge of the shade on the right side, with the outer edges of the end tabs even with the outer edge of the shade and spaced evenly. Baste in place. Pin facing to the lower edge of the shade, right sides together, matching raw edges and hemmed ends. Stitch a ⅜" seam through all layers.

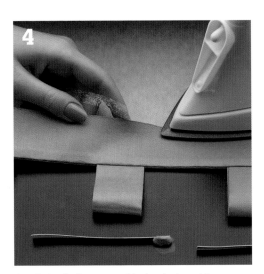

Turn facing to the wrong side; fuse in place at the upper edge and ends of facing using fusible web. Cut the dowel ⅛" shorter than the finished width of the shade. Paint the dowel and finials, or apply stain and clear finish.

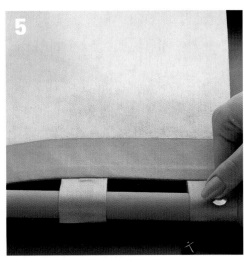

Insert the dowel into the tabs. Attach the finials. Secure with thumbtacks on the back sides of the first and last tabs. Mount and install the roller shade on the brackets.

Coach Shades

These shades recall the window coverings on early twentieth-century stagecoaches; when installed in the home, however, coach shades are quite elegant and versatile. Fabric rolls up from the bottom and is controlled with loops of cord. Pair the shade with a top treatment to hide the mechanism, or make a shade and valance all in one.

In this project, one fabric shows on the face of the shade; the other shows on the valance and the bottom roll. Two cords, strung through screw eyes on the underside of the mounting board, raise and lower the shade and wrap around an awning cleat to hold the shade at the desired level. Use firmly woven, lightweight to medium-weight fabric and avoid glazed or treated fabrics, which will not bond well with the fusible adhesive. Before you begin, cut, cover, and secure the mounting board above the window frame using angle irons and nuts and bolts. Measure for the finished size of the shade and remove the nuts and bolts that hold the mounting board to the angle irons.

This coach shade plays a playful role in this aquatic-themed bathroom. Tied only in the center, the shade bends to create a relaxed, casual mood.

Cutting Guide ▸

	Length	Width
Decorator Fabrics	Finished length + 20"	Finished width + 1"
Fusible Backing	Finished length + 20"	Finished width + 1"
Cord 1	Finished length × 3 + finished width	
Cord 2	Finished length × 3	

How to Make a Coach Shade

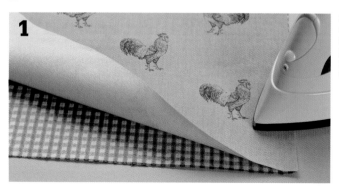

1

Fuse the adhesive to the wrong side of one of the fabrics, following the manufacturer's instructions. Remove the paper backing. Fuse the second fabric to the first, wrong sides together. Allow the fabric to cool completely.

Mark the finished width on the shade. Square off the upper and lower edges, using a carpenter's square. Draw a decorative, symmetrical upper edge (this will become the bottom of the valance). Cut along the marked lines and apply liquid fray preventer or diluted fabric glue along the cut edges. Glue decorative trim to the valance edge on the side that will face the room. Drill pilot holes and insert three screw eyes, centered on the underside of the mounting board. Insert one screw eye 1" from the end on the side of the shade where you want the cords to hang. Insert the other two screw eyes 3" from each end. Staple the shade over the top of a mounting board, allowing the desired length to hang forward for the valance. Pierce the fabric with an awl over the mounting holes.

Cut the dowel to the shade width, paint if desired, and staple the shade bottom to the dowel with the back of the shade facing up. Roll the shade around the dowel until the shade is the desired finished length. Staple along the back of the dowel.

Tie a small loop in one end of both Cords 1 and 2, leaving 6" tails. Staple the cords to the top of the mounting board with the loops over the bolt holes.

Mount the shade on the angle irons, making sure the bolts go through the cord loops. Just before tightening the bolts, secure the loops with two or three knots.

Wrap the cords under the rolled dowel, up over the shade front, and through the screw eyes. String Cord 1 also through the opposite screw eye and both cords through the end screw eye on the draw side. Knot the cords together just outside the last screw eye. Attach a small drapery pull to the ends. Secure an awning cleat to the edge of the window frame or to the wall. Pull gently on the cords to raise the shade. Wind the cord around the clean to hold in position.

Flat Roman Shades

Flat Roman shades are tailored window treatments that are flat and smooth when down. When raised, however, Roman shades pleat crisply instead of roll. The shade design is minimal—lining provides added body, prevents fabric from fading, and creates a uniform appearance from the outside. A system of evenly spaced rings through which cords are run on the back of the shade make it possible to raise and lower the shade. Rings are spaced in even columns and rows so the shade will fold neatly at regular intervals when raised.

Choose sturdy decorator fabric for a crisp look. Roman shades show off large, allover prints nicely, but all patterns and styles work. Mount Roman shades on a board either inside or outside the window frame. For the project shown, follow the directions for installing a mounting board on page 359 before you begin.

With a large pattern and warm, earthy colors, these tailored shades are the perfect solution for these challenging large windows.

Cutting Guide ▸

	Length	Width
Decorator Fabric	Finished length + 7"	Finished width + 2"
Lining Fabric	Finished length + 3½"	Finished width

How to Make a Flat Roman Shade

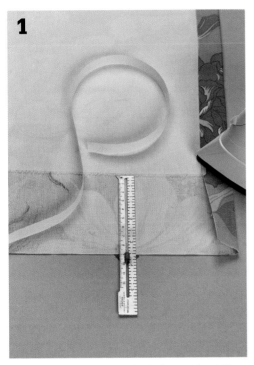

Press under 1" on the sides of the shade. Cut strips of ¾" paper-backed fusible adhesive the length of each side. Turn back the hem and place the strips near the cut edge. Press over the strips to fuse them to the hem allowance, following the manufacturer's directions. Place the lining over the shade fabric, wrong sides together, with the lower edge of the lining 3½" above the lower edge of the shade fabric. Tuck the lining under the side hems. Remove the paper backing from the fusible adhesive and press to fuse the hems in place.

Press under ½" at the lower edge, then press under 3" to form the hem pocket. Pin the hem in place. Edgestitch along the top fold of the hem through all layers. On the lining side, draw a line across the top of the shade at the finished length. Draw a second line 1½" above it (equal to the board projection). Cut off excess fabric along the top line. Pin the layers together and finish the upper edges with wide zigzag stitches or serging.

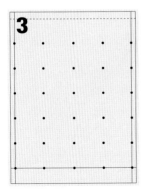

Finished width of shade - 1½" / 12 =	# of spaces between columns
# of spaces between columns + 1 =	# of columns
Finished length of shade (from top of hem to upper marked line) / 8" =	# of spaces between rows
Finished length of shade (from top of hem to upper marked line) / # of spaces =	Distance between rows

Diagram the back of the shade on graph paper, indicating the finished length and width. Mark the hem 3" from the lower edge. Plan the locations of rings in columns spaced 8 to 12" apart, with the outer columns ¾" from the edges of the shade. Space them in even horizontal rows 5 to 8" apart, with the bottom row at the top of the hem and the top row on the marked line. Mark the placement for the rings on the lining side of the shade, following the diagram. Pin horizontally through both layers of fabric at each mark.

(continued)

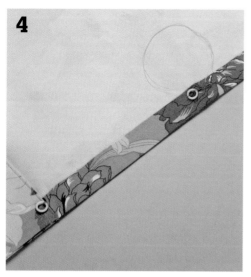

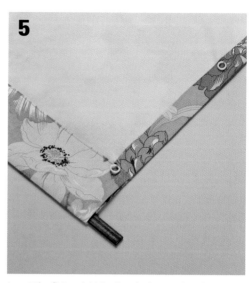

Stitch a ring at each mark through both layers of fabric, stitching either by machine or by hand. Reinforce the rings in the bottom row with extra stitches because they carry the weight of the shade.

Insert the flat weight bar into the hem pocket. Slipstitch the side openings closed.

Staple the shade to the top of the mounting board, aligning the marked line to the front edge of the board. Drill pilot holes and insert screw eyes, centered on the underside of the mounting board, aligning them to the columns of rings.

On the side where you want the cords to hang, run cord through the first column of rings, through the top screw eye, and at least halfway down the side. Cut the cord at the desired length and tie a nonslip knot at the bottom ring. Repeat for each column in order, running the cords also through the previous screw eyes. Apply glue to the knots for security. Install the mounting board.

8

Adjust the cords with the shade down so the tension on all cords is equal. Tie the cords in a knot just below the first screw eye. Braid the cords, insert them through a drapery pull, if desired, and knot and trim the ends. Secure an awning cleat to the edge of the window frame or on the wall. Pull gently on the cords to raise the shade and wind the cord around the cleat to hold in position. Train the shade by raising it and pulling the excess fabric forward to form gentle rolls. Leave the shade in the raised position for a few days to set the folds.

Roman Shade Variations ▸

Flat roman shades can be customized in countless creative ways. Pair them with matching goblet-pleated draperies (left) or add a beautifully shaped hem with decorative trim or tassels, as in the example at right. Mounted on French doors, these shades sit close to the glass but clear most of it when raised, giving the illusion of added height to the room's centerpiece.

Butterfly Shades

A butterfly shade has the smoothness of a flat Roman shade with draped softness at the lower edge. As the shade is drawn up, the folds stack in the center and flare at the sides, creating a butterfly effect. Choose firmly woven lightweight to medium-weight decorator fabric for this project. Butterfly shades should be mounted so the finished length from the top of the mounting board to the highest point of the hem is evenly divisible by six. The swagged fabric at the bottom of the shade will hang below the sill.

Before you begin, cut the mounting board and cover it with fabric. Secure angle irons to the bottom of the board, near the ends, and in the center, if necessary. Mount the board, centered above the window frame, as on page 259. Measure for the finished size of the shade, and then remove the screws that hold the mounting board to the angle irons, leaving the angle irons in the wall.

Cutting Guide ›

	Length	Width
Decorator Fabric	Finished length + 26" + mounting board length	Finished width + 2× mounting board width + 2"
Lining Fabric	Cut length of decorator fabric + 1¼"	Cut width of decorator fabric − 3"

When your view isn't beautiful, a well-dressed window is especially important. This plaid shade is mounted inside the deep frame, showing off the decorative wood trim. Bead trim along the lower edge of the shade draws attention to the dramatic curve of the fabric.

How to Make a Butterfly Shade

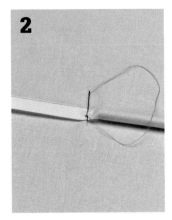

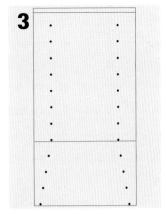

Mark a line across the wrong side of the lining 26⅝" from the bottom. Fold the lining, right sides together, along the marked line; pin. Stitch ⅝" from the fold, forming the dowel pocket. Press the pocket toward the bottom. Insert the dowel into the pocket and slide it to the center of the lining.

Tack through the dowel pocket at the ends of the dowel to hold the dowel in place. Press under ¾" twice on the sides of the shade fabric. Place the lining on the shade fabric, wrong sides together, matching edges; with the lining tucked under the side hems, pin. Blindstitch side hems. Press up 1" of the lower edge twice; pin. Stitch. Finish upper edge. Mark a line from the upper edge a distance equal to the projection of the mounting board.

Mark placement for two columns of rings, each positioned one-sixth of the shade width from the sides. Space rings 6" apart vertically. Place two rings at the dowel; top rings should be 6" below the upper marked line. Mark placement for two rings in the center of the lower hem, at the edge of the side hems. Space the remaining three rings evenly between the dowel pocket ring and the bottom ring.

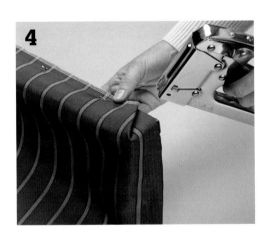

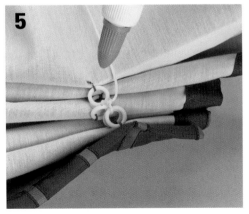

Center the shade on top of the mounting board, aligning the marked line to the top front edge of the board. Staple the shade to the mounting board; wrap the sides over the ends of the board and staple in place forming squared corners. Drill pilot holes and insert screw eyes, centered on the underside of the mounting board, aligning them to the columns of rings. Install a third screw eye 1" from the end of the board on the draw side. Run cords as in step 7 on page 370.

Tie the lower five rings of each row together securely. Apply glue to the knots and ends of the cords to prevent them from slipping. Reattach the mounting board and finish as in step 8 on page 371.

Cloud Shades

A cloud shade is gathered across the top and hangs as a softly shirred, translucent panel when lowered full length. When raised, the bottom of the shade forms soft, cloudlike poufs. Cloud shade headings are gathered or softly pleated using a styling tape. Several styles are available; select a style for the amount of fullness your shade will require. This shade is also made extra long to create the "cloud" effect. Space poufs evenly or create one large pouf in the center, framed with smaller poufs. An odd number of poufs generally looks more appealing than an even number. Choose lightweight, soft fabric for a cloud shade. Lining is not necessary.

Before you begin, cut and cover the mounting board, and secure with angle irons above the window frame. Remove the screws that hold the mounting board to the angle irons, leaving the angle irons on the wall.

Ring Placement ▸

Width of hemmed panel - 2" / # of poufs desired =	Distance between ring columns
Length of shade (top of hem to bottom of styling tape) / 8" =	# of spaces between rows (round up)
Length of shade (top of hem to bottom of styling tap) / # of spaces between rows =	Distance between rows

Use the table above to determine the placement of rings. Mark ring placement on the panel. Stitch a ring at each mark through both layers of fabric, with a machine or by hand. Do not stitch rings at the base of the styling tape. Reinforce the rings in the bottom row with extra stitches.

Cutting Guide ▸

	Length	Width
Decorator Fabric	Finished length + 15"	Finished width + (2 × projection of the mounting board) × fullness required for styling tape + 4"
Weight Rod Cover	1" larger than rod circumference	Finished width + 1"

The softly gathered, casual appearance of this cloud shade and the tone-on-tone color scheme make for a quiet, relaxing living area.

How to Make a Cloud Shade

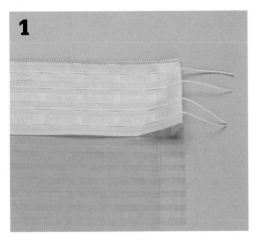

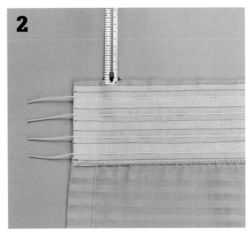

Seam panel as necessary using French seams. Press under 1" twice on the sides and stitch. Press under a 1" double-fold hem pocket at the lower edge. Stitch along the upper edge of pocket. Cut styling tape to the width of the hemmed panel plus 2". Turn under 1" on the ends, keeping the cords free. Place the tape right side up on the right side of the panel, aligning the lower edge of the tape to the upper edge of the panel. Finish the edges together using overcast stitches.

Fold the tape and panel to the wrong side, forming a ¼" fold above the upper edge of the tape. Press the fold. Pin the tape in place and stitch to the panel, stitching next to the cords. Stitch all stitching lines in the same directions to avoid ripples.

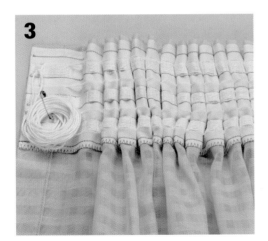

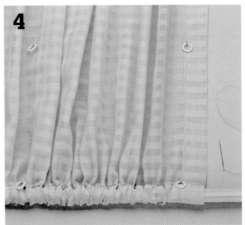

Knot the cords together or in pairs at each end of the styling tape. At one end, pull evenly on the cords to gather the fabric, adjusting the width of the heading to the finished width of the shade, including returns. Knot the cords together to close the shade. Cut off excess cords or wrap them in a circle and safety-pin them behind the heading. Fold the weight rod cover strip in half lengthwise, wrong sides together. Stitch along the long side; turn the tube right side out. Insert the rod and stitch the ends closed.

Insert the covered rod into the hem pocket, distributing fullness evenly. Stipstitch the hem ends closed. Tack the hem to the rod cover at the ends and near each ring to hold spacing. Cut the hook and loop tape to the finished width of the shade; attach the hook side to the mounting board and the loop side to the upper edge of the styling tape. Follow steps 7 and 8 on pages 370 to 371 to finish. In step 8, leave a long tail at each bottom knot. Using the tails, tie together the bottom three rings of each column to secure the bottom poufs.

Balloon Shades

Tailored box pleats meld with luxurious poufs to create the ever-popular balloon shade. With its split personality, a balloon shade can be equally at home in a living room, a breakfast nook, or a child's bedroom. Box pleats give this shade controlled fullness when lowered and a billowy, soft effect when raised. Evenly spaced pleats should be about 12" apart. Lightweight, soft fabrics work best for the gentle gathers of this shade. Lining is optional. Mount the shade on a mounting board outside the window frame. Attach the mounting board to the wall, then remove the screws that hold the board to the angle irons, leaving the angle irons on the wall.

The gentle swags that form at the bottom of this balloon shade as it is raised accent the structured architecture of the room.

Cutting Guide ▸

	Length	Width
Decorator Fabric	Finished length + 12" + projection of mounting board	2 × finished width + 4" (do not cut until step 2)
Facing Strip	2"	Finished width + 1"
Adding Machine Paper		Decorator fabric cut width

How to Make a Balloon Shade

1

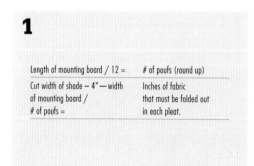

Length of mounting board / 12 =	# of poufs (round up)
Cut width of shade − 4" — width of mounting board / # of poufs =	Inches of fabric that must be folded out in each pleat.

Cut the strip of adding machine paper; this will be a pattern to help determine the pleats. Mark a 2" hem allowance at each end of the pattern. Mark pleat lines, as determined by the chart above. Fold the pattern into pleats and measure to check for accuracy.

2

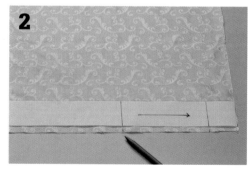

Seam fabric widths together. Trim the seam allowances to ¼", finish them together, and press to one side. Place the pattern on the fabric, aligning the seams to points in the pattern where they will be hidden in pleats, and mark the fabric at the pattern ends. Cut the fabric to the width of the pattern. Press under 1" twice on the sides of the panel and stitch the hems. Place the pattern on the shade at the lower edge. Mark the pleat fold lines. Repeat at the upper edge.

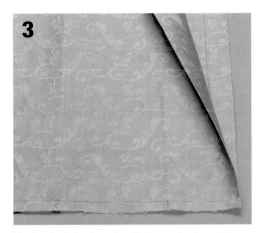

3

Pin the pleats in place along the lower edge; the side hems will be hidden under the half-pleats at the sides of the shade. Stitch ½" from the lower edge to secure the pleats.

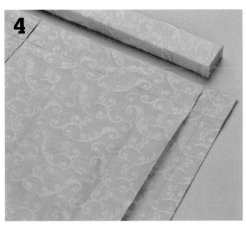

4

Pin the pleats in place along the upper edge. Extend the hemmed edges away from the pleat fold a distance equal to the projection of the mounting board. Stitch a distance from the upper edge equal to the projection of the mounting board. Finish the upper edges together. Pin pleats in place from top to bottom. The shade will be slightly wide at the top. Press pleats. Press ½" under on the long edge of the facing strip. Pin the raw edge to the bottom of the shade, right sides together, with the ends extending equally. Stitch a ½" seam.

5

Press the seam toward the facing. Turn the ends over the seam allowance, then turn the facing to the wrong side. Edgestitch along the fold, forming a weight rod pocket.

6

Length of shade (top of the pocket to stitching line at the top) / 6" =	# of spaces between rows (round up)
Length of shade (top of the pocket to stitching line at the top) / # of spaces between rows =	Inches between rows

Mark the placement for the rings in columns at the side hems and at the center of each pleat. Mark the bottom row at the upper edge of the pocket and space rings according to the chart above. Stitch rings to the shade at the marks, taking care not to catch the pleat fabric in the stitches. Insert the weight bar into the pocket. Slipstitch the ends closed. Staple the shade to the mounting board; wrap the sides over the ends and staple in place.

7

Finish as in steps 6 to 8 on pages 370 to 371. In step 6, insert the end eye screws 1" from the ends of the mounting board. In step 7, leave a long tail at each bottom knot. Using the tails, tie together the bottom three rings of each column to secure the bottom poufs.

Curtain Styles

Before you decide what style of curtain will work the best for you, consider the functional requirements of the room. For example, lined curtains that extend above and beyond the window block the most light, and may be the best choice for bedrooms. Use the same style with a sheer fabric in a sitting room or breakfast nook to invite light to pour in, while protecting your privacy. Café curtains frame a window without interfering with the sunlight that makes a kitchen so inviting. Experiment with color, fabric choice, and pairing curtains with blinds, shades, or top treatments to best suit the form and function of any space.

Tools & Materials ▸

Decorator fabric	Curtain hardware,	**Optional Materials**	Fusible interfacing
Lining fabric (optional)	as needed (grommets,	Swinging extender	Grommet heading tape
Decorative rod	decorative hooks, clip-	rod set	Decorative rod
or mounting board	on or sew-on rings)	Safety pins	with finials or elbows
Installation hardware	Drapery weights (for	Double-stick	Tieback holders
Stapler and staples	floor-length curtains)	carpet tape	or wooden blocks
Sewing notions			

Curtain colors and patterns affect a room's overall feel dramatically. Dark colors absorb light and therefore pull a room in, making it feel smaller (left photo). This is a good effect for formal dining areas or spaces you wish to feel cozy or warm. White curtains reflect light, making rooms feel bright and therefore more spacious (right photo). This effect is good for areas you would like to feel clean, cheerful, social, or contemporary.

Styles to Consider

Basic curtains are panels with clip-on or sew-on rings. There are many styles of rings and clips. Depending on the rings or clips you pick, the curtains can hang from a rod or from high-tension string.

Tab-top curtains are panels of fabric trimmed with tabs, loops, or ties that slip over decorative rods. They can be pulled open and closed, but the tabs don't always slide smoothly. Attach tabs to rings or clips to remedy this problem.

Rod-pocket curtains are held in place by inserting a curtain rod into a pocket sewn into the header (the top of the curtain). Although they can be opened and closed fairly easily, they are mostly considered stationary because it is time consuming to arrange and rearrange their pleats each time they are moved. Many sheers are constructed with rod pockets.

Café curtains cover only a portion of the window—usually only the lower half. They're often made of sheer fabric and hung by rings on small metal rods mounted inside or directly on the window frame. Café curtains create a stylish look but don't interfere with the light or view from the window. They can be opened and closed easily, but by design they are not handled often.

Stationary curtains don't close at all and serve no function beyond decoration. Typically, they consist of one or two panels—with or without valances—hanging on each side of a window. Stationary curtains are easy to make, easy to hang, and inexpensive because they use so little fabric.

Hanging Curtains

Hanging curtains is a simple project that can be finished quickly and cleanly with careful measurements and preparations. Before you begin, decide whether you'd like your curtains to open and close, or if they will be stationary curtains; this will help determine what kind of hardware you will select. Also, pay careful attention to the finish and style of decorator hardware to ensure a good match with other hardware in your room.

Tools & Materials ▸

Curtain rods
Curtain
Sheer
Decorative curtain clips
Decorative curtain rod
  hardware
Self-tapping hollow
  wall anchors
Sheer rod hardware
Painter's tape
Tape measure
Drill

Choose your curtains and hardware carefully to ensure a smooth installation. Here, the rod-pocket curtain rod needed to be shorter than the decorative rod so that only the decorative rod is seen in the finished installation. Planning out such details will save you time and money.

How to Hang Curtains

1

Measure the height and width of the window. Make a quick diagram of the window and note the measurements you took. Before purchasing curtains or hardware, decide where you want the curtains to start and stop, and indicate those measurements on your diagram. Attach the brackets for the sheer rod. Place the sheer rod and check for level. Adjust if necessary.

2

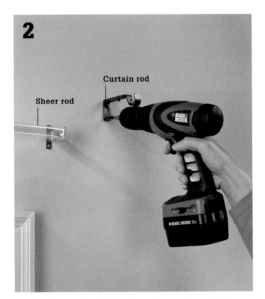

Curtain rod

Sheer rod

Attach the brackets for the decorative curtain rod a few inches outside and above the sheer brackets. Use wall anchors if the bracket is not located over a stud.

3

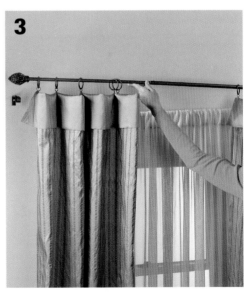

Place the curtain over the sheer rod, and then place the rod for the sheer into the mounting plate. Repeat for the decorative curtains and rod.

Draped Window Treatments

Soft, draping window treatments beautify your window as they invite light to spill into the room, and can be made quickly from sheer or lightweight reversible fabrics. These treatments are made without side hems or seams, so it's important to use fabrics with neat, narrow selvages. Lace fabrics with finished side edges work nicely for this project. The number of fabric widths needed vary from window to window; experiment with inexpensive fabric to determine the number of lengths you'll need before you begin.

Mount this style of treatment on a decorative rod just above the window frame, or tie the fabric to decorative knobs or hooks for a unique flair and innovative draping style.

Tools & Materials ▸

Sheer to lightweight reversible fabric with narrow selvages or lace with finished edges
Decorative rod or pole

Mounting brackets, or decorative hooks or knobs
Decorative tieback holders
Coordinating ribbon or cord

Draped window treatments have a casual feel and simplistic beauty. Add drama by using heavier fabrics or lush silks.

Cutting Guide ▸

	Length
Pole or rod-mounted, to puddle on the floor	2× desired finished length + 40"
Pole or rod-mounted, free-hanging straight lower edges	Hang a length of twill tape over the pole to desired length with the lower edges even. Cut fabric 2" longer than tape.
Hook or knob-mounted, to puddle on the floor	2× desired finished length + 40"
Hook or knob-mounted, free-hanging uneven lower edges	2× desired finished length + 2"

How to Install a Draped Window Treatment on a Rod or Pole

Press cut edge under ½" twice; stitch to make double-fold hem. Repeat for opposite cut end, pressing fabric in opposite direction.

Hang fabric over rod, and then form two panels, with lower edges even and hem allowances facing the window.

How to Install a Draped Window Treatment on Hooks or Knobs

Install decorative hooks or knobs on or just above the window frame; predrill holes to avoid splitting woodwork and use appropriate anchors if installing hanger bolts into drywall. Position one at each outer edge, with the remaining hooks or knobs evenly spaced. Tie a decorative cord or ribbon to each hook or knob, leaving long tails.

Hem the cut edges of fabric, as in step 1, above. Fold the fabric in half, forming two panels, with the lower edges even and hem allowances facing the window. Grasp the outer edge at the fold; tie to the hook or knob, 2 to 3" from the fold. Repeat at the opposite side and again at the center. Repeat for any additional panels.

Draped Window Treatment Finishing Styles

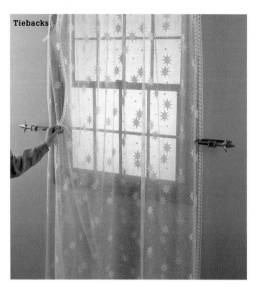

Tiebacks

Install tieback holders at the desired height, even with outer edge of the window treatment. Grasp the outer edge of the front fabric panel even with the holder.

Gather up fabric to the opposite edge at a 45° angle toward the floor. Secure gathered panel to holder. Repeat for the opposite side of back panel, if desired. This finished look can be used with draped treatments on knobs or hooks as well.

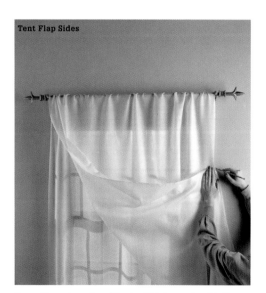

Tent Flap Sides

Grasp the outer edge of the front fabric panel; pull to the opposite side, adjusting position of the pulled-back edge as desired. Mark the wall for placement of tieback holder or tenter hook; mark fabric edge with pin.

Install the tieback holder or tenter hook; tie the fabric edge to the holder using ribbon or cord. Pull back and secure the opposite edge of the back panel, if desired.

Center Knot

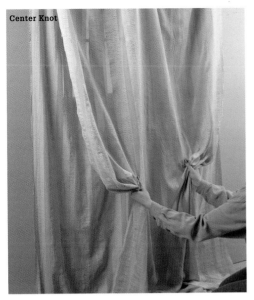

Grasp outer edges of the front fabric panel about 18" below the desired knot position. Gather up fabric on each side toward the center, and upward toward the desired knot position.

Tie a knot in the gathered front panel; adjust sides of the panel above the knot as desired.

Side Knots

Install tenter hooks at desired knot height, even with the outer edge of the window treatment. Grasp the outer edge of the front fabric panel even with the holder.

Gather up fabric to the opposite edge at a 45° angle from floor. Tie a knot in the panel; secure the knot to a tenter hook. Make a side knot for the opposite side of the back panel, if desired.

No-Sew Side Panels

For a no-sew window treatment with a light, unstructured appearance, drape soft, lightweight fabric panels over swinging extenders or crane rods, to create a deep valance and elegant floor puddles. This treatment is suitable for full coverage on narrow windows or as side panels on wider windows.

Swinging extender rods are mounted to a bracket on one end and can swing out to expose the window view. Decorative utility crane rods are available from specialty window hardware suppliers, through decorators, or sometimes at antique shops or thrift stores. Choose a soft, lightweight, reversible fabric that has an attractive or minimal selvage. If the fabric ravels, you may want to finish the lower edge of the drapery panel.

Side panels like this are a perfect project for the decorator with no sewing experience and drape beautifully around any window that needs dressing up.

No-sew Side Panels Cutting Guide ▶

	Length	Width
Decorator Fabric	Top of rod to the floor + 60"	Width of fabric

How to Make Draped Side Panels

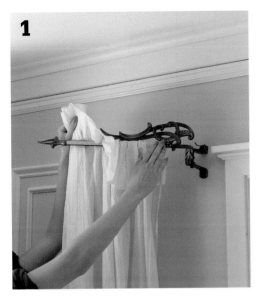

1

Cut and apply double-stick tape to the back side of the rod. Drape the upper edge of fabric over the rod, with about 4" folded to the back side; secure fabric to the tape, distributing fullness evenly.

2

Gather fabric loosely about 36" below the rod, using hands; fold the bottom of the panel up and over the rod, with hand gathers at the top of the rod forming an 18" valance.

3

Arrange the valance, distributing the fullness evenly and folding in the selvages.

4

Arrange the bottom of the panel on the floor, draping it loosely and concealing the raw edges and selvages of the fabric.

Basic Curtains

Flat-panel curtains are one of the most basic, easy-to-make window treatment styles. Surprisingly, they are also one of the most versatile. Adjust fullness or ring placement for very different looks, from flat to neatly folded; from controlled dips to softly swooping curves. Fabric selection also plays a large role in your finished look: Firm, medium-weight fabrics create a simple, tailored look with an upper edge that dips gracefully. Sheer, lightweight fabrics swing gracefully and fall in soft puddles. Choose to line or not line your panels for privacy and light filtration, depending upon the needs of your room. Hang curtains from the rod with clip-on or sew-on curtain rings, which are available in many styles. Whatever your window treatment needs, many different looks can be achieved with these simple panels.

For a simple, controlled look, only one and one-half times fullness is used for basic curtains.

Fabric Fullness & Hardware Spacing ▸

For a flatter panel, 1½-times fullness is used (left), meaning the width of the curtain measures 1½-times the width of the rod. For a fuller panel, use 2-times fullness or more (right).

For a controlled look along the top of the curtain, use more rings and space them closer together (left). For a soft look, use few rings spaced farther apart (right).

Cutting Guide ▸

	Length	Width
Decorator Fabric	Finished length + 22 to 28" (depending on desired floor puddle)	Finished width × desired fullness

How to Sew a Curtain Panel

Unlined panel. Seam the fabric widths, if more than one width is desired for the panel. Press under 1" twice at the lower edge of the panel; stitch a double-fold hem. Repeat for a 1" double-fold hem at the upper edge, then at the sides.

Plan and pin-mark the spacing for the rings or grommets at the top of the curtain panel. As shown opposite, if fewer rings or grommets are used, spaced farther apart, more fabric drapes between them. For a more controlled look, use more rings or grommets, spaced closer together.

Check the drape of the panel by securing it at pin marks to the side of an ironing board, with markings spaced the desired distance apart. Adjust the number of rings or grommets and the spacing between them, if necessary. Use an even number of grommets if a rod will be inserted through them.

Attach the grommets to the top of the panel at the markings, following the manufacturer's directions. Insert hooks into the grommets, or attach sew-on or clip-on rings. Hang panels from the decorative rod.

Arrange the fabric to puddle onto the floor, if desired.

Grommet Curtains

Flat curtain panels with grommets in the top hem can be hung from a decorative rod with cording laced through the grommets or with fancy S-hooks. Grommet curtains with large grommets can be speared by the rod, as in the project shown here. In this technique, it's important to have an even number of grommets so both sides of the curtain turn toward the wall. How close or far the grommets are spaced to one another is completely up to you: wide spacing will allow the curtain to slouch between grommets, closer spacing will hold the upper edge in a straighter line, or use grommet tape, which determines the grommet spacing for you. Use medium-weight fabric for this project.

Cutting Guide ▶

	Length	Width
Decorator Fabric	Finished length + lower hem allowance + 2"	Grommet tape + 6"
Grommet Tape	Standard	Finished width × 2. Measure this length of tape: you must have an even number of grommets and must begin and end 2" beyond a space tab on each edge.

These grommet curtains combine sheers and sun-blocking panels for a multipurpose window treatment. The casual puddling on the floor adds to the carefree attitude.

How to Make Grommet Curtains

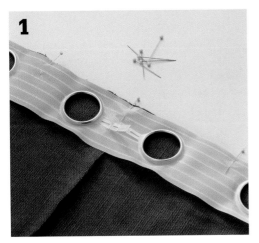

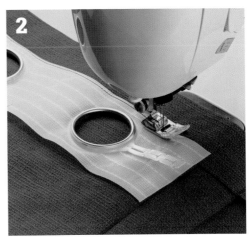

Seam the fabric widths together for each panel. Finish the seams together and press toward the side of the panel. Lay out grommet tape along the upper edge. Adjust placement so the seams fall between pairs of grommets. Mark the curtain panel 3" beyond the ends of the tape and trim excess fabric evenly down the sides. Press under the lower edge the full amount of the hem allowance. Unfold and turn the cut edge back to the fold line. Press. For floor-length curtains with more than one width, tack a drapery weight at the base of each seam. Refold lower edge and stitch. Press under 3" on each side, then unfold and turn the cut edge to the fold line. Press outer fold and repeat on the other side. Unfold side hems.

Turn under the upper edge 2" and press, then pin the grommet tape tabs up, on the wrong side of the panel, aligning the cut ends to the inner folds of the side hems, with the upper edge of the tape 1½" from the upper pressed fold. Stitch close to the top and bottom edges of the tape. Insert a drapery weight between the layers of the lower hem and tack in place. Stitch side hems, using a blindstitch or straight stitch. Straight stitch the hems over the grommet tape, keeping the spacer tabs free.

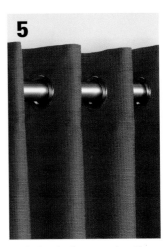

Trim away the fabric from inside the grommet openings.

Working on a flat surface, clip the decorative rings over the grommet openings, encasing the raw edges of the fabric.

Hook the plastic spacers together to ripple-fold the curtain. Insert the rod through the grommets and hang.

Loop-tab Curtains

Tab curtains draw the eye upward with the no-frill appeal of fabric tabs, loops, or ties that hold this style of curtain to the rod. Tab curtains effortlessly blend form and function and are easy to make and install. This style is not intended to be opened and closed repeatedly, as the friction would put too much strain on the tabs; usually, tab curtains are stationary panels on the side or are drawn to one side on a tieback to let light into the room. Tab curtains can be lined or unlined, depending on the fabric selection and the degree of light control and privacy required. Medium-weight fabrics will keep the upper edge of the curtain in a tailored line, whereas lightweight or sheer fabrics will drape elegantly between tabs.

Earth tones of cream, brown, and yellow create a calm and inviting space. Add button accents for understated detail.

Cutting Guide ▶

	Length	Width
Decorator Fabric	Finished length + bottom hem allowance + 3"	Finished width × 2
Tabs	Desired length (see step 2, below)	Desired tab width × 2 + 1"
Facing strip	3"	Cut width of curtain panel

How to Make Loop-tab Curtains

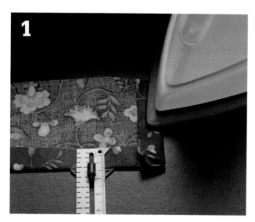

On the facing strip, press under ½" on the long side and each short end. Press double-fold lower and side hems of curtain. Stitch lower hem only.

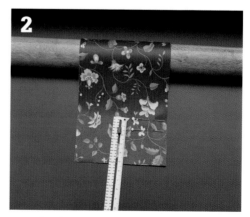

Determine the tab length by pinning a strip of fabric over the rod and marking the desired length with a pin. Add ½" for seam allowance. Cut tabs to the measured length and two times the desired width plus 1".

Fold each tab in half lengthwise, right sides together. Stitch ½" seam along cut edge; sew from one tab to the next, using continuous stitching. Cut tabs apart and turn right side out. Center the seam in back of each tab; press.

Fold each tab in half so the raw edges are aligned. Pin or baste tabs in place on the right side of the curtain, aligning raw edges of tabs with upper edge of curtain. Place end tabs even with side hem fold line of curtain.

Pin facing to the upper edge of the curtain, right sides together, so the raw edges are aligned and the tabs are sandwiched between the facing and the curtain. Stitch a ½" seam with the curtain side hems extended.

Press facing to the wrong side of the curtain so tabs extend upward. Fold curtain side hems under facing, covering the seam allowance. Stitch the side hems. Slipstitch facing to the curtain. Insert the curtain rod through tabs and hang.

Rod-pocket Curtains

Rod-pocket curtains are often chosen for a stationary window treatment that is understated and easy to sew. With ample fullness and a deep, ruffly heading, classic rod-pocket curtains take on a feminine, romantic appearance. With less fullness and a shorter heading, the look becomes tailored and robust. Or eliminate the heading ruffle altogether for relaxed curtains that fit snugly over the rod with a sleek, streamlined appearance.

The rod-pocket is the "tunnel" where the rod or pole is inserted; stitching lines at the top and bottom of the rod-pocket keep the rod in place. Rod-pocket curtains are extremely versatile and work with a wide variety of fabrics and rod styles. Use a rod with elbows to create returns, where the sides of the curtain wrap around the panel toward the wall. Or use a rod with finials for a decorative finish. Sheers or medium-weight fabrics drape and ruffle very differently, and lining can be added for light control and privacy.

Add a ruffle to the sides of panels for a romantic, airy flair.

Cutting Guide ▸

	Length	Width
Decorator Fabric	Finished length + lower hem allowance + depth of heading and rod pocket + ½"	Finished width × desired fullness

How to Make Rod-pocket Curtains

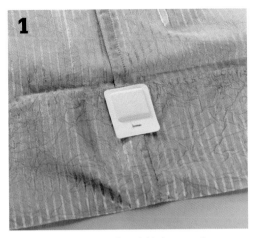

Seam fabric widths together. Finish the seam allowances together, then press toward the side of the panel. Press the lower edge the full amount of the hem allowance; unfold pressed edge and turn cut edge back, aligning it to the fold line. Press. If making floor-length curtains with more than one width, tack a drapery weight to the upper layer of fabric at the base of each seam. Refold the lower edge, encasing the weights. Pin. Stitch.

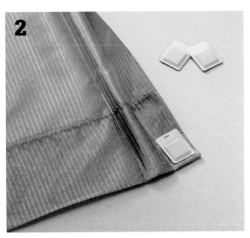

Press under 3" on one side, then unfold the pressed edge and turn the cut edge back, aligning it to the fold. Press. Tack a drapery weight between the layers of the lower hem. Refold the edge. Blindstitch. Repeat for each curtain panel side. Press under ½" on the upper edge. Then press under an amount equal to the rod-pocket depth plus the heading depth. Measure the distance from the wall to the center of the rod. Unfold the upper edge of the curtain on the return side of the panel. Measure from the side of the curtain a distance equal to this measurement; mark the center of the rod pocket on the right side.

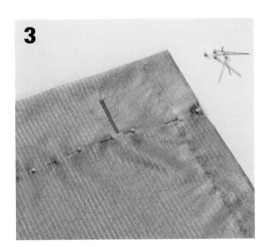

Cut a 1 ft. strip of fusible interfacing, 1" longer than the depth of the rod pocket. Fuse the strip to the wrong side of the curtain panel, centering it directly under the mark made in step 2. On the right side of the panel, stitch a buttonhole at the mark, from the top to the bottom of the rod pocket. Refold the upper edge of the panel along the pressed lines; pin.

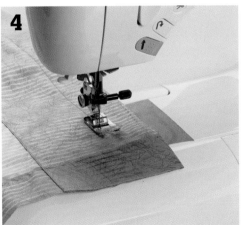

Stitch close to the first fold; stitch again at the depth of the heading using tape on the bed of the sewing machine as a stitching guide.

Tent-flap Curtains

Trim, tailored tent-flap curtains are great for bedrooms, bathrooms, or home theaters, where you want optimum light control and privacy. These flat panels are lined with decorative fabric because both sides show when the flaps are open, and are a great way to use two coordinating prints!

Tent flaps can be drawn back in a variety of ways and are typically secured by slipping a buttonhole, grommet, or metal ring over a button or small wall hook. Choose medium-weight, firmly woven decorator fabrics for both the front and the lining. If you choose two print fabrics, layer them and hold them up to the light to see if the pattern from the back fabric shows through. You may need to interline the two layers with drapery lining or blackout lining to minimize this issue. Install tent-flap curtains on a mounting board and angle irons.

The simple styling and decorative drapery holdback dress up this window with a deep ledge.

Cutting Guide ▸

	Length	Width
Decorator Fabric	Top of mounting board to desired finished length + mounting board projection + ½"	Mounting board / 2 + return + 2"

How to Make Tent-flap Curtains

Pin face fabric to lining, right sides together, and stitch three sides in ½" seam, leaving the upper edge open. Press one seam allowance back to make it easier to turn a crisp, sharp edge. Trim the seam allowance across corners, turn panels right side out, and press.

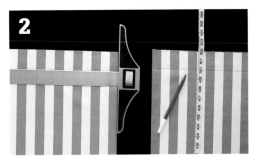

Mark finished length across the top of the panels, making sure that both panels are exactly even and that the end is at a perfect right angle to sides.

Align panel length marking with the front edge of the mounting board. Staple panel to board, starting at return. At the corner, make a diagonal fold to form a miter. Panels overlap about 1" at the center.

Mount the board with angle irons positioned at the edge of window frame.

Fold the front edges of the panels back to the side edges and adjust the opening. Measure to be sure they are even on both sides.

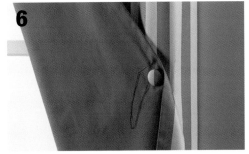

Hand-tack two layers together and finish with decorative or covered button. Or hand-tack ties at the front edge and sides. To maintain projection at the sides, attach the panel to the a tieback holder or wooden block attached to the window frame behind the ties.

Tie-top Curtains

Tie-tops are a refreshing, casual way to dress up a window heading; they draw the eye up to highlight crown molding or decorative trim and highlight your color and fabric choices. Choose matching or coordinating fabric for ties, or save time by using 1½- to 2"-wide ribbon instead. Tie-top curtains slide open easily, but bear in mind that opening and closing frequently will wear quickly on the ties. Use lightweight to medium-weight fabrics for best results, and add a lining for more light control.

Determine the number of ties needed by placing one pair at each end of the curtain panel, one pair in the center, and spacing the remaining pairs every 6 to 8".

These tie-top sheers have a casual, soft look that is perfect for bedrooms.

Cutting Guide ▸

	Length	Width
Decorator Fabric	Finished length + 6½" (for 3" double hem at lower edge)	1½ to 2 × Finished width + double side hems
Facing	4"	Finished width
Ties	4"	10" to 18"

How to Make a Tie-top Curtain Heading

Fold strip lengthwise, right sides together, and stitch across one short end and along long edge with ½" seam allowance; or overlock. Use continuous stitching. Trim corner, turn right side out, and press.

Pin pairs of ties to right side of the curtain with raw edges even. Overlock one long edge of facing, or hem with narrow hem. Pin facing strip over ties, with right sides of facing and curtain together. Stitch ½" seam at top of facing.

Turn facing to wrong side, so ties are free at the upper edge. Fold raw edges of facing under ½" on each side. Fuse side and lower edges to curtain with fusible web.

Making Tiebacks ▸

Tiebacks are a decorative, sleek way to hold curtains open. They are usually 2 to 6" wide; experiment with the best length by pinning fabric around curtains before cutting.

Center fusible interfacing on the wrong side and fuse. Press short ends under ½" fold in half lengthwise, right sides together. Stitch ½" seam, leaving short ends open. Press open. Turn tiebacks right side out. Center seam down back and press. Turn pressed ends inside and slipstitch closed.

Hand-tack a ring on the back seamline at each end, ¼" from edge (a), or press corners diagonally to the inside to form a point; slipstitch or fuse in place and attach a ring (b).

Drapery Styles

Draperies are one of the most functional, durable window treatments available. This traditional style does require more advanced sewing techniques, but the end result is an elegant, refined treatment that will stand the test of time. Attach draperies to a decorative rod and use elegant tiebacks and tailored details for a final treatment that is effectively functional and refined, especially on tall windows or doors. Use medium-weight to heavyweight fabrics with or without lining for a classic look, and choose from a wide variety of pleating styles to best complement your existing décor.

Tip ▶

The secret to an opulent look in curtains or draperies is a flannel interlining. A must with decorator silks, which would look limp and skimpy otherwise, interlining can also give other fabrics a body-building boost. Stitch interlining between the decorator fabric and lining to boost the volume of any window treatment.

Experiment with multiple fabrics when constructing your drapery panels. These color-blocked panels in red and taupe provide a colorful solution for this family room patio door.

Styles to Consider

Pinch pleats: The most common drapery style, pinch pleats gather neatly at the top of a window when closed and remain gathered in pleats when open for a professionally tailored look.

Goblet pleats: Open tubes that are pinched into pleats at the bottom resemble wine glasses—thus the name goblet pleats—and add a dressed-up finish. Detail the base of each goblet with a tassel or covered button.

Inverted box pleats: Most often used for valances, dust ruffles, or skirts on upholstered furniture, box pleats are also a beautifully tailored accent for full-length draperies, especially in rooms with a clean, modern style. In the inverted style, fullness is folded out to the back of the heading, creating a smooth line on the front.

Cartridge pleats: Stitch the heading into cylinders to create soft, rounded folds throughout the panel. Cleverly placed wide fringe trim calls attention to the heading and transforms the drapery from a quiet backdrop to an energizing accent to the room's warm décor.

Attached valances: Add depth and layers to your drapes by sewing a valance to the heading of your panels. This style is an easy way to add detail, such as trim or tassels, or to incorporate complementary fabric without building an extra treatment.

Banded panels: Banding helps define the edges of a curtain or drapery. A solid-color band can accent a patterned panel, adding visual weight to the sides and anchoring the lower edge. In the treatment shown, the dark-colored banding frames the box pleats as the dark wood frames on the furniture pieces complement their clean, neutral fabrics.

Pinch-pleated Draperies

Classic pleated draperies are the ultimate window treatment for versatility and style. Installed on traverse rods, they easily open to reveal the full window view. When closed, they offer privacy, light control, and insulation from the weather.

When designing the treatment, allow for the stacking space at the sides of the window, so the draperies will clear the window when they are open. The actual stacking space varies, depending on the weight of the fabric, the fullness of the draperies, and whether or not they are lined—but a typical stacking space is about one-third of the width of the windows, divided evenly between the two sides. A wide variety of fabrics, from sheers to medium-weight, can be used. Most common is 2½-times fullness, but for very light fabrics or sheers, 3-times fullness may be best.

Tools & Materials ▸

Decorator fabric
Lining (optional)

Decorative traverse rod
4"-wide buckram

The different styles and sizes of doors and windows in this bedroom posed a decorating problem solved by the pinch-pleated, traversing draperies. Choosing a lighter color drapery than the wall draws the eye around the room's clean, inviting décor.

Estimating Drapery Yardage ▸

Drapery Length	
1) Desired length as measured from rod	
2) 8" for heading	+
3) 8" for double hem	+
4) Cut drapery length	=

Drapery Width	
1) Rod width (from end bracket to end bracket on conventional rods; from end ring to end ring on decorative rods)	
2) Returns	+
3) Overlap [standard is 3½"]	+
4) Finished drapery width	=

Drapery widths per panel	
1) Finished width times 2, 2½, or 3 (fullness)	
2) Width of fabric	÷
3) Fabric widths needed: round up or down whole width	=
4) Divide widths by 2	÷
5) Number of widths per panel	=

Total Drapery Fabric Needed	
1) Cut drapery length (figured above)	
2) Fabric widths needed (figured above)	×
3) Total fabric length	=
4) Number of yd. needed: total fabric length divided by 36"	yd.

Lining Length	
1) Finished length of drapery (from top of heading to hem)	
2) 4" for double hems	+
3) Cut lining length	=

Lining Width	
1) Number of widths per panel (figure as for drapery widths per panel, above)	
2) Multiply widths by 2	×
3) Total fabric widths	=

Total Lining Fabric Needed	
1) Cut length (figured above)	
2) Fabric widths (figured above)	×
3) Total fabric length	=
4) Number of yd. needed: total fabric length divided by 36"	yd.

Calculating Drapery Pleats

After fabric panels have been seamed and hemmed, use the table to determine the number and size of pleats and spaces per panel; the recommended amount of fabric required for each pleat is 4 to 6", and space between pleats should be 3½ to 4". If your calculations result in pleats larger than 6" or spaces smaller than 3½", adjust the number of pleats to ensure that your measurements are within the recommended range.

Pleats Worksheet ▸

Finished Panel Width

1) Finished drapery width (figured left)	
2) divided by 2	÷
3) Finished panel width	=

Space between Pleats

1) Number of widths per panel (figured left)	
2) Times number of pleats per width*	×
3) Number of pleats per panel	=
4) Number of spaces per panel (one less than pleats)	
5) Finished panel width (figured above)	
6) Overlap and returns (figured left)	−
7) Width to be pleated	=
8) Number of spaces per panel (figured above)	÷
9) Space between pleats	=

Pleat Allowance

1) Flat width of hemmed panel	
2) Finished panel width (figured above)	−
3) Pleat allowance	=

Pleat Size

1) Pleat allowance (figured above)	
2) Number of pleats in panel	÷
3) Pleat size	=

* Figure five pleats per width of 48" fabric, 6 pleats per width of 54" fabric. If you have a half width of fabric, figure 2 or 3 pleats in that half width. For example, for 48" fabric, 2½ widths per panel = 12 pleats.

How to Sew Pinch-pleated Draperies

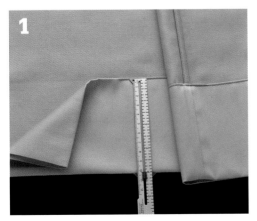

Seam widths together as necessary. (Remove selvages to prevent puckering.) Use French or serged seams. Turn under and blindstitch or straight stitch double 4" bottom hems.

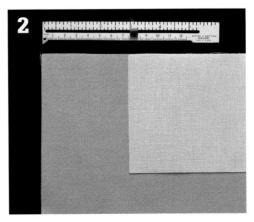

Cut 4"-wide buckram 6" shorter than the width of panel. On wrong side of drapery panel, place buckram even with the top edge and 3" from the sides.

(continued)

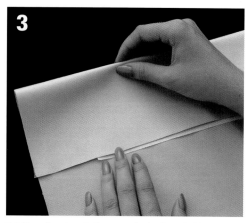

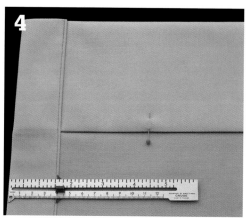

Fold heading over twice, encasing buckram in fabric. Press; pin or hand baste in place.

Turn under and blindstitch or straight stitch double 1½" side hems. Determine size of pleat and space between pleats from worksheet (page 403).

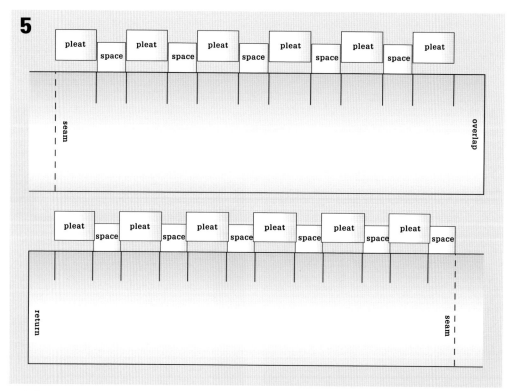

Mark the returns and overlaps on each panel; then mark the pleats and spaces. Mark a pleat just before the return and another next to the overlap. Mark pleats next to any seams on the opposite side of the panel from the return. Bear in mind that pleat size can vary slightly within each fabric width. Spaces between pleats must stay uniform. Spaces between pleats should be 3½ to 4".

6

Fold individual pleats by bringing two pleat lines together and pinning. Crease buckram on the fold.

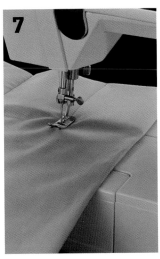

7

Stitch on pleat line from top of heading to ½" below heading; backstitch to secure.

8

Divide into three even pleats. Crease the fold of the pleat with one hand while opening the pleat at the top of the heading. Press the fold straight down to meet the pleat stitching line. Two pleats form at the sides. Pinch outer folds up to meet the center fold (inset). Finger press three pleats together, making sure they are all even.

9

Tack pleats with machine bar tack in center of pleat, ½" from bottom of buckram. Set machine for widest stitch and stitch four to five times.

10

Insert drapery hooks. On a conventional traverse rod (a), top of hook is 1¾" from the upper edge of drapery. On a ringless decorator traverse rod (b), the hook is ¾" to 1" from the upper edge. On a wood pole set (c), hook is ½" from upper edge.

Drapery Lining

Lining adds body and weight to curtains to help them hang nicely. A lining also adds opaqueness, prevents fading and sun damage to decorative fabric, and provides some insulation. For lined curtains with a 2" double-fold hem, cut lining the finished length plus 2½" and the finished width minus 6".

How to Line Curtains

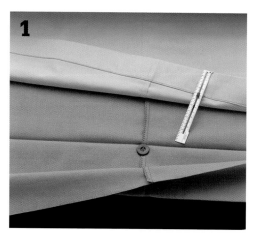

Turn, press, and stitch 2" double-fold hem in lining. Turn and press double-fold hem in curtain. Tack weights inside fold of curtain hems at seams and stitch curtain hems.

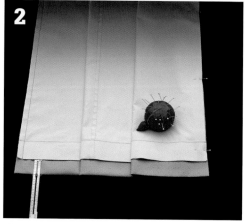

Place lining on curtain right sides together so the lining is 1½" above curtain hem. Pin and stitch ½" seams on sides.

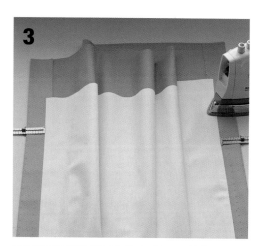

Turn curtain right site out. Center lining so side hems are equal width. Press side hem with seam allowance toward the center. Continue to the top edge of the curtain.

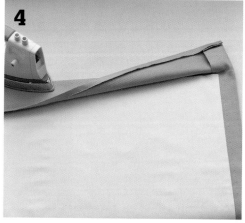

Press ½" seam allowance across the upper edge of the curtain. Fold the upper edge of the curtain down an amount equal to the depth of the casing and heading. Lining ends at fold line.

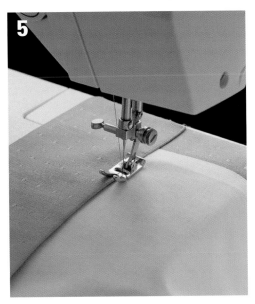

Stitch close to the folded edge to form casing. For curtains with headings, stitch the heading the desired depth.

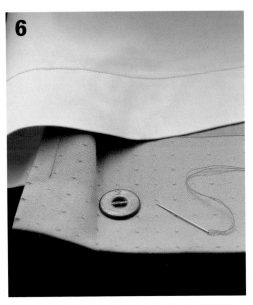

Hand-tack weights along lower edge of the curtain inside side hems.

Turn side hems back diagonally below lining to form a miter. Slipstitch miter in place.

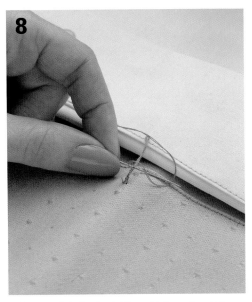

Make French tacks about 12" apart between hem and lining using double thread. Take two stitches near the top of the hem and directly across the lining, leaving 1" slack in thread. Make blanket stitch over thread; secure with knot in lining.

Using Pleater Tape ▶

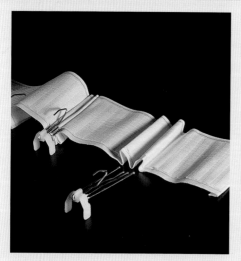

Prepleat pleater tape to finished width of drapery panel. Leave space unpleated at one end of tape for overlap and at other end for return.

Position the pleater tape on installed traverse rod and adjust pleats if necessary. Fold ends under ½". Remove hooks. Cut drapery panels using pleater tape as a guide.

After double-fold hem on lower edge and side hems are finished, pin the upper edge of pleater tape, pocket side up, ½" from the upper edge on the right side of the drapery (so the pleater tape overlaps ½"). Stitch ¼" from the edge of the pleater tape. Fold to inside of drapery and press. Stitch lower edge and both sides.

Insert hooks. Push prongs all the way up into pleats. Adjust folds between hooks.

How to Sew Lined Pleated Draperies

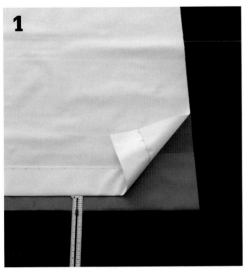

Stitch drapery fabric as on page 403. Repeat for lining, pressing under 2" double-fold hem. Place drapery panel on large flat surface, then lay lining panel on top, wrong sides together, with the lower edge of lining 1" above the lower edge of the panel; raw edges will be even at sides.

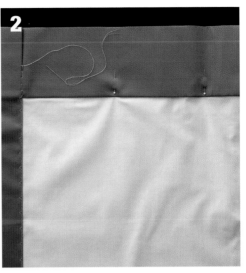

Mark lining panel 8" from upper edge of drapery panel. Trim on marked line. Cut buckram the width of each panel. Place buckram even with upper edge of panel on wrong side. Fold heading and buckram to wrong side; press.

Fold again, encasing the buckram, and then press. Pin or hand baste in place. Press under 1½" twice on sides, folding lining and drapery panels as one fabric. Stitch double-fold side hems. Finish draperies as on page 405.

Dressing Draperies ▸

When draperies are finished, draw into stacked position and guide pleats into soft folds. Staple paper around drapes at the hemline and halfway between the hem and the rod to hold draperies in place; leave them to hang straight from the rod in this fashion for five to seven days. The humidity will encourage the setting process, so the soft folds will continue to hang nicely in the future.

Valance Styles

A window valance is a top treatment that can be used alone or paired with curtains, blinds, or draperies. Window valances have traditionally been used as an attractive covering for window hardware, but today are often primarily a decorative accent that can draws together complementary fabrics used throughout the room. Valances are also a great outlet for your creativity—whether you prefer tailored pleats or softly draping clouds of fabric, complete your window treatment with one of these popular styles, or a variation of your own.

Tip ▶

Modify the technique of making the balloon shade (page 376) to make this stationary valance, which adds an attractive focal point to the sunny décor of this bathroom.

A single inverted box pleat at the middle of a deep, banded valance makes a strong statement in this formal area. While centering the attention on the window, the valance also hides the hardware for the draperies and roman shade.

Styles to Consider

Rectangle Valance: Lined Rectangle Valances are simply a length of fabric lined to the edge with the same or contrasting fabric. Multiple looks can be achieved by changing the dimensions of the rectangle or the way the valance is hung, either clipped to a decorative rod or stapled to a mounting board.

Rod-pocket Valance: Use the technique employed in rod-pocket curtains to create these attractive top treatments; choose to shape the bottom edge to complement your window (shown) or leave the bottom edge in a straight line for a classic look.

Buttoned Valance: These box-pleated valances are tailored and simple; however, fold the lower corners back in this decorative style to highlight the contrasting fabric of the pleat inserts for stylistic flair.

Cloud Valance: Feminine, romantic, and eye catching, a cloud valance is a great way to draw attention to a well-dressed window. This style is gathered across the top, either by making a rod pocket and mounting on a curtain rod or by gathering the top with shirring tape and securing it to a mounting board.

Upholstered Valance: This formal, tailored top treatment is made by covering a wooden frame with fabric. First, cover the frame with batting to round the corners, then cover with decorator fabric. For added detail, apply welting to define the upper and lower edges.

Shelf Valance: Think creatively, and add a shelf to the top of your window instead of a fabric valance. Placed in the window's light, these shelves are a great place for an herb garden, flowering plants, or soft pieces, such as children's stuffed toys.

Buttoned Valance

The lower corners of the box-pleated valances are buttoned back in this project, revealing the contrasting fabric of the pleat inserts. These valances are self-lined, eliminating the need for a lower hem. If the valance or insert fabric is patterned, it's best to interline the valance with lining fabric to prevent the pattern from showing through in the sunlight.

Unless the projection of the mounting board is less than 5", pleats should always be positioned and buttoned back at the outer front corners. The number of remaining pleats and spaces between them will vary, depending upon the design that will best suit your window and room. In some cases, it may be desirable to align pleats with existing divisions in the window space created by moldings. It's also smart to consider the fabric you're using when planning the number of pleats and spacing. You may want to repeat a large motif in each space between the pleats, or perhaps a series of stripes. In general, a solid-colored fabric, or a fabric with a small print, can be divided into smaller spaces than a fabric with a large print.

Tools & Materials ▸

Decorator fabric(s)	Mounting board
Lining fabric	Angle irons
Covered buttons	and screws
or decorative	Staple gun
buttons	and staples

Fold back your pleats in large diagonal strokes, or in small corner flaps (above) for varied shape and design. You may also choose to align pleats with window molding to add to the overall consistency of the window treatment.

Cutting Guide ▸

	Length	Width
Main Valance Fabric Sections	Finished length × 2 + 3"	Width of each space between pleats + 1"
Valance Returns (2)	Finished length × 2 + 3"	Projection of mounting board + 1"
Pleat Inserts (Contrasting Fabric)	Finished length × 2 + 3"	If mounting board projection is 5" or more: All pleat inserts = 21"
		If mounting board projection is less than 5"
		Corner Inserts: Mounting board projection × 2 + 11"
		Remaining Inserts: 21"
Interlining (optional)	Finished length + 1½"	Finished width of valance

Calculating the Spaces & Pleats ▶

To calculate the spaces between pleats, diagram the window treatment, including any undertreatments. Label the finished length and width of the valance, then determine where you would like pleats (if aligning with window molding) or the number of pleats that will work best for your design. Always place the first and last pleats on the outside corners. The size of the spaces between pleats can either align with the window molding or can be divided evenly across the width of the valance. To do this, first determine the approximate spacing between pleats, and divide into the width of the valance, rounding up or down to the nearest whole number. This is the number of spaces between pleats. Remember, there should always be one more pleat than the number of spaces. Divide this number into the valance width to determine the exact measurement of each space.

How to Sew a Valance with Buttoned Pleats

Pin the pleat insert for left end of the valance over the left return section, right sides together; stitch ½" seam.

Pin a space section to the pleat insert, right sides together; stitch ½" seam. Continue to join sections, alternating pleat inserts and space sections end with the right pleat insert and the right return section. Press seams open.

Fold the end of the valance in half lengthwise, right sides together. Sew ½" seam on outer edge of returns; turn valance right side out, and press. Repeat for the opposite end of valance.

Press valance in half, matching raw edges and seams. Machine baste layers together, ½" from raw edges at the top of the valance.

(continued)

Mark center of each pleat insert along upper and lower edges. If return is less than 5", measure from inner seam of return a distance equal to twice the return; pin-mark.

Fold under pleats at all seamlines; press. Bring the pressed seams together to pin marks; pin pleats in place along upper and lower edges.

Press folded edges of all pleats, turning valance back and pressing only on the pleat to avoid imprinting edges to right side of valance.

Stitch pleats in place across the valance, 1½" from upper edge. Finish the upper edge, using overlock or zigzag stitch.

Fold back lower corners of pleats at desired angle to expose pleat insert. Pin in place; press, if desired.

Determine button placement. Sew the buttons in place through all layers. For shank-style buttons, cut a small slit in the fabric, through corner layers only. Insert the shank through the slit; sew button through remaining layers.

Cover mounting board. Position the valance on the mounting board using stitching line as guide to extend upper edge 1½" onto top of board; position end pleats at the front corners of board. Clip fabric at corner pleats close to stitching line. Staple the valance in place, beginning with returns; ease or stretch valance slightly to fit the board, if necessary. Mount the valance.

How to Sew an Interlined Valance with Buttoned Pleats

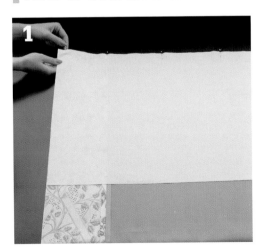

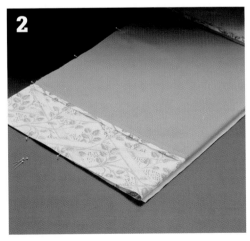

Follow steps 1 and 2, page 413; measure the width of seamed valance. For interlining, cut the lining fabric to this measurement, seaming widths together as necessary. Pin interlining to wrong side of valance, matching upper edges and ends.

Complete valance as in steps 3 to 11, pages 413 to 414. The lower edge of interlining extends to the lower fold of valance.

Cloud Valance

Cloud valances are soft and feminine and draw the eye to window treatment details. The headings of cloud valances are typically gathered, either using a rod pocket and decorative rod or shirring tape, and the lower edge is raised into soft billows by sewing in a column of rings and tying them together.

The pouf sizes can be all the same, or they can vary in width and length, depending on the needs of your window. Columns of ring should be placed at seams between fabric widths and then 18 to 24" apart. Depending on the width of your treatment, there will be two to three poufs per width. Lightweight fabrics and soft, medium-weight fabrics work best for cloud valances. Depending on your fabric and desired look 2½-times or 3-times fullness can be used.

Tools & Materials ▸

Decorator fabric
Lining fabric (optional)
Plastic rings
Shade cord
Two utility curtain rods of equal projections
Installation hardware and tools

An extra-wide pocket rod creates a grand top for this sheer cloud valance. Three graceful swags of different depths are created by tying the two inner columns of rings tighter than the outer columns.

Cutting Guide ▸

	Length	Width
Each Valance Section	Finished length + (rod pocket depth × 2) + (Heading height × 2) + 18"	Full valance: rod length + (projection of rod × 2) × desired fullness Valance section: divide full valance width by number of valance sections, round to nearest whole number
Lining	Finished length + (rod pocket depth × 2) + (Heading height × 2) + 18"	Full valance: rod length + (projection of rod × 2) × desired fullness Valance section: divide full valance width by number of valance sections, round to nearest whole number

How to Sew a Cloud Valance

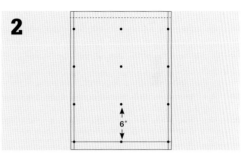

Seam fabric widths together. Repeat for the lining, if necessary. Pin valance and lining wrong sides together, aligning edges. Trim any excess, turn under and stitch 1" double-fold side hems, handling pieces as one fabric. Press under ½" on the upper edge. Then, press under an amount equal to the rod-pocket depth plus the heading depth. Stitch close to the first fold; stitch again at the depth of the heading. Turn under and stitch a 1" double-fold hem at the bottom.

Lay the valance face-down. Mark positions for rings in columns at the side hems and at each seam, placing the bottom marks at the top of the bottom hem. Space one or two additional columns of marks between seams. Place four marks in each column, spaced 6" apart.

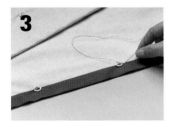

Seaming Fabric Widths ▸

Use only full and half widths. Add half widths at the sides. If an even number of full widths are needed, divide one in half and add a half width to each side of the center full width to avoid a seam in the center of the valance.

Stitch a ring at each mark, stitching through the lining and valance fabric.

Thread a length of shade cord through the rings of the first column and tie the rings together. Leave long tails of cord. Repeat for each column. Insert the curtain rod in the upper rod pocket and mount the valance. Adjust fullness evenly. Mount a second rod under the valance, even with the clusters of tied rings. Tie the cording tails to the rod to keep the poufs in position.

Upholstered Valance

An upholstered valance is a style of cornice: a formal, tailored top treatment made by covering a wooden frame with fabric. The frame, which is a box with an open back and bottom, is first padded with foam or batting to round the corners for a soft, upholstered look. Fabric-covered or cord welting can also be used to define the edges of the valance.

Building the valance frame takes only very basic carpentry skills—and any imperfections will be covered with the padding and decorator fabric. Design your cornice to clear the curtain or drapery hardware by 2 to 3" and extend at least 2" beyond the end of the drapery or window frame on each side. Medium-weight, firmly woven decorator fabrics and upholstery fabrics are suitable for this project; railroad the fabric to eliminate seams or place the seams inconspicuously, never in the center.

To mount the cornice to the wall, remember to first attach the angle irons to the frame and mark their positions on the wall. Then, remove the angle irons from the frame and attach them to the wall at your marks. Finally, reattach the frame to the angle irons. Following these instructions will ensure that you don't get in to a sticky spot trying to screw a narrow frame to the wall.

Tools & Materials ▸

Decorator fabric
Lining fabric
Welting cord
  and fabric
½"-thick plywood
  or pine boards
Carpenter's glue
Finishing nails
Stapler and staples

Polyester upholstery
  batting or ½"-thick
  polyurethane foam
Cardboard upholstery
  stripping
Spray foam adhesive
Installation hardware
  and tools

These dramatic arched valances are a grand focal point for this formal dining area. Apply antique details to the finished cornice, such as the metal medallions in the corners here, for added character.

Cutting Guide ▸

	Length	Width
Face Piece	Height of frame + 3"	Front + sides of frame + 6"
Inner Lining Strip	4"	Front + sides of frame + 6"
Lining Strip	Height of frame – 2"	Front + sides of frame + 6"
Dustcover	Top of frame + 1"	Width of frame top
Batting or foam	Height of frame	Front + sides of frame
Welting	Length of all welting edges + 6-8"	1½"

How to Make an Upholstered Valance

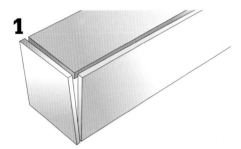

Measure and cut the cornice top. Cut the front the same width and the desired finished height. Shape the lower edges, if desired. Cut sides pieces the same height as the cornice front plus the depth of the top piece, plus the thickness of the wood. Glue the top to the front board and nail to secure. Attach the sides, first gluing in place, then securing with nails. Allow glue to set.

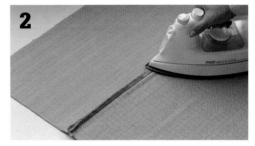

Stitch welting to the lower edge of the face piece with a ½" seam, then sew the lower (welted) edge to the inner lining strip, right sides together. Sew the free edge of the inner strip to the lining strip. Press seam allowances toward the lining. Mark the center at the top and bottom on both the face piece and the frame. Place the wrong side of the fabric on the outside of the cornice, with the lower (welted) seam on the lower front edge of the frame, matching center markings. Staple in place at the center.

Pull the seam allowances taut to the corners of the cornice and staple in place. Staple every 4" from the center to the ends, keeping the lower (welted) seam aligned to the front edge of the frame.

Place cardboard stripping tight against the lower (welted) seam. Staple every 1 to 1½". Cut and overlap the stripping at the corners. Fold lining to the inside. Fold under the raw edge and staple at the inside of the box where the top and face meet. At the lower corners, miter the fabric and staple close to the corner. Tuck excess fabric into the upper corners and staple.

(continued)

5

Open the welting seam back to the edge of the frame. Trim welting to 1". Trim out the cording even with the cornice back edge to reduce bulk. Staple the lining to the back edge of frame; trim excess lining. Staple the welting end to the back edge of the frame. Turn cornice face up and apply spray adhesive to the front and sides. Place padding over the glued surface and smooth it taut over the front and sides. Allow glue to set, then fold face fabric over the padded front. Gently smooth toward the top, keeping the padding tucked snugly into the corners and lower edge.

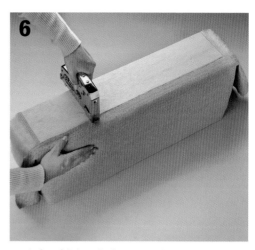

6

Staple face fabric to the frame top at the center and ends. Starting at the center, turn under the raw edge and staple it to the cornice top. Smoothing the fabric as you go, work first toward one end and then the other, placing staples 1½" apart. Pull fabric around the frame end to the top back corner, removing any slack; staple. Fold side fabric to the back edge; staple. Trim excess fabric at the back edge.

7

Fold the fabric diagonally at the corners to form miters. Staple at the corners and across the ends.

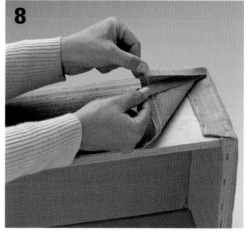

8

Staple welting to the sides and front of the cornice top, with the welting stitching line along the front and side edges. Place dustcover over the welting on cornice front, with right sides together and raw edges event. Staple cardboard stripping at the front. Fold under the sides of the dustcover even with the sides of the frame. Insert cardboard stripping into the folds. Staple dustcover to the top of the frame, close to the folds. Fold the back edge under and staple in place.

Cornice Variations ▶

If you love the look of upholstered valances but are intimidated by the frame construction and upholstery techniques, don't fret! You can achieve the look and feel of upholstered cornices without building a frame by using one of these clever techniques.

Soft cornices are mounted on a board with side extensions instead of a full frame and result in a similar shape with a lighter look. Soft cornices can be made as either a single panel of fabric with a shaped lower edge or with overlapping panels. Welting defines the lower edge of the soft cornice and can also trim the upper edge.

Rod-pocket mock cornices are mounted on flat curtain rods that are 4½" wide. Fusible fleece applied inside the rod pocket gives the treatment a padded look. The top and bottom of the rod pocket are accented with welting to add to the illusion. Add a pleated or gathered skirt below the rod pocket for extra length.

Hanging Shelf Valance

Think creatively about your window treatments, and replace a traditional valance with a hanging shelf to house collectibles, toys, or plants. This functional piece can also be a delightful decorative addition to kitchens, bathrooms, and bedrooms. Hang a single shelf near the top of a window as a valance, or hang multiple shelves for additional privacy.

The shelves in this project are made from 1 × 6 stock lumber, braced with parting stop at each end, and suspended with a rope from a wooden pole. If mounting a shelf over a window that is more than 36" wide or if you will be displaying heavy items, add an additional brace and rope to the center, along with a center support bracket for the pole. Ropes are knotted just below the pole and under each brace to keep the shelf hanging level.

Tools & Materials ▸

1 × 6 board for each shelf, cut to the width of the window frame
Two 7"-lengths of parting stop for each shelf
Sponge applicator
Drill with ⁵⁄₁₆" drill bit and ³⁄₃₂" combination drill and countersink bit
1" flat head screws
1³⁄₈" wood pole with finials
180-grit or 220-grit sandpaper
Pole brackets with 4 to 6" projection
Latex paint or wood stain and clear acrylic finish
³⁄₁₆" nylon or polyester rope (cut twice as long as the distance from the pole to the bottom of the last shelf, plus 6 to 10" for each knot)

How to Make a Hanging Window Shelf

1

Mark placement of holes for rope on the wide side of braces ½" from each end; drill holes using a ⁵⁄₁₆" drill bit. Sand all wood surfaces using 180-grit or 220-grit sandpaper; round corners of the shelves and braces slightly.

2

Mark lines on underside of shelf 2" from each end. On wide side of braces, mark placement for screws, 1½" from ends. Place braces, wide side up on shelf with outer edges along lines and ends extending equally on each side of shelf. Position a third brace, if needed at center of board. Repeat for braces on any additional shelves.

3

Adjust ³⁄₃₂" combination drill and countersink bit so head of drywall screw will be recessed below the surface of wood when inserted into drilled hole, then predrill screw holes, holding the brace firmly in place as positioned. Drill through brace and into underside of shelf, up to point on drill bit indicated by the white line. Insert screw and repeat for remaining braces.

4

Paint the shelves, if desired, or stain shelves and apply clear acrylic finish.

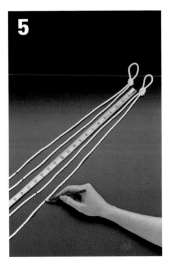

5

Fold the ropes in half. Tie each folded rope together in an overhand knot near the folded end, leaving a 2½" loop; tie all knots in the same direction so they look the same. Measure from the overhand knots to the desired location for the first set of shelf support knots, allowing 1¼" for the thickness of the shelf and braces and mark the ropes.

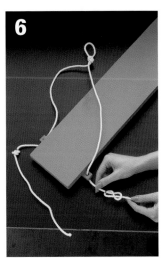

6

Thread the rope down through the holes in the braces of the shelf until the pencil marks are below the braces. Tie a figure-eight knot at each location, just under the mark. Repeat for any additional shelves, measuring from previous knots.

7

Mount brackets for wood pole on or just outside the window frame. If a center support bracket is needed, mount it with one side of the bracket at center.

8

Slide the pole through loops in the rope, and attach finials to ends; mount the pole on brackets. Check to see that shelves are level and resting on knots; adjust the knots if necessary. Trim excess rope under the knots for the bottom shelf.

Swag Styles

Swags are elegant and versatile and are easily employed by decorators of all skill levels. As a top treatment, they are the perfect way to introduce an accent color or pattern to your window décor. Consider adding a swag in a complementary color to your curtains or draperies to tie together various elements of your room's color scheme.

For a polished designer look, be sure to take proper measurements and style the fabric over the window throughout the process. Avoid directional prints, such as birds or flowers that only look right in one direction: you don't want to have upside down tulips on one side of your window. Consider semisheer decorator fabric for a soft, airy look. For a more formal, traditional look use medium-weight decorator fabric and consider trimming the edges with bullion fringe. Bias swags made from striped or plaid fabric can add interest, tie the window treatments in with other patterns and colors in the room, or just add a fun focal point with a burst of pattern or color.

Tip ▶

For a reversible option or to tie in a prominent color or scheme in the room, consider lining the backside of the fabric.

Making a decorator window treatment is easier than you may have thought! Here a white semisheer freeform swag cascades to the floor for formal, yet fresh softness.

Tools & Materials ▶

Decorative rod and
  mounting hardware
Long cord or string
Tape measure
Decorator fabric
**Depending on the
project you choose,
you may also need:**

Paper for
  pattern making
Drapery lining
Fringe
Clip-on or sew-on
  drapery rings
  (ten per 36")
Twill tape or ribbon

Swag Styles to Consider

Freeform scarf: This swag style is classic and uninhibited, draping effortlessly across a window frame. Made of a full-width, unshaped length of fabric, this style can be sewn and draped in minutes. Add trim or decorative swag holders to accent the fabric

Bias: Cut with the true bias running through the center of the swag, bias-cut swags drape in smooth, graceful folds.

Tapered: Floral print is draped through scarf rings to form this easy single swoop treatment. There are hidden seams at the points where the swag goes through the rings, so a directional print like this can run upward on both tails.

Tailored: The tailored version is more structured has a formal, pleated look. This swag style is not formed at the window, but rather created with a muslin pattern to fit the window perfectly.

Rod pocket: This softly gathered swag is versatile and can be tailored multiple ways. Add fringe or decorative trim for a formal finish, or add a ruffle for country charm.

Multiple swoops: Shape your swag with multiple swag holders to unify windows of multiple heights, accent a vaulted ceiling, or to add variety to a large bay window.

Shirred: This lined swag is adorned with multicolored rope trim and is created with jabots, or side panels. The trim simply drapes through the swag and hangs over the jabots on each side.

Butterfly: A stationary treatment, the butterfly swag can be made in any length. Its tan-folded fabric is held in place with decorative straps, which helps the fabric to swag in the center and flare at the sides.

Scarf Swag

This elegant top treatment is versatile and requires very little sewing; in fact, a scarf swag is simply a long length of fabric that is hemmed at the ends. If the selvages are neat and unpuckered, they can be left intact as finished edges for the long sides of the swag. You will use the entire width of a decorator fabric, running the lengthwise grain up one side, draping across the rod, and down the opposite side. Avoid directional prints when creating swags in this style.

How to Make a Scarf Swag

Mount the rod above the window frame, with the outer brackets beyond the frame sides. Drape a cord in the path you want the lower edge of the swag to follow. Cut fabric 2" longer than this length.

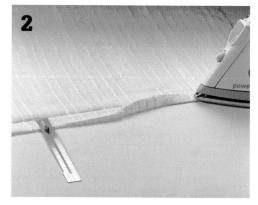

Fold and press 1" from the outside edge of swag end, and then unfold it. Turn the cut edge back, aligning it to the first foldline (shown), and press.

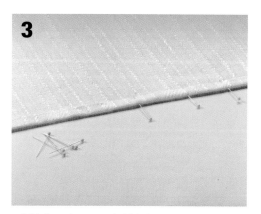

Refold along the pressed 1" foldline to create a double-fold hem. Pin the hem as shown. No-sew alternative: fuse or glue the final hem instead of pinning it.

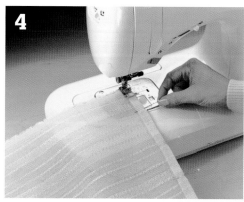

Align the selvage edge under the presser foot, with the needle aligned just inside the inner fold. Straight stitch the entire length of the swag edge, removing pins as you go. Be sure to backstitch at the start and finish. Repeat for the hem at the opposite end.

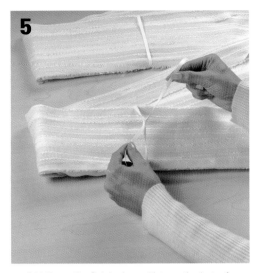

5

6

Fanfold the entire finished panel into gentle pleats of consistent depth, keeping the right side facing out on the first and last folds. Tie the folded fabric at regular intervals using ribbon or twill tape.

Drape the folded fabric over the rod, remove the ties, and arrange the folds. Tug gently at the center of the lower folds to shape the swag into a gradual curve.

Variation: Freeform Swag with a Knot

1

2

3

Measure and mark the point in which the swag will fold together near pole ends. If you want an exact placement for the fold, use a fabric pencil. Fan fold the swag along the marked lines, keeping the number and depth of folds consistent. Secure with a Velcro strap or twill tape.

Hang the swag over the rod. Secure the upper edge to the rod with double-sided carpet tape so that it doesn't move.

Tie the fabric between bundles into a large, loose knot over the rod. Pin the bundles together inside the knot. If you'd like to use multiple knots, begin in the center and work out toward each side.

Bias Swag

This style of swag is cut with the true bias of the fabric running through the center of the piece, which enables the swag to drape in smooth, graceful folds. Bias swags can be light and airy when made in semisheer fabric, or formal and refined when made with medium-weight fabric and decorative trim. Drape one bias swag per window, or make multiple swags to overlap as you mount them.

The striped fabric in these swags hides the gap between the top of the window and the decorative rod. The stripes echoed in the upholstered chair cushions pull the overall design together.

How to Make a Bias Swag

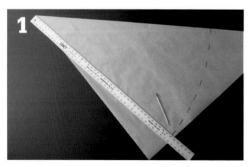

Measure your window to determine how much fabric you need. Take a square measurement based on the farthest edges top to bottom and right to left (typical size is 42"). Cut a square piece of paper to match your desired measurement. Fold the square diagonally from corner to corner. Using a string and pencil, draw an arc between the square corner and the fold, marking the lower edge of the swag. Cut along the marked line.

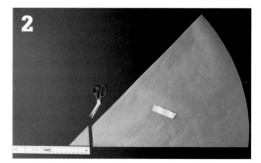

Mark the folded edge 5" from the upper point. Draw a line from the mark to the opposite edge (as shown) and cut along the line. Use this template for the swag and the lining.

Fold under 2" on the long straight edges. Trim the lower area that is folded under, following the curve. Unfold the pattern. This pattern can be used for the lining and swag. Test it out by hanging it in place on the rod.

With right sides together, align and stitch the fabric and lining together at the curved edge with a ½" seam. Turn the swag right side out.

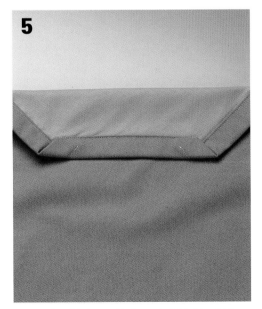

Press under 1" twice on the long straight sides, folding the decorator fabric and lining together. Stitch close the inner fold. Repeat at the upper edge.

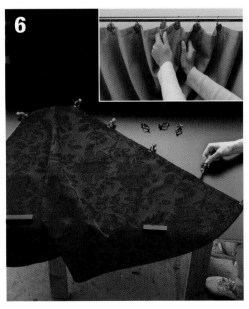

Attach drapery rings to the upper straight edges of the swag as shown. Hang the rings on the decorator pole. Arrange the swag as desired (inset).

Rod-pocket Swag

Modeled after traditional rod-pocket curtains (page 394), this swag style is simple to make and can be detailed to match many décor styles. Style the swag to fall in one deep, graceful half-circle, or in multiple swags of equal depths. Or divide the swag further to create a deeper swag in the center, framed by smaller swags on the sides. Lightweight, sheer or medium-weight decorator fabrics all work well rod-pocket swags.

Whatever your styling, this top treatment will always be constructed from a half-circle of fabric. Surprisingly, the straight edge of the half-circle will become the lower curved edge of the valance to which the ruffle or fringe is attached. Before you begin, install the rod and drape a piece of string or twill tape from the rod to simulate the final appearance of the swag(s). Mark the swags on the string and use this piece to help determine your final measurements.

This rod-pocket swag has been gathered along the pocket and the top portion is folded over, resulting in a cloud-like fullness at the top.

How to Make a Rod-pocket Swag

Determine the depth of the heading and rod pocket. Fold the decorator fabric in half crosswise. Mark an arc using a straightedge and pencil, measuring from the outer edge at the fold, a distance equal to ½ the measured length of the lower edge of the valance plus the depth of the heading and rod pocket plus ½" for seams. Cut on marked line through both layers. Cut lining to this same size.

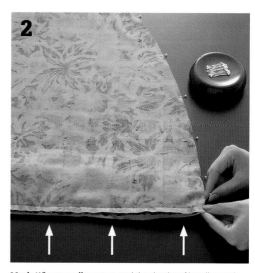

Mark ½" seam allowance and the depths of heading and rod pocket on the wrong side of the valance fabric (arrows), at each end of the straight edge. Pin valance to lining, right sides together, matching raw edges.

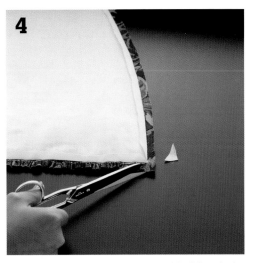

Stitch valance to lining in ½" seam, stitching with valance face up. Leave an opening for the rod pocket at each end of the straight edge, and an opening near the center of the straight edge for turning.

Press the lining seam allowance toward the lining. Trim the corners diagonally.

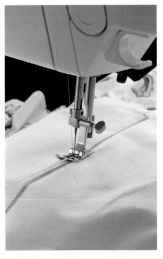

Turn valance right side out; press seamed edges. Stitch the center opening closed. Mark chalk lines for depth of heading and depth of rod pocket on curved edge of valance. Pin layers together. Stitch on marked lines.

Insert the curtain rod or pole into the rod pocket, gathering fabric evenly. Install rod on brackets. Adjust folds of valance as desired. *Note: Swag shown has a ruffle attached to the straight edge. Attach ruffle to long straight edge before beginning project, if desired.*

Variation: To gather swag, follow steps 1 through 5 then mark gathers on the wrong side of the fabric. Zig-zag stitch over a length of cord down one side of the line. When you reach the end, pivot and continue stitching over cord on the opposite side of the line and secure at the end. After mounting swag, draw up cords to gather swag to the desired height, then tie cords together and trim.

Stained Glass

Hanging stained glass panels in a window is a dramatic way to add color to the brightest places in your home. Custom order a new panel or search for a unique find at an antique store or salvage yard. If you are refurbishing an older panel, follow these simple tips to make sure it looks its best. Or, if you can't afford (or can't find) the perfect panel for your window—make an imitation panel yourself! Use this simple painting technique to add a colorful, removable design to your window glass.

Tools & Materials ▶

Hooks and chains
Mineral spirits
Paintbrush
Vinegar
Razor blade
0000 steel wool
Glass cleaner
Finishing compound
    or furniture polish
Painter's tape
Spray stained glass
Felt-tip marker
Paper
Liquid leading

To hang a stained glass panel, secure hooks to the top of the panel frame and to the top of the window frame, predrilling holes. Hang from chains secured to the hooks. Ask for help selecting hardware that will be strong enough to support the weight of your piece.

Refurbishing Stained Glass Panels

Remove old paint by applying mineral spirits to the area covered with paint using a paintbrush; wait a moment and scrape away paint with a razor blade. Remove putty or glazing compound using vinegar and a razor blade.

Clean dirty lead by rubbing 0000 steel wool over it, taking care not to scratch the glass; then wipe the lead with a dampened cloth.

Clean glass using a commercial-grade glass cleaner and polish with finishing compound. Wipe the polish on, allow it to dry and buff the surface. You can also use furniture polish to shine the glass. Either kind of polish will protect the glass with a wax coating.

How to Make Imitation Stained Glass

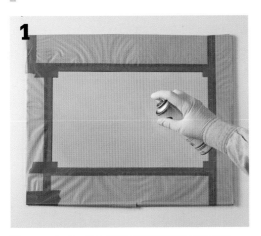

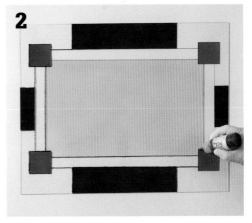

Plan your design on a piece of paper, then place your drawing behind the glass panel and trace over your guidelines with a marker on the front of the glass. Mask off your first color, and apply Spray Stained Glass in short sweeping motions. Repeat for each color.

When all colors have been applied and have dried, apply liquid leading materials following your marker lines.

Frosted Glass

Frosted glass spray paint provides a durable finish that cuts the glare of strong sunlight and provides privacy for windows in bathrooms or entrances. Spray paint over a masking stencil of self-adhesive vinyl to leave spaces of clear glass in a decorative shape. Or, reverse the stenciling process and apply frosted glass in a decorative pattern to imitate etched glass detailing. Unlike true frosted glass, however, frosted glass spray paint can be removed, using a razor blade or lacquer thinner.

Tools & Materials ▸

Frosted glass
   spray paint
Self-adhesive
   vinyl, such as
   Con-Tact®
Mat knife

Graphite paper
   or pre-cut stencil
Masking tape
Paper
Glass cleaner
Lint-free cloth

Frosted glass can add privacy to doorway windows or bathrooms along with decorative flair. Or, apply frosted glass to small stenciled areas to imitate etched glass (above).

How to Apply a Frosted Glass Finish with a Clear Design

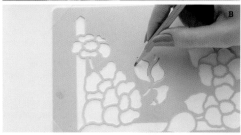

Clean the window thoroughly using glass cleaner and a soft, lint-free cloth. Cut self-adhesive vinyl 2" larger than design. Remove paper backing; affix vinyl to window in the desired location, pressing out any air bubbles. If more than one width of vinyl is needed overlap the edges slightly.

Position design on window, with carbon or graphite paper under design, tape in place. Trace design onto vinyl (A). Or tape precut stencil to vinyl in desired position; trace design areas with pencil (B).

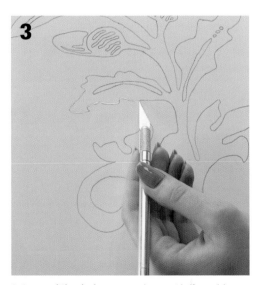

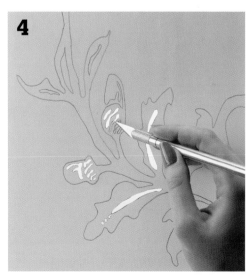

Cut around the design areas using a mat knife, applying just enough pressure to cut through the vinyl. Overcut corners or curves into surrounding areas, if necessary, but do not cut into design areas.

Remove vinyl surrounding design areas using tip of mat knife to lift edge of vinyl.

(continued)

5

Press firmly on all areas of the design; rub away any traces of adhesive left on glass, using glass cleaner and soft, lint-free cloth.

6

Mask off the woodwork around window and surrounding wall area using masking tape and paper to protect from overspray of the paint.

7

Check to be sure the glass surface is free of dust. Follow the manufacturer's instructions for applying paint. Spray paint onto the window in sweeping motion, holding can 10 to 12" away from glass, lightly respraying surface several times in one application. Allow to dry for 15 minutes. Repeat two or three times for good coverage.

8

Remove vinyl in design areas using tip of matt knife to lift edge of vinyl. Gently rub away any traces of adhesive left on the glass, using a soft cloth dipped in glass cleaner.

How to Apply a Frosted Design with Surrounding Clear Glass

Follow steps 1 and 2 on page 435. Cut around the design areas to be frosted using a mat knife, applying just enough pressure to cut through the vinyl. At the corners, do not cut past point of the intersecting lines, onto the area surrounding design.

Remove vinyl in design areas to be frosted using tip of mat knife to lift edge of vinyl.

Follow step 5, opposite. Mask off woodwork, walls, or any areas of the glass not protected by the stencil using masking tape and paper.

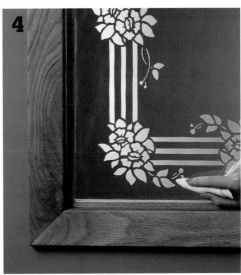

Follow step 7, opposite, spraying over design area. Remove vinyl, masking tape, and paper. Gently rub away any traces of adhesive left on glass using a soft, lint-free cloth dipped in glass cleaner.

Shoji-style Screen

Traditional Japanese screens, called shoji, are made with an intricate wooden lattice framework backed with rice paper. Shoji-style screens filter muted light through the transparent paper backing, adding sophisticated elegance and an aura of tranquility to any room. Shoji-style screens are especially suited for windows that cannot be opened and closed and that have a less-than-perfect view.

These shoji-style screens are made from parting stop and rice or decorative paper. Parting stop measures ½" × ¾" and can be painted or stained, if desired. Paper backing can be applied in one sheet or in multiple sheets. Mount the screen inside or in front of your window frame. Careful measuring and cutting is important, especially if you plan an inside-mount. Make your screen ¼" narrower and shorter than the inside of the frame. Take accurate, detailed measurements of the window and draw a full-size pattern of the screen framework before cutting any of the wood pieces.

Japanese shoji-style screens are timeless, and filter light softly in to any room for simple, classic elegance.

Tools & Materials ▸

Parting stop
Rice paper or decorative paper
Double-stick transfer tape
1⅝" drywall screws
Wood filler
Wood glue
Sandpaper
Paint, or stain and clear acrylic finish
    (optional)
Mat knife
⅛"-thick self-adhesive bumper pads
    (for inside mount)
Two shoulder hooks and screw eyes
    (for outside mount)
Spring clamps
Drill with ⅛" combination drill
    and countersink bit
Small miter box and backsaw

Anatomy of a Shoji ▸

Shoji-style framework has an inner frame, consisting of two vertical stiles (a) and top and bottom rails (b), a slightly offset outer frame (c), and interior lattice strips (d).

How to Make a Shoji-Style Screen

Measure window frame; determine outer measurements of screen (¼" narrower and shorter than window frame). Draw outline of screen on large sheet of paper; use accurate measurements and square corners.

Draw the outer frame of screen ½" wide; sides run full length of frame, with top and bottom sections abutting sides at inner edges.

Draw stiles and rails ½" wide, inside outer frame; stiles run the full length between top and bottom sections of outer frame, with rails abutting stiles at inner edges.

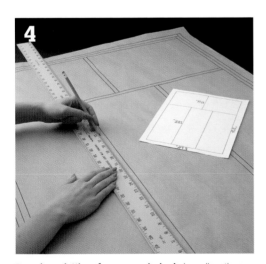

Draw inner lattice of screen as desired; draw all sections ½" wide, abutting the ends of lattice sections to inner edges of stiles, rails, or other lattice sections. Sections should abut each other at right angles. To allow for the insertion of screws, stagger placement of ends that abut opposite sides of the same section. It is helpful to plan the design of the lattice by sketching it on another piece of paper before drawing it on the pattern.

Tape the finished pattern to the window frame, checking for accuracy. Measure pattern for the length of each wood section, including the stiles, rails, lattice, and outer frame sections. Keeping the ½" side of the parting stop face up, mark and cut for each section; cut on the outside of the line using a miter box and backsaw, leaving each section slightly longer than the desired finished length.

(continued)

Check the lengths of outer frame sections by placing sections of parting stop over pattern. Sand the ends of sections until they fit the pattern exactly. Reposition on the pattern. Repeat for stiles, rails, and all lattice sections until the entire framework is laid out (inset).

Remove left stile from pattern and place it face up near the edge of a flat work surface. Abut bottom rail to stile, face up, with lower edges even; clamp. Mark placement for screw on outside of stile in line with the center of the rail.

Adjust ⅛" combination drill and countersink bit so head of drywall screw will be recessed below surface of wood when inserted into drilled hole, then predrill screw hole, drilling through the side of the stile and into the center of the end rail. Countersink the hole up to point on bit indicated by white line. Insert drywall screw.

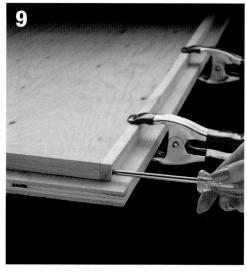

Repeat steps 7 and 8 for top rail. Attach right stile to the opposite end of rails, abutting ends of rails to side of stile; countersink holes and insert screws.

Position the stiles and rails over the lattice pieces on pattern. Align all pieces for perfect fit. Make small pencil lines at every abutting location.

Join sections of lattice, working from center outward and aligning penciled markings. Keep lattice flat on work surface, and predrill holes in line with center of section being joined; insert screws.

Fit lattice inside the framework of stiles and rails. Join the stiles and rails to lattice, countersinking holes and inserting screws.

Apply wood glue to upper side of top rail and top ends of stiles. Place the framework face up on flat surface; place straightedge of about ⅛" thickness next to top rail. Rest the top section of outer frame on straightedge to offset it slightly; glue to the top rail, aligning ends. Clamp in place. Repeat for bottom section. Then, glue side sections of outer frame to stiles.

(continued)

14

Cover exposed screw heads in lattice with wood filler, if desired. Allow to dry. Sand filled areas until flush with wood surface. Sand any rough areas of the screen. If desired, paint or stain framework.

15

Cut paper 1" longer and wider than outer frame. Apply double-stick transfer tape to all stiles, rails, and lattices.

16

Center piece of paper, right side down, and affix center of each side to frame. Pull paper taut and affix sides of paper to stiles and rails. Then, affix paper to all lattice sections.

17

Fold back the excess paper at the edges of inner frame; crease. Trim using mat knife.

Attaching Paper Using Multiple Sheets ▸

Divide original screen pattern into areas that can be covered with one piece of paper. Trace each area onto tracing paper, planning for paper pieces to overlap each other on the back of the lattice sections, hiding seams. Cut each piece of paper using the traced patterns. Add 1" margin on each side.

Affix paper to frame using double-stick transfer tape, one area at a time. Always apply to outer edges first, and then to any lattice strips. Center paper over the area and affix to frame as in step 16. Trim, using mat knife, and move on to the next section, overlapping pieces on the back of any adjoining lattice strips (inset).

Mounting a Shoji-Style Screen

Inside Mount: Adhere self-adhesive bumper pads to outside edge of outer frame, 2" from each corner, and then every 18 to 24", around the entire frame. Push the screen into place inside the window frame until the front of the screen is flush with the front of the window frame. Stack additional pads, if necessary.

Outside Mount: Attach screw eyes to the top of the outer frame, 2" from the corners. Hold screen in place and mark placement for shoulder hooks. Attach shoulder hooks to window frame and hang the screen, hooking the screw eyes over the shoulder hooks.

Reference Charts

Metric Conversions

To Convert:	To:	Multiply by:
Inches	Millimeters	25.4
Inches	Centimeters	2.54
Feet	Meters	0.305
Yards	Meters	0.914
Square inches	Square centimeters	6.45
Square feet	Square meters	0.093
Square yards	Square meters	0.836
Ounces	Milliliters	30.0
Pints (U.S.)	Liters	0.473 (Imp. 0.568)
Quarts (U.S.)	Liters	0.946 (Imp. 1.136)
Gallons (U.S.)	Liters	3.785 (Imp. 4.546)
Ounces	Grams	28.4
Pounds	Kilograms	0.454

To Convert:	To:	Multiply by:
Millimeters	Inches	0.039
Centimeters	Inches	0.394
Meters	Feet	3.28
Meters	Yards	1.09
Square centimeters	Square inches	0.155
Square meters	Square feet	10.8
Square meters	Square yards	1.2
Milliliters	Ounces	.033
Liters	Pints (U.S.)	2.114 (Imp. 1.76)
Liters	Quarts (U.S.)	1.057 (Imp. 0.88)
Liters	Gallons (U.S.)	0.264 (Imp. 0.22)
Grams	Ounces	0.035
Kilograms	Pounds	2.2

Converting Temperatures

Convert degrees Fahrenheit (F) to degrees Celsius (C) by following this simple formula: Subtract 32 from the Fahrenheit temperature reading. Then, multiply that number by $5/9$. For example, 77°F - 32 = 45. 45 × $5/9$ = 25°C.

To convert degrees Celsius to degrees Fahrenheit, multiply the Celsius temperature reading by $9/5$. Then, add 32. For example, 25°C × $9/5$ = 45. 45 + 32 = 77°F.

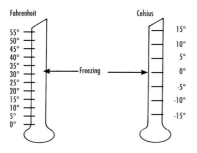

Lumber Dimensions

Nominal - U.S.	Actual - U.S. (in inches)	Metric
1 × 2	¾ × 1½	19 × 38 mm
1 × 3	¾ × 2½	19 × 64 mm
1 × 4	¾ × 3½	19 × 89 mm
1 × 5	¾ × 4½	19 × 114 mm
1 × 6	¾ × 5½	19 × 140 mm
1 × 7	¾ × 6¼	19 × 159 mm
1 × 8	¾ × 7¼	19 × 184 mm
1 × 10	¾ × 9¼	19 × 235 mm
1 × 12	¾ × 11¼	19 × 286 mm
1¼ × 4	1 × 3½	25 × 89 mm
1¼ × 6	1 × 5½	25 × 140 mm
1¼ × 8	1 × 7¼	25 × 184 mm
1¼ × 10	1 × 9¼	25 × 235 mm
1¼ × 12	1 × 11¼	25 × 286 mm
1½ × 4	1¼ × 3½	32 × 89 mm
1½ × 6	1¼ × 5½	32 × 140 mm
1½ × 8	1¼ × 7¼	32 × 184 mm
1½ × 10	1¼ × 9¼	32 × 235 mm
1½ × 12	1¼ × 11¼	32 × 286 mm
2 × 4	1½ × 3½	38 × 89 mm
2 × 6	1½ × 5½	38 × 140 mm
2 × 8	1½ × 7¼	38 × 184 mm
2 × 10	1½ × 9¼	38 × 235 mm
2 × 12	1½ × 11¼	38 × 286 mm
3 × 6	2½ × 5½	64 × 140 mm
4 × 4	3½ × 3½	89 × 89 mm
4 × 6	3½ × 5½	89 × 140 mm

Metric Plywood Panels

Metric plywood panels are commonly available in two sizes: 1,200 mm × 2,400 mm and 1,220 mm × 2,400 mm, which is roughly equivalent to a 4 × 8-ft. sheet. Standard and Select sheathing panels come in standard thicknesses, while Sanded grade panels are available in special thicknesses.

Standard Sheathing Grade		Sanded Grade	
7.5 mm	(5/16 in.)	6 mm	(4/17 in.)
9.5 mm	(3/8 in.)	8 mm	(5/16 in.)
12.5 mm	(½ in.)	11 mm	(7/16 in.)
15.5 mm	(5/8 in.)	14 mm	(9/16 in.)
18.5 mm	(¾ in.)	17 mm	(2/3 in.)
20.5 mm	(13/16 in.)	19 mm	(¾ in.)
22.5 mm	(7/8 in.)	21 mm	(13/16 in.)
25.5 mm	(1 in.)	24 mm	(15/16 in.)

Liquid Measurement Equivalents

1 Pint	= 16 Fluid Ounces	= 2 Cups
1 Quart	= 32 Fluid Ounces	= 2 Pints
1 Gallon	= 128 Fluid Ounces	= 4 Quarts

Resources

American Society of Interior Designers (ASID)
202 546 3480
www.asid.org

The Bradley Collection Limited
44 (0) 845 118 7224
info@bradleycollection.co.uk
www.bradleycollection.co.uk

Color Association of US
www.colorassociation.com

Encyclopedia of Fabrications
by Ethel Mahon
see WCAA entry

US Environmental Protection Agency (EPA)
202 272 0167
www.epa.gov

Esteban Interiors
7605 Girard Avenue
La Jolla, CA 92037
858 729 0045
www.estebaninteriors.com

IKEA Home Furnishings
610 834 0180
www.Ikea-USA.com

International Furnishings and Design Assoc. (IFDA)
610 535 6422
www.ifda.com

International Interior Designers Association
888 799 4432
www.iida.org

National Kitchen & Bath Association (NKBA)
800 THE NKBA
www.nkba.org

National Association of Remodeling Industry (NARI)
847 298 9200
www.nari.org

Room and Board
800 301 9720
www.roomandboard.com

Wallcovering (paper) Resources
www.creativewallcovering.com (919 384 1994)
www.jocelynwarner.com
www.madisonandgrow.com
www.mardero.com
www.pottokprints.com
www.tracykendall.com (info@tracykendall.com)
www.wallpaperstore.com (406 541 2091)

WCAA | Window Coverings Association of America
Window coverings & home furnishings standards.
Publications, certification programs, and training to maintain quality standards, definitions of industry terms, and standardization of window treatments.
Publisher and distributor of the *Encyclopedia of Fabrications* by Ethel Mahon.
2646 Hwy 109, Ste. 205
Grover, MO 63040
636 273 4090
www.wcaa.org

Photo Credits

p. 230 Naill McDiarmi/Alamy
p. 234 Beateworks Inc./Alamy
p. 237 Armstrong
p. 238 (top) Armstrong
p. 250 Room & Board
p. 261 Shelley Metcalf
p. 301 (lower) iStockphoto
p. 338 (left) Brian Vanden Brink
p. 349 Eric Roth
p. 355 (top left, lower right) iStockphoto, (top right, lower left) Hunter Douglas
p. 357 (lower right) Louvolite
p. 360 IKEA
p. 361 (top two, middle left) Louvolite, (middle right, lower left) Tony Giammarino, (lower middle) ADO USA, (lower right) Waverly
p. 362 Louvolite
p. 366 (top) Photolibrary
p. 368 Louvolite
p. 371 (lower left) photo/design Kathie Chrisicos, (lower right) Marcia Wright/design Carol Stearns
p. 372 Tony Giammarino
p. 374 David Duncan Livingston
p. 376 (top) ADO USAi
p. 378 (left, right) IKEA
p. 379 (top left & top middle), (top middle) IKEA, (top right) ADO USA, (lower right) Interiors by Decorating Den and D. Randolph Foulds/design Adrian Halprin
p. 382 iStockphoto
p. 388 (left) IKEA
p. 390 ADO USA
p. 392 (top) IKEA
p. 394 Jessie Walker
p. 396 Conso Company
p. 398 Shutterstock
p. 400 (lower) Interiors by Decorating Den/design Sally Giar, (top) iStockphoto
p. 401 (top left) Color Association of US, (top middle) Jessie Walker, (top right) Interiors by Decorating Den and D. Randolph Foulds/design Connie Thompson, (lower left) Carol Stearns/design Barbara Tabak, (lower middle) Interiors by Decorating Den and Doug Barnett/design Janet White, (lower right) Interiors by Decorating Den and Doug Barnett/design Marisa Lupo
p. 402 Interiors by Decorating Den/Casa Fiora
p. 410 (top right) Richard Leo Johnson/design Carlette Cormier/CC's Designs, (lower) Hunter Douglas
p. 411 (top left) iStockphoto, (top middle) design T. Comer, (lower left) Jamie Gibbs & Associates, (lower middle) design Cheryl McLean
p. 416 David Duncan Livingston
p. 418 GetDecorating.com
p. 421 (top left) Carol Stearns/design Connie Thompson, (top right) David Duncan Livingston
p. 425 (top left) Hunter Douglas, (middle left) Interiors by Decorating Den/design M. Anquetil, (middle right) Cotdooorating.com, (lower right) Interiors by Decorating Den/design Rebecca Shearn
428 (top) Interiors by Decorating Den/design Beverly Barrett

Photography Resources
ADO USA, Fine fabrics/www.ado-usa.com/
888 766 5895
p. 361 (lower middle), 376 (top), 379 (top right), 390

Alamy/www.alamy.com
p. 230 Naill Mcdiarmid/Alamy; 234 Beateworks Inc./Alamy

Armstrong, Flooring, ceiling, cabinets/
www.armstrong.com
p. 20 (lower), 193, 198, 237, 238 (top)

The Bradley Collection Limited/www.bradleycollection.co.uk/info@bradleycollection.co.uk/
44 (0) 845 118 7224
p. 23 All window rods courtesy of Bradley

Bratt Décor, Baby cribs and children furnishings/
www.brattdecor.com
p. 182 (top)

Brian Greer's Tin Ceilings, Walls and unique metal work/www.tinceiling.com
p. 201

Ceramic Tiles of Italy/www.italytile.com
p. 83 (top two)

Chrisicos Interiors/www.chrisicos.com/617 699 9462
p. 371 (lower left) photo/design Kathie Chrisicos

Color Association of US/www.colorassociation.com
p. 379 (top left)

Conso Company/www.conso.com
p. 396

Corbis Corporation/http://pro.corbis.com
p. 19 (lower two), 204 (top), 218

Esteban Interiors/www.estebaninteriors.com/
858 729 0045/info@estebaninteriors.com
p.19 (top left), 166 James Hiebling, Esteban López

Fireclay Tile, Inc./www.fireclaytile.com
p. 187 (lower right)

FLOR, Modular carpet squares/www.flor.com
p. 8, 246 to 249 carpet squares courtesy of FLOR

GetDecorating.com
p. 418, 425 (middle right)

Tony Giammarino, photographer/
www.tonygiammarino.com
p. 3 (Giammarino & Dworkin), 13 (top left), 361 (middle right, lower left), 372, 401 (top left)

Gilded Planet/www.gildedplanet.com
Gold leaf, copper leaf, silver leafing & gilding supplies.
p. 206, 207 (top left)

Hakatai/www.hakatai.com/888 667 2429
p. 244 glass mosaic tiles courtesy of Hakatai

Hunter Douglas, Window fashions/
www.hunterdouglas.com
p. 355 (top right, lower left), 410 (lower), 425 (top left)

IKEA Home Furnishings/www.ikea.com
p. 90, 222, 360, 378 (both), 379 (top middle), 388, 392 (top)

Interiors by Decorating Den/www.decoratingden.com
p. 379 (lower right) D. Randolph Foulds/design Adrian Halprin, 400 design Sally Giar, 401 (top right) design Connie Thompson, 401 (lower middle) design Janet White, 401 (lower right) design Marisa Lupo, 402 Casa Fiora, 411 (top middle) design T. Comer, 411 (lower middle) design Cheryl McLean, 425 (middle left) design M. Anquetil, 425 (lower right) design Rebecca Shearn, 428 (top) design Beverly Barrett

iStockphoto/www.istockphoto.com
p. 5, 7, 20 (top), 68, 87, 100 (top), 105, 132 (top), 141, 146 (top), 147 (lower), 175, 176, 301 (lower), 355 (top left, lower right), 411 (top left)

Jamie Gibbs & Associates, Interior designers and landscape architects/www.jamiegibbsassociates.com
p. 411 (lower left)

Jocelyn Warner, Wallpaper, lighting, rugs/www.jocelynwarner.com
p. 10 (lower left), 12 (top left & right), 13 (lower left & right), 91 (top two, lower right & left), 92 (top)

Richard Leo Johnson
p. 410 (top) design Carlette Cormier/CC's Designs

Kimberley Seldon Design Group/
www.kimberleyseldon.com
p. 19 (top right) photo Ted Yarwood

David Duncan Livingston, photographer/
www.davidduncanlivingston.com
p. 374, 416, 421 (top right)

Louvolite, Window blind systems and fabrics/
www.louvolite.com
p. 25 (lower), 357 (lower right inset), 361 (top two, middle left), 362, 368

Madison & Grow, LLC/www.madisonandgrow.com
Eco-friendly designer wallcoverings: Modern, chic, sustainable, green, handmade.
p. 208 (Elizabeth design)

Marvin Windows and Doors/www.marvin.com
p. 128

Deron E. Meranda/http://deron.meranda.us
p. 124

Shelley Metcalf, photographer/tele. 619-281-0049, email Shelley.Metcalf@cox.net
p. 12 (lower right), 62, 74

Modern Seed/www.modernseed.com
p. 181 (top)

Oceanside Glass Tile/www.glasstile.com
p. 83 (lower left)

Photolibrary/www.photolibrary.com
p. 12 (lower left), 24 (lower), 25 (top), 78 (top), 180 (top), 366 (top)

Pottok, Wallpaper artist prints and patterns/
www.pottokprints.com
p. 13 (top right), 91 (lower middle)

Eric Roth, photographer/www.ericrothphoto.com
p. 83 (lower right), 349

Room & Board, Modern furniture and accessories/
www.roomandboard.com
p. 9 (both), 10 (middle & lower right), 11 (top), 18, 24 (top), 250

Shutterstock/www.shutterstock.com
p. 59, 261, 398

SieMatic Corp., High-end kitchen features/
www.siematic.com
p. 211

Carol Stearns/www.decoratingden.com
p. 371 (lower right) design Marcia Wright, 401 (lower leftdesign Barbara Tabak, 421 (top left) design Connie Thompson

Brian Vanden Brink, architectural photographer/
www.brianvandenbrink.com
p. 187 (lower left), 338 (left)

Jessie Walker, photographer/www.jessiewalker.com
p. 394, 401 (top middle)

Waverly, Fabrics, wallcoverings, window treatments, paint, and more/www.waverly.com
p. 361 (lower right)

Woodharbor, doors and cabinetry/
www.woodharbor.com
p. 228

Ted Yarwood, photographer/www.tedyarwood.com
p. 19 (top right), design Kimberley Seldon Design Group

Index